WITHOUT FEAR OR FAVOUR

WITHOUT FEAR OR FAVOUR

A FREE-WHEELING ACCOUNT
OF LIFE ON THE THIN BLUE LINE

JACK S. TINSLEY

GREAT PLAINS
PUBLICATIONS

Great Plains Publications
420–70 Arthur Street
Winnipeg, MB R3B 1G7
www.greatplains.mb.ca

Great Plains Publications gratefully acknowledges the financial support provided for its publishing program by the Government of Canada through the Book Publishing Industry Development Program (BPIDP); the Canada Council for the Arts; as well as the Manitoba Department of Culture, Heritage and Tourism; and the Manitoba Arts Council.

Design & Typography by Relish Design Studios Ltd.

Printed in Canada by Friesens Printing

LIBRARY AND ARCHIVES CANADA CATALOGUING IN PUBLICATION

Tinsley, Jack S., 1952-
    Without fear or favour: a free-wheeling account of life on
the thin blue line / Jack S. Tinsley.

ISBN 978-1-894283-91-5

    1. Police—Manitoba—Winnipeg. 2. Winnipeg Police Service.
I. Title.

HV7911.T55A3 2009   363.2097127'43   C2008-907073-9

ENVIRONMENTAL BENEFITS STATEMENT

Great Plains Publications saved the following resources by printing the pages of this book on chlorine free paper made with 100% post-consumer waste.

TREES	WATER	ENERGY	SOLID WASTE	GREENHOUSE GASES
20	7,473	14	960	1,800
FULLY GROWN	GALLONS	MILLION BTUs	POUNDS	POUNDS

Calculations based on research by Environmental Defense and the Paper Task Force.
Manufactured at Friesens Corporation

For Theresa

Foreword

I t took me forever to write this book. More than thirty years ago, it occurred to me that one day I might actually consider doing it, so I began leaving scribbled notes on anything handy and I kept them all in a shoe box. It was my opinion that the camaraderie, the sense of humour and the level of dedication within the ranks of the Winnipeg Police Department in those times should never be forgotten. The box survived three decades and in January of 2007—just over two years after I retired—I finally found that I had the time to start it. One memory always lead to another memory so it was nearly impossible to maintain an exact chronological order of the events in this book, but the majority of it is focused on the first half of my thirty-three-year career that started in 1971.

Most of us who have served as police officers have made it to the finish line with our minds and bodies still relatively intact. We're surely all a bit more worn but a whole lot wiser to the ways of the world than when we started out. One doesn't, however, completely retire from it. We still think like cops until we die—analytical and objective—but knowing that just when we think we have seen it all, something else will come along and prove that we haven't. By this point we are on a first name basis with our strengths and weaknesses and have become just sage enough to know that we have both.

In the end, all retired police officers—regardless of rank or career paths—ask themselves the same question. "Did I make a difference?" In my own case I have to say that most likely I did not. I may have cured a few individuals from continuing in their evil ways, but the stark reality is that the true spirit of the institution has always been—and always will be—driven by the combined efforts of the majority of the men and women in the ranks who cared. This book is not about me but about the characters I worked with and came to respect for their ability to "make it right." It is written in the language of the time and the environment that we worked in and I've made no attempt to change that.

Policing was, and will always be, a job that never gets done. There is no end. The beginning is too far back to remember. It is simply an existence of smaller and bigger occurrences that are dealt with and then filed. It is a place of overwhelming frustration and immense satisfaction. We dealt with each day's events as they occurred and then moved on to something else. You're there until you're not. It goes on without you.

There is no institution without people. Because we are merely humans, there has been treachery, petty jealousy, hypocrisy, politics and gossip on the force, just as there are in any other place where people exist in numbers. More importantly, I saw that the nucleus of honour, integrity, dedication to duty and mutual support was always there and most often stood a head higher than any of our failings. I hope I was able to capture a little of it in this book. I wasn't always right, but I did make a concerted effort at not overdoing it if I had to be wrong. At some point I learned that you could come to respect people that you didn't particularly like and that it wasn't necessary to become enemies with a person whose opinion varied from your own.

I suppose it is considered proper when one becomes an author to dedicate the fruits of his labour to the people who provided the motivation for the work. My list is short, but these are the people that made the difference for me.

- My mother and father, Robert and Hazel (deceased). They were Law and Order all the way and supported me in every single endeavour of my life, including my decision to seek out a career in law enforcement.

- Sergeant of Detectives Bill Hrycyk (deceased) who gave me my very first tour of the Winnipeg Police Department headquarters in May of 1971 just days before I applied to join and introduced me to Chief Constable Norman M. Stewart.

- Chief of Police Norman M. Stewart (deceased) who hired me, was one of the truly great leaders I have ever known, and who became the standard by which all later Chiefs of Police have been judged.

- Chief of Police Ken Johnston (deceased) for always supporting his troops.

- Chief of Police Herb Stephen who in the most difficult days of his office during the Aboriginal Justice Inquiry learned of my mother having been stricken with her first bout of cancer and sent her flowers and a personal note of support to her hospital room.

- Deputy Chief Joe Gallagher for the quality and integrity of his leadership. After learning that my mother could not survive long enough from her illness to be present at the next scheduled Awards Day Ceremony, Joe arranged for the entire chain of command between the Chief of Police and myself to be present in my parents' home on very short notice for the presentation of my Exemplary Service Medal. My mother lived but ten more days. Joe attended her funeral.

- Deputy Chief Lawrence Klippenstein for his legacy of fairness and wisdom in his leadership. He always called them exactly as he saw them despite political pressure and the opinions of others. He left big boots to fill.

- Superintendent Wayne King for his mentorship, leadership and support during the formative years of the Emergency Response Unit and who will always be "one of the boys."

- Chief of Police Dale Henry for his poised presentation of my Exemplary Service Medal on very short notice. Chief Henry quoted my Service File from memory and brought the entire chain of command between us in ceremonial dress to my parents' living room. Words cannot express my gratitude.

· My wife Theresa for putting up with my tirades during the months that I worked on this book through computer crashes, long hours of typing and lost notes. Always for her unwavering support and encouragement.

· Gordon Sinclair Jr. for his words of encouragement when I first asked him to proof-read a small excerpt of the book. Also for his work in helping me find a publisher.

· Lou-Anne Buhr for her very valued suggestions and explanations of the many options facing a new author. Most especially for her motivation to "go for it."

· Ron Drysdale, president of Antech Computer Services Inc., for keeping the whole project afloat through his technical wizardry.

CHAPTER 1 The Spark

It must have been Easter, or maybe Christmas, because those were the only two times between September and June that my sister and I were out of school long enough to make the trip to Texas. I remember that the cotton was already a few inches high—so that and the fact that it wasn't drizzling rain pretty much ruled out Christmas. It was 1958.

My grandmother had loaded me, lunch, and two old fishing rods into an aging Ford pickup. We were hurtling down the South Texas two-lane toward the San Bernard River at her usual breakneck speed of thirty miles an hour. The two of us were singing old cowboy songs from her youth and discussing what kind of fried pies we'd have when we got back home. Then I saw something up ahead. From a quarter mile away and using up my six-year-old brain's spectrum of possibilities, I decided it had to be Roy Rogers rounding up a herd of zebras.

It wasn't. Not hardly. A Hulk Hogan clone with a hat wider than a hula-hoop was sitting high on twenty hands of stallion as black as his stovepipe mule-eared boots. As he nudged the big stud around the front of the stopped pickup I couldn't help but notice that he and the horse carried more firepower than the *Red October*. In a hand-tooled belt around the man's ample waist were a matched pair of Colt single-actions with carved horn grips. Between them rode five full boxes of .45's in the back cartridge loops. A 1911 Army automatic hung in an open shoulder holster under his left arm and there was a Winchester jammed in the rifle boot under his leg. A ten-gauge hammerless double rested easily across his lap and a long bandolier of green paper-tube "double-ought" buckshot loads hung off the saddle horn with a canteen. The bores of the big scattergun looked like the gates to The Abyss.

The monster black stallion bobbed his nose about six inches from my grandmother's as the giant astride him swept off his hat in a signature of Southern gallantry and bowed deeply at the waist. In a voice like deep, rolling thunder he exclaimed: "Good morning, Miz Tinsley...and a beautiful one it is, ma'am!" Goddamn! My Granny knew this gunfighter! As she scratched the big horse's snout, she smiled back, "Good morning to you, Mr. Pink!" I was vibrating on the seat beside her. The giant Mr. Pink then allowed: "I'll have these boys across in just a minute, ma'am."

They weren't zebras. They were men. Mainly black men. And all carrying hoes. And all chained together. And all wearing dirty black and white pajamas and rubber boots that looked pretty leaky. But the strangest thing was that they were all stopped, looking straight ahead as if the man and his horse and our pickup weren't even there. It was too much! The giant swung the huge horse as he replaced his hat and barked "Hup" or "Yup" or something like that and in a nanosecond the prisoners clinked double-time across the blacktop and into the field on the other side where they stopped again. Not a man looked to the side. We drove away with me turned around in the seat and I watched them until they vanished. I had seen Texas justice for the first time.

About seven hundred questions later, I had learned from my Granny that these were "bad" men, and that not all bad men were black—just most of them. She alluded that they were trucked out each morning to work in different fields according to the Lone Star State's self-supporting penal system. A water truck came by once in the morning and once in the afternoon...maybe twice if the temperature nudged over a hundred. And no, they all didn't get their own Dixie cup. Lunch was a fifteen-minute break for a slab of sow-belly, a chunk of cold cornbread and a lukewarm ladle full of pintos or navies, depending on which was the bean of the day. The call of nature was answered on the spot, which I recall struck me as a bit of a challenge for the modest.

I never forgot it. After haranguing my Granddaddy later in the day I learned little more, but years after his death I was enlightened to the fact that he had often hunted escaped convicts in those South Texas swamps with dogs and a Stevens single-trigger twelve-gauge. It was fifty dollars of the state's money whether they came back walking in front of his horse or laying behind the saddle. Rumour had it that he only explained the two options but one time. Most drowned or got snake-bit and he got them after the turtles and possums did, but he ran quite a number of Brazoria County's runaways to ground when the need arose.

There was one interesting account of him resting in the cane-brake after a couple of days' worth of hot-footing it after one particular runner of notable stamina. His hunter's ears tipped him to some soft but unnatural rustling in the cane. When the convict with the hog-killing knife slid up to him the first thing he saw was the front bead on Granddaddy's double about six inches from his nose. The second would have been the smile behind it.

So, that was I believe, the roots of it. From this one incident was spawned the drive to uphold the law and I never really wanted to do anything else from that day on. My father always addressed every peace officer he ever spoke to as "Sir" and he left no doubt that he had ultimate respect for the law and those that enforced it. I knew it went way past just his good Southern manners, and that worked for me. However, the unseen total immersion in all the madness and bullshit that a thirty-three-year career in police work entailed must have been in the fine print when I first signed up.

I should explain some of the bizarre twists of fate that led me to the Winnipeg Police Department. The first was the fact that my father—Robert Porter "Buddy" Tinsley—weighed thirteen pounds when he was born (a seventh-generation Texan) and this was likely an early clue into his later occupation. I myself was supposed to be born a Texan. The original land grant for the family cotton plantation on the Brazos River was written in Spanish so the smart money was probably on us staying there forever—especially after the kinfolks had gone to great lengths in settling assorted neighbour squabbles with the Mexicans, the cannibalistic Karankawa Indians, the Union Army and rustlers. However, my old Dad blossomed into a serious running back, kicker and blocker and got himself noticed when his 1941 Barbers Hill Eagles high school football team won the Texas state championship. No one even scored on them during their twenty-four regular season games, and they waltzed through the big city schools during the playoffs all the way to the top.

Dad graduated high in his senior class and made the first of many decisions that ultimately led to me being the family's first Canadian. He passed on the "paying job" that awaited him on the drilling floor of an oil rig close to home and, despite the protests of his parents, he took up Baylor University on their full-ride football scholarship offer. He was just getting used to the cafeteria food and the two-a-day football practices at Waco when the war in the Pacific put his life on hold for the next four years. Barely eighteen, Dad told the administration at Baylor that he'd see them when the war was over. Again it was strange how it worked out. He'd signed up to be a U.S. Navy fighter pilot but was promptly rejected as he was too big and heavy to fit into the cockpit of anything the Navy had. It was just as well, as the statistical probability of his survival as a fighter jockey in the Pacific in those early years of conflict with Japan was grim at best.

Dad was posted in the Seaman Guard at Corpus Christi and rose quickly in rank to become a Sergeant-at-Arms at that naval base for the duration of the war. As such, he oversaw the basic training of one of the thousand-man barracks of new recruits. He also got in four years of very tough Navy football. When he requested to be discharged some months after the war so that he could return to college, the Navy had other ideas for him and put a lot of pressure on him to stay in the service. He was recommended to Annapolis for officer training and a full Navy career. Another decision—but he had told Baylor University that he would be back and his word on it was the bottom line.

The four years of Navy football and the fact that he was still growing when he'd left college brought him back in the physical condition of his life—and some thirty pounds bigger than when he had left. At six foot four and two hundred and sixty-five pounds, with all of his previous running back's speed, his college coaches moved him to tackle—and there he stayed unless the team REALLY needed a yard or two and he was a fullback for one play.

The most important decision he made came one summer when he was back home working in the oil field for his extra living money for the upcoming year at college. He met my mother and they took a shine to each other. They married in 1949 around the time the Los Angeles Dons of the old American Football League snared my Dad after he graduated. My folks were living in the bright lights of Hollywood in a rented mansion with two other football couples and life was pretty exciting during his outstanding rookie year in professional football.

At the end of the 1949 season, the American Football League and the National Football League amalgamated and although he was a free agent, Dad was drafted to Pittsburgh. However, the Winnipeg Blue Bombers had scouts across the United States and late one night Ralph Misener, who was the Bombers' team president at the time, called Dad in Los Angeles. The belching smoke stacks of the Pittsburgh steel mills hadn't appealed to him much more than had the prospect of spending thirty years on a drilling rig. A deal was struck on the telephone and according to plan, Dad met quarterback "Indian" Jack Jacobs—a full-blooded Oklahoma Creek Indian who had been lured from Green Bay—at Emerson just before the commencement of the 1950 training camp. They drove into Winnipeg together for the first time and stayed at the Fort Garry Hotel. My mother and older sister Cindy joined him shortly thereafter. Eleven football seasons as the team's perennial captain and fifty-eight years later he is still here. I arrived in Winnipeg in Year Two.

Legendary CFL fullback, punter and close family friend Charlie Shepard told me: "Your Daddy was the strongest white man I have ever seen." Bud Grant spoke at a recent Blue Bomber event in Winnipeg in October 2007 and stated my Dad was the toughest football player he had ever coached. Affable lineman Angelo Mosca of Hamilton Tiger-Cat fame laughingly recalled: "He almost killed me in my rookie year."

I have always been very proud of him and his legacy of always making the right decision, but sometimes I wished he had asked a little more about the weather when he first struck that telephone deal with Mr. Misener. Texans have historically never had any concept of forty below zero. At seventy-two degrees Fahrenheit they reach for jackets and anything less than sixty-five is declared a "Blue Norther" by some scientific formula known only to Texans. Once or twice a century actual freezing occurs in South Texas, and all three of the South's official religious denominations—Baptist, Methodist and Any Form of Organized Football—declare it to be the return of The Ice Age.

CHAPTER 2 Twenty Years Later

I t was a shit job. I was a narc for Christ's sake—a Drug Squad guy! And my partner for the late evening shift, Frenchie, worked Bookmaking. It was Christmas night and the only reason we were working at all was because one team and a Sergeant were the minimum strength for holiday shifts.

As it turned out, I was junior man in the whole division and my temporary partner hated his wife's family, so there we were. The real bitch of it was that we got a Morals guy for the Sergeant. I think he was the original Pussy Posse cop in Canada. Short, fat, bald and bespectacled, he was a raving fanatic about massage parlours, indecent acts, any exposure of body parts or movies that didn't have Annette Funicello in them. He'd foam at the mouth at the mere mention of films like "The Stewardesses" or "The Valley of The Dolls" and he had shrieked with triumph as he literally tore the reels of "Last Tango in Paris" from the movie theater projector.

I don't know it for sure, but I had been told that no one brought any lost children down the same hallway as the Vice Division when he was working because he'd be out there quizzing them about their maybe having been involved in some oral sex or shit like that. Anyway, right after my partner and I decided that we would just quietly slide out onto the street and disappear for a few Christmas cocktails, and before we could do just that, we were informed that we would be bringing in a Morals arrest for his sheet—OR ELSE. With due consideration of his request and respect for his superior rank, we told him to fuck off. I argued that some of my best snitches were hookers and I added that I felt it was important for lonely people to get their nuts licked on Christmas if not at any other time of the year. It was just the Christian thing to do. My partner agreed, adding that there was probably at least one of his bookmaking targets that was taking action at that exact moment and was using the profit to buy drugs.

The Old Boy wasn't buying it. But, he was willing to negotiate. *If* we brought in a Morals arrest for his sheet, which without doubt would raise his status with our Inspector—of whom he was scared shitless—he would then allow us the rest of the shift to ourselves without further interruption *and* buy the first round. Deal.

Minutes later, in the heart of "The Main Street Drag," we secreted ourselves as best as possible in our undercover four-door Plymouth with black wall tires and the visible radio antenna—which was bearing the same series AE license plates as the rest of the city's marked police units, buses and ambulances. We would drive down residential streets in them and six-year-olds would yell "Hi Narcs!" None of the high-class ladies were even working so we didn't bother with a cruise of the Exchange District. Our target was a svelte, five foot three, two hundred and thirty pounder in red Spandex pants perched on the curb near Henry and Main. The black heels would have been a nice touch—except for the hockey jacket—but they appeared to be a crush fit so she was wobbling a bit. Or, it could have been the booze. She was it. There wasn't another bit of action for twelve blocks in any direction.

It took about ten minutes. A delivery van cruised past her slowly, taking a gander, but as soon as the over-zealous lover-for-hire stepped off the curb to move on him he chickened out. Some Grampa-looking type in a ski jacket. In five minutes he was back. This time there was the usual hurried negotiation and nodding and our gal had her date and jumped in. Now we knew they would go to one of three or four places to get the exchange of body fluids underway, so we hung back and followed at a leisurely pace. Sure enough, it was the old marina parking lot and they pulled in and shut off the lights and engine.

Now this was the tricky part. You had to gauge the exact, correct moment to spring into action and actually catch them in some form of sexual act. A little too late and they were already done and zipped back up. But you had to allow enough time for the business of money to be concluded and things to get rolling. So we waited, until Frenchie said: "They're sawing one off. I can see the van jiggling." We commandoed up on the side of the van, which was conveniently windowless and in one swift motion, I fired open the side sliding door while my partner illuminated the entirety of the interior with his fifteen cell Maglite as we yelled "Police!" I don't know why we bothered, because I had hair down to my ass and a beard and my partner had a goatee, fifty jailhouse-looking tattoos and an orange Hawaiian shirt. They wouldn't have believed us anyway.

Perched on a little wooden milking stool was our anxious "john" with his pants appropriately pulled down to his ankles. Kneeling in front of him was our princess, head-bobbing with obvious enthusiasm, to the point where she was oblivious to the two million candlepower light which was by then melting the snow on the van. We had to yell at her to stop as the john was unable to dislodge her on his own. Obviously, his attempts to disengage were misconstrued by our lady as throes of passion on his part and she bore down with even more intensity. Finally, we dragged her loose and out of the van where my partner commenced a very standard line of police questioning, as follows:

"What the fuck were you doing in there?"

"I was putting a blowjob on him."

"Oh yeah? Let me smell your breath!"

With that, the lady coyly puffed a small breath at him through pursed lips. He sniffed deeply and nodded his head.

"Yup. That's cock! You're under arrest!"

Deferring to his obvious expertise in this line of questioning, I felt free to leave the proper wording of the charge and the explanation of rights to him while I attempted to keep from pissing my pants from laughing. We dutifully paraded the pair before our by then outraged Sergeant as we explained the heinous criminality of this offence and the sordid details of our observations.

He sucked an inch off his perpetual stogie with every breath as he took in the details, his lips quivering in disbelief of the level of perversion and dementia we had saved the city from. When he finally addressed them, he began a forty-minute tirade on their having sunk into the deepest depths of infamy and degradation and how a whole nation had become defiled by their vile sexual perversion. As he began to tire, we released them both on Appearance Notices for later court dates and went drinking.

The Sergeant was still preaching after they were long gone. His soliloquizing often prompted written presentations to Parliament and the Supreme Court on the evils of recreational sex. As we rode down the elevator, Frenchie alluded to the fact that we had something to celebrate in that we had just become bona fide Porcupine Hunters. The quizzical look on my face must have prompted his clarification. "Oh, yeah! If she'd had as many sticking out of her as she'd had stuck IN her, she'd look like a fucking porcupine!"

CHAPTER 3 Cadet

I had started in the department as a police cadet six days out of high school—for the princely sum of $161.42 every two weeks. I came to learn that the homeless had a higher standard of living. The hiring procedure had consisted a British Sergeant with impeccable manners coming to my high school where my principal told him I was an honest kid from a good family. He said that though I wasn't the best brawler in the school's history, I had a lot of heart. The medical took only slightly longer. I had to get naked and cough while the city doctor grabbed my balls, and then look at one of those Chinese puzzles and tell them what coloured number I saw. The job interview itself consisted of two questions. I fucked one of them up.

But now I was a Cadet, which meant I was still too young to be a real police officer. However, as such, I did receive some black ankle boots, new shirts with the police crest on the sleeves and two pairs of hand-me-down issue uniform pants. The hitch was that Cadets' pants did *not* have the red stripe which—back in the day— were on Constables' pants. Sergeants also did not have the red stripe, so it meant that the "hand me down" pants usually came from older, retired Sergeants who had, with age, become somewhat more rotund in comparison to their recruitment physiques. I was a hundred and eight-five pounds soaking wet with a thirty-two-inch waist. My pants came from a certain retired Patrol Sergeant who weighed three-twenty in his shorts. When trying them on in the old "Stores" office, I remember that I could fold them around myself almost three times. The stone-faced old gold-striper that was in charge informed me to "get them altered" and gave me a slip to have that work performed. I went to the department tailor, who was moonlighting from his blacksmith job, and received my pants back in short order. I did notice that the back pockets now overlapped and they were still about three inches too short but I donned them with pride along with the rest of my new uniform and was taken before the Chief in the token "parade" when one got hired.

The first words out of the Chief's mouth were: "Where the fuck did you get those pants?" The Inspector who had paraded me received a terse instruction to see that I got some new pants immediately and I was good to go. Before I left, the Chief unfolded his six and a half feet from behind his desk, walked over and gave me a crushing handshake along with a little advice. He looked me square in the eye and said: "Son, as long as you have a little common sense, at least a small degree of human compassion and a sense of humour, you'll do just fine." He was never more right. I was marched back to Stores to see the same gruff sociopath that had given me the tent-pants and he was ordered to give me *two* new pairs, which he grudgingly did, and now hated me for life.

The thing that really hit home on my first day was that as a Cadet, you were the lowest form of life on the Police Planet. You were snake shit with white-walls on your new, ugly haircut. The second thing I noticed is that Sergeants yelled pretty loud. I soon learned not to take any of it personally, because they ALL yelled at you with the exception of a very few who actually treated you like a human, cared if you learned anything and answered all your stupid questions. I'm also quite certain that in 1971 the "Bullying in the Work Place" concept was still in an unlit hookah pipe someplace. Many of the department's veterans who were forty-five years plus in age had chewed a lot of the same dirt in Europe during The Big One, and the "Sergeants Are God" mentality of the combat units had naturally carried over into the post-war paramilitary make-up of the nation's police forces. Few of we newer recruits had served anywhere, so we were deemed by many of the Old Guard to be doubly worthless.

I managed to get through my first two weeks of orientation working 8:00 A.M. to 4:00 P.M. before I was plunged headfirst into shift work. Those first two weeks were pure Hell. I was at the mercy of a manual filing system in Central Registry where several Cadets rotated through at a time on their way to becoming Constables or to becoming civilians again in short order. Thank Christ I had taken typing in high school as I was a virtual whiz with my forty words per minute. Contrary to any type of logic, we were under the direct supervision of a couple of elderly clerks who had about eighty-five years of service between them. Hawkish, unsmiling old prudes with treachery in their hearts, they would rat you out in a flash to the equally poker-faced civilian head of the division who was mostly occupied with displaying the interpersonal skills of Vlad the Impaler.

Night shift changed all that. I arrived at midnight and humped it all night filing a couple of thousand or so contact cards that had been pulled during the day for manual data entry. Then there were the disposition cards from final court decisions, and police reports by the millions while answering the hundreds of phone calls for manual "want" and "record" checks and attending the numerous officers who attended to the front counter for copies of records, etc. for their reports. It had been made perfectly clear that it *all* better be filed by 8:00 A.M. and the overnight Major Incidents typed up neatly and copied for all the Divisional Inspectors.

Despite having to move at the speed of light to complete this myriad of duties in eight hours, I found the nightshift Cadet was always running across the hall into the Detective Division to deliver requested paperwork to the nightshift Sergeant of Detectives who was a mythical figure and a source of awe and respect bordering on terror. On my first trip, I pushed open the swinging door into the back of the Detective Office and was somewhat amazed to see a small, weasel-faced and sobbing individual teetering on a metal garbage can which had been inverted on a wooden chair.

Curiously, his hands were bound behind his back and a noose was firmly secured to his neck, over the door and was hitched to the door handle on the other side. A quick mental calculation left no doubt that if he fell off the garbage can, he would be hanged by the neck until dead. There was no one around. I stood, as previously instructed, outside the open Sergeant of Detectives door waiting for him to notice me. One did not speak to him unless spoken to first. I was also amazed that he had seemingly not noticed the fellow perched on the garbage can right behind me, but prudence prevailed and I kept my mouth shut.

He looked up and said: "Who the fuck are you?" As his small office was nearly greyed-out with cigar smoke, I could only make out the fact that he was huge and unhappy. Before I could answer, two boisterous middle-aged men in suits had appeared and after announcing to the individual on the chair he was a "piece of lying shit" loud enough for people in the hotel across the street to hear, they booted the chair out from under the garbage can and weasel-face was dangling a foot off the floor. After a couple of convulsive jerks, I could just hear him croak: "Okay! Okay! I'll talk! Fuck!"and he was dragged away into a nearby interview room.

Defying logic, the Sergeant of Detectives had noticed the folders in my hand but had failed to see any part of the preceding incident right behind me. It must have been the smoke. With growing animosity he bellowed: "Are you going to stand there like a pillar of shit or are you going to give me those fucking papers?" I'd wager that was the longest personal address I ever received from anyone in the Detective Division for the next five years until I went into plainclothes myself.

Guys in harness would spend three to four hours meticulously typing their two-pages-with-carbon reports on the old manuals and then trudge up from the basement of the old Public Safety Building to the second floor and the open door of the Sergeant of Detectives only to find this same Mountain of Malice on duty inside. Besides choking out the lower atmosphere with his Lapalina Lillies, it seemed his sole delight in life was the intimidation of anything with a uniform on. All criminal investigation reports of the day had to be signed off by the Sergeant of Detectives before the reporting officer retired from duty. It was then assigned to a "team" in the applicable Detective Investigative Unit for follow-up as uniform cops were deemed too stupid to actually investigate anything. After a seven or eight second perusal of five-page report, it was a common occurrence to have him announce: "It's a piece of shit. Do it over," and then casually rip the entirety of the report into postage-stamp pieces and fix you with a stare that would freeze water in the glass.

Another of our extremely important duties as Cadets was to insure—at all costs—that the enlarged map of the city in the Detective Division's general office was accurately plotted with assorted coloured-coded pins on each shift. It was a well-known fact that if a wrong coloured pin was used or any pin was placed incorrectly, the entirety of the Detective Division would be thrown into a state of general mayhem for an undetermined period of time. Strangely, it was my immediate personal observation that few, if any members of the Detective Division even looked at the map, or even knew what it was for.

In any case, the red pins were for residential break-ins, green ones for commercial break-ins, yellow ones for armed robberies, blue ones for strong arm robberies and white ones for sexual offences. On several occasions, I had attended the Detective Office on the later shifts with my little box of coloured pins in their own color's compartment and stood for eons reading off the Major Incidents from the previous shift and insuring that I got all the pins just right. Usually only a few minutes into this chore, one or more jovial detectives would stroll over, call you a Fucking Retard and slap the box of pins out your hand. Then I'd get to spend the next twenty minutes or so on my hands and knees picking them all up while everyone in the office threw phone books and abandoned overshoes at my head. On one occasion, a slightly tipsy old veteran grabbed a handful of the spilled pins and began jamming forty or fifty of them indiscriminately anywhere on the map. I knew that my career had just ended. I was *totally* screwed. I attempted to intervene, but he slapped me in a headlock while his partner stole my tie and kicked me in the ass. Then they dumped me head-first into the paper bin and left. Not ten seconds later, the Sergeant of Detectives was hanging over me, bellowing "Stop fucking around and get the FUCK out of the paper bin!"

A full analysis of the Detective Division's personnel in those days would have most likely ended up with one thinking that it was a hockey team. It consisted of Thumpers and Thinkers, a few real super stars, and several shifts of hard-charging, tough-beyond-belief types who were as professional as the times allowed. Stick-handling shit calls and other undesirable assignments were skills learned at the earliest stages of uniform patrol, but only in plain-clothes could they be honed to perfection. Their successes didn't come from DNA comparisons, video surveillance or Crime-Stoppers because no one had even heard of any of them in those days. It was their gumshoe grit and tenacity that got it done.

The Special Squad, I had been informed, was the elite bunch in the Division and all the important stuff like Bank Robberies and Murders fell to them for solution. They had the polyester suits with the cowboy boots. Their awe-inspiring expertise was only diminished by their virtual lack of marksmanship, but the clause "will maintain absolute control of police fire power" probably wasn't in the Procedure Manual. This had never been more evident that when the fifth floor windows of an office building were machine-gunned during one of their stake-outs at a main floor financial institution. As time went on, I never did see anything more special about them than the rest of the second floor suits, including the Morality and Juvenile dicks, except that they played a bit harder. A few of them thought they were pretty special, and one or two might have actually qualified for Special Olympics, but the truth of it was that more than a couple of the department's best managers and administrators came out of there.

CHAPTER 4 The Drug Squad

Six or seven years later, when I was still on my first tour in the Vice Division and working Drugs, I actually inherited my former Sergeant of Detectives as the new Divisional Commander in his new rank of Staff Inspector. I had been rocking along pretty well for several months and had already made quite a few street purchases of assorted dope by the time he arrived. The whole division moaned like they were gut shot when we heard the news that he was coming.

The Inspector's somewhat spartan office had the usual metal frame desk with about four or five feet of space between it and a row of stackable chairs that backed against the wall under a big Westclox office clock. The big guy's office always smelled like a Havana whorehouse from all those cigars he smoked and the dime store perfume wafting in from the back when all the working girls got dragged in for a bi-weekly roust. His twelve-inch steel issue ashtray was always brimming with butts and about a half an ice cream pail full of ashes. The same wall that sported the clock in his office was the dividing wall between the office and Interview Room #1 in the back.

It was that one, single, seemingly unimportant fact that got me as close to being killed INSIDE the police station as I ever came—and by my own boss.

Big Mike had been a classmate of mine and was a fat-free two hundred and fifty pounder. He was an ex-railway cop and had spent a few years bonking hobos and throwing them off moving trains before he got on with the city. Despite being an affable guy, he was not to be fucked with.

The buy went like clockwork. I scored a pound of Mexican El Ropo for two hundred bucks from a four-time loser whose I.Q. and shoe size were probably interchangeable. The cover team had to lay back a ways as it was pretty wide open and I did the deal through the open window of the dirt bag's Challenger. I touched my glasses—the signal to pounce—and three of the less-than-secret looking Plymouths were closing like sharks on a floundering tuna. It was going really well until I heard the Challenger's three-eighty-three rev up to about ten grand and the clutch came out. Shitbreath had seen them a little too early and the chase was ON with Big Mike running a tight second place amongst the police units. The first red light took out the lead Vice car with a spectacular crash and a month's supply of Injured on Duty reports. The Challenger took a ninety degree turn about ten blocks down and skidded sideways at sixty miles an hour on the April puddle that had frozen at night and not yet re-thawed completely. Big Mike was on him and T-boned the Challenger right in the driver's door-at warp speed. I didn't see it, as I was still on foot back at the bus stop where I bought the dope but the other boys said it was spectacular. The Challenger flipped sideways five times, took out a light standard which fell on a bus and then chewed down fifty feet of picket fence that belonged to a couple of somewhat excitable Filipino immigrants.

Numbnuts came out of the wreck fighting and Big Mike casually dislocated his right shoulder and handcuffed him—tightly—behind his back. The blessed uniforms appeared and we dumped the whole mess on them with blood oaths of renumeration involving liquor on the next pay night at the Police Club.

I had to sit on the thrashing dope dealer all the way back to the station in the borrowed black and white as two of our three Vice units were now going to be the next year's Toyotas. The Nut Hold barely slowed him. Several calls came in about three hippies fighting in a stolen police car. By the time we all made it back to the office, The Boss had been tipped by the dayshift Detective Sergeant to our little fiasco, and he awaited the pleasure of our company in his office.

I was trying to figure out some diplomatic way of explaining that:

1. the dealer had eaten the two hundred dollars in marked bills during the chase which was going to be a bit of a continuity issue in our chain of evidence
2. two Vice cars were written off along with a civilian's Audi Fox and the bus people were pretty pissed, too
3. two of our guys were being treated for "cuts and abrasions" which COULD also be internal injuries and trauma
4. the prisoner was most likely going to have to do one armed pushups in the lockup for a bit
5. Manila MIGHT not be a good choice for a vacation spot for him and the missus

Just as I was getting it together in my head we hit the backroom of the Vice office with the Wild Man of Borneo who had just attempted to kick Mikey square in the Love Cluster. I DID see this crash. We were still ten feet from the open door of Interview Room #1 when Big Mike launched the screaming drug dealer by his long hair and the back of his jeans through the air and across the interview room to where he stuck headfirst into the drywall sheet on the rear wall. What I DIDN'T see was the frying-pan sized Westclox on the other side sail off the wall and with an impact of three point four on the Richter Scale, explode into the boss's overfilled ashtray. To somewhat complicate matters, The Boss was sitting in his chair two feet away. All Divisional Commander's of the day wore WHITE police shirts with dark blue trousers and a matching tie.

It started as a low, guttural Cro-Magnon growl and as it was at least fifteen seconds long, the crescendo perfectly mimed a twelve thousand pound enraged bull elephant at about the same moment he popped into view from the front office area. His perfect military haircut and parade-square uniform looked like he had just hangglided into Mount St. Helens. I remember thinking we were about to be attacked by an overweight, rabid angel. The first recognizable sound he made sounded a lot like "JESUSFUCKINGCHRISTONAFUCKI NGCRUTCH!!!" although I couldn't be sure as he was hyperventilating badly. However, the "WHOTHEFUCK??" that followed immediately after was perfectly clear.

He KNEW it was all MY fault because it was MY buy. Period. He had overheard us talking about how the buy was supposed to go down earlier that morning in the back office, but Big Mike was the REAL focus of his ferocity at that particular moment. To somewhat worsen matters, if that was in fact possible, Mike casually said "Jesus, Inspector...what IS that shit all over your uniform?" They went toe-to-toe in the boss's now somewhat untidy office for over ten minutes. They were both the same size, but Mike had an age advantage if things got really ugly. They took turns hammering the desk. You could hear them in the lunch room on the fifth floor. When they came out, Mike was transferred back to harness and a caretaker came and cleaned the office.

Looking back on it, I think what REALLY pissed him off was the very senior detective who would have been the mandatory retirement age in another week, who feared no one and didn't give a rat's ass about anything and had witnessed the whole thing. He was howling uncontrollably and lost it so bad he actually toppled over backwards in his swivel chair in the front office. Cops passing in the hallway were rushing in and throwing the Heimlich maneuver on him.

Just about everything we did was weed, hash and acid. They were just the standards of the day. Very occasionally, the odd few grams of magic mushrooms or real PCP would turn up and we knew all about cocaine, but no one ever really saw any. Up until then, the only street coke I ever seized was some crap that dentists use and had been stolen in a break-in. We had a Heroin Squad for several years and they pulled in exactly dickola. I read some of their reports. "We SAW a known junkie at 09:30 hours today." I remembered thinking, "Good. Making real progress there."

However, a bunch of our more worldly and affluent shit-heads were, on good information, starting up what we were lead to believe was a pretty lucrative cocaine mini-organization in the city. You have to admire that entrepreneurial spirit. One of them was a semi-pro hockey player languishing on and off an assortment of NHL farm teams, or sitting on his ass back in the city getting wasted, but he had hooked up with some real coke people in the U.S. who were mailing the snort to him. There were a couple of other goofs with him along with their assortment of squeezes all of whom were holed up in a big three-story house downtown. It was quite a joint—all refurbished with high-end furniture and assorted big dollar trappings. We did surveillance and sure as shit they LOOKED guilty. So, it was time for Big Brother to get to listen in. We called an obliging Mountie who was a wizard at electronics and on a Saturday night when the rats were out playing we decided to sneak in and bug the place. I'm sure that someone in our group had thought to get a search warrant. Anyway, our lock guy did the door and we were in.

In order to install the listening devices, the power had to be shut down for eight or ten minutes in the house. These were then state-of-the art little units that were hard-wired directly into the wall plugs and were pretty much invisible after the plate covers were replaced. The rub came when my partner and I were assigned to head down into the basement and turn off the main breaker. When I opened the basement door, the first thing I noticed was the overwhelming stench of dog shit. Being a dog guy myself, I wasn't really too concerned until we had both descended the basement stairs and found ourselves surrounded by a slavering pack of eight full grown, hundred and thirty pound dogs with fully curled lips and a face full of bone-white scimitars. There were NO tails wagging. At a casual glance, they closely resembled Siberian wolves. By coincidence, like Siberian wolves, they didn't bark, and they were obviously smart. They were waiting, partially hidden behind the furnace and assorted junk until we had gotten far enough from the stairs to preclude any form of retreat. My partner pulled his snubbie. I told him to shoot me first.

The excrement, old and new, was at least six inches thick on the concrete floor and it was twenty feet from the bottom stair to the breaker panel. There was no fucking way. I made a mental note to serve the owner with a summons under the Pound By-Law for having more than three adult dogs in his premises at one time—if I lived. We retreated backwards up the stairs with the drooling pack creeping a stair below us. The Mountie informed us that he was NOT going to risk electrocution because of our cowardice. We both whispered a "Fuck him" but it was back to the stairs. As I cracked the door a few inches a lightning quick snapping of jaws protruded in three places above the floor.

Then, I spied them—a full five-pound bag of Dad's Oatmeal Cookies. I cracked the bag and flipped one into the two-inch opening past the edge of the door. It never hit the floor before it was inhaled. I followed it up with another, and then another. I had their attention, and they were, for the time being, more focused on snagging a cookie than gnawing a twenty-pound roast off each of our asses. We backed them down the stairs by flipping cookies over their heads until we re-gained the basement floor. With experimentation, I quickly learned that about every six or seven seconds a new cookie had better be airborne or they pressed right into us, their noses a foot from our nuts. We inched to the panel box, snapped on our flashlights, and yelled upstairs to get ready. My partner hit the main breaker and my ass slammed shut when the basement went black. The hounds' eyes were then all green pinpoints of light shining in our anemic pocket-lights as the seconds ticked by. It was death by werewolves. I couldn't hold the cookie bag, throw a cookie and hang onto the six-inch Colt Python that I reserved for serious social occasions all at the same time, so the Colt got jammed into the front of my jeans. If the rush had come, it was at least a small comfort to know that one of those satanic motherfuckers would have busted a tooth.

The Mountie was an amazing technician and he moved even quicker having been encouraged by our near hysterical squeals for speed. He got five of the "ears" in the walls in under six minutes. He yelled that he was nearly done and I yelled back for him not to go for a smoke or a shit or anything because we were running desperately low on cookies. When he yelled "OKAY" my partner hammered the main breaker back on…and we began our retreat to the stairs. We weren't going to make it. There were only THREE cookies left. I screamed for someone to throw ANYTHING edible down the stairs, and after five or six seconds to absorb the humour value of our dilemma, someone flung a half eaten pepperoni and mushroom pizza that had been laying on the kitchen counter over our heads and into the mass of steadily advancing cookie-snatchers. When they all pounced on it, we made the twenty-odd steps to the top in two bounds and dove into the safety of the kitchen. The dogs ate the pizza and then the box.

The near brush with death by dismemberment seemed to have an unsettling effect on my partner Pig Pen. He was a portly, dirty brute who looked like he rode with Attila The Hun, but he was normally rock steady through anything. Without speaking, he strolled into the dining room where a splendid assortment of fine liquors were displayed and he snatched up a jug of Remy Martin and chugged off the top half in one hit. This wasn't at all out of character for him, because he did this at just about every place we ever did a ticket on. However, directly after replacing the jug, he heaved his two hundred and sixty pound carcass up onto the hand-polished antique walnut dining room table, hauled out his equipment, and began urinating into the forty gallon tank full of piranhas which were a full eight feet away. He never spilled a drop. Looking back on it, I suspected that this must have been some form of Post Incident Stress Syndrome—before it was identified by science.

In the end, our weeks of surveillance and listening-post duty were rewarded with a seizure of THREE AND A HALF grams of cocaine which we plucked from an ice cube tray in the freezer on a legitimate search warrant. One of the first conversations we had taken in—the day after we bugged the place—was the hockey-head whining on the phone to somebody that his mutts were suffering from Advanced Squirt-Bum and a shroud of brown mist had engulfed his basement.

Some bars were tougher than others. It was a fact of life on the streets that each element which makes up the whole of a big city's night life end up in their own preferred places of recreation. It was just water seeking its own level. The bars on The Main Street Drag catered largely to the Aboriginal trade. The older crowd in from the reserves were wooed by the neon jungle's early opening hours, cheap draft beer and live fiddle music. There was rarely any trouble excepting the usual short duke-outs over women, suspected infidelity, money and perceived insults—which occurred in ALL bars. The odd filleting knife got run into a rib-cage or a beer bottle got smashed into an eye socket. It was just good, clean fun and the next day everyone was usually buddies again because no one could remember shit from the night before, anyway.

Understandably, when the heavily-lubricated drinkers ran out of money after being short-changed for four or five hours straight by the human rodents that posed as waiters, they got the heave-ho pretty quick and many of them didn't like it. A night in the Drunk Tank usually cooled them off. The younger crowd on The Drag had a couple of choices for DJ's with canned music or a struggling live rock band here and there and it all worked out pretty good.

Drugs changed all that. Unfortunately, we didn't see it coming. Today, the lure of way too much easy money, notoriety, social acceptance, building a "rep" or whatever else Maslow's Theory of Hierarchy says causes it, far too many kids are hitting the bright lights with a nine millimeter and something to prove. Hydroponic weed, Ecstasy, crack, coke, meth and a plethora of pharmaceuticals have invaded every type of lifestyle and the insatiable drive for more cash and more drugs fuels crime at every level. It ALL runs on dope today and those who are really raking it in defend their enterprise at all costs. It stands to reason that a couple of the Asian boys that have been found dumped in the snow on the city's outskirts and sporting a third eye did not give due consideration to this fact. Anyone who claims to be a social scientist or a knowledgeable peace officer and denies this is just plain stupid and is not even fooling himself. It is plainly The Have Nots seeing The Haves, and the stairway to heaven is paved with dope.

As far as tough bars went at the time, the old St. Vital was a No Man's Land for drug enforcement on a good day. It had it all—bikers, hoods, junkies, and every form of low-life known to modern man and the dope flowed like the beer. Occasionally, we could pick off the odd barf-bag in the rear parking lot doing a deal or smoking up in a car, but we weren't taking the fight to them in a big way and it was time. It sounded good in theory, anyway.

Pig Pen had been at the game a couple of years longer than I had, so whenever we went anywhere, we always went in separately in case he got burned from some piece of shit he had already busted. He had changed his appearance somewhat, by gaining another thirty or forty pounds and a three-day growth. He was two hundred and sixty pounds of pure narc.

Pig Pen went in first. I waited about fifteen minutes after we had stashed our not-so-undercover four-door Plymouth narcmobile in the rear parking lot wedged between a Blazer and rusted out Dodge van. When I strolled into the bar through the front doors, I already knew that Hound Dog was playing as we had heard them from three blocks away. It also occurred to me that the hotel may have exceeded the allowable numbers of patrons in the bar by about two hundred and fifty people. The lead guitar's Stratocaster was plugged into an old Fender tube amp as big as a shithouse and it was killing the termites in the rooms upstairs. I pinballed through the crowd until I spotted an empty chair at a table with a good view of most of the bar. The California blonde with the grey roots and eyes that couldn't focus motioned me to go ahead and sit down as any attempt at conversation was doomed anyway. One look at her and I knew it was definitely Bong Night at the St.V.

I had barely located my partner's whereabouts and had taken the first glug off a cold one when I saw two dudes at the next table doing some wild gesturing and yelling into each other's ears. One was a stocky younger Eskimo or Inuit kid with a short haircut. The other looked like something you'd donate to cancer research—a filthy, long-haired, mobile cadaver with rotten teeth. When he was born the doctor probably had slapped his mother. Then the cadaver hiked up his jean's leg. Rammed into his bio-hazard sock were about a dozen foil-wrapped little missiles of Thai-sticks. Without further ado, they were both up and heading for the can. I gave them a bit of lead and then stood up, giving my partner a subtle nod in that direction. I strolled into the can like I owned it, and Mr. Personal Hygiene was just grabbing a mitt full of cash from Nanook of The North. I stepped up to the urinal after a casual nod at them, and was relieved to see they were the only two rats in the can. I heard Pig Pen lumber in the door behind me and as I turned, badge in hand, I saw his was already out.

Badge flashing was always a sort of art form in the Drug Squad. You had to get it out and then back into your pocket in a micro-second as you ALWAYS needed both hands free in the seconds that followed. Fighting, running, slapping on handcuffs and strip-search-ing dirt bags in the middle of the street seemed to be the automat-ic result of a couple of shit-heads seeing that tin in the middle of their dope deal. However, sometimes the suspect you had jumped on after flashing your tin would say "Let's see those badges again" —like we had just fished them out of a cereal box that morning. Pig Pen had a special ritual for those types. He'd open up his badge and warrant card folder again, and then ram it at a thousand miles an hour straight into the wise ass's head, usually leaving a perfect outline of the badge imprinted somewhere in their face. Then, he would enquire if they were able to see it okay the second time. He got a lot of snot on his badge but it was funny.

Both of them were kissing the tile about a second later and we ripped a wad of cash, two dozen Thai sticks and a bonus strip of blotter acid off the crud-ball. The native kid was only holding the stick he had just bought. I cuffed the stinky one behind his back and casually suggested to my partner that he might get around to cuffing the other one so we could get the FUCK out of there before we got killed. After a few bumbling starts, he managed to inform me that he had forgotten his handcuffs back at the office. It really wasn't an appropriate time to kill him, so I unhooked one wrist on my guy and cuffed the pair together. Just as I was explaining how we were going to very casually stroll out of the bar in a happy four-some and that if either one of them gave us even a hint of trouble on the way I was going to blow both of their fucking brains out, the band stopped playing and washroom door swung open. Another member of The Great Unwashed caught it all. He turned and ran back into the crowd yelling "NARCS!!!!" as loud as he could.

The cacophonous din that had just moments before been nearly excruciating was gone. You could have heard a cricket fart outside the door. I cracked it for a little peek and there were about four hundred serious-looking scrotozoids all staring back. It looked like one of those zombie movies. I turned to my partner and told him to push. I'd pull. He had already established a nice rapport with our prisoners whom he was by then affectionately referring to as Blubber Burner and Cheese Dick, and he encouraged them to participate to the very best of their athletic abilities.

We hit the crowd so fast that we were nearly half way to the panic bar on the rear exit door to the parking lot before they could even react. Pig Pen's oak-stump thighs were whirring like a twenty-eight speed blender stuck on puree. Then I saw it—a hundred and fifty or so full, empty and partially filled beer bottles and glasses all airborne at once and rolling in on us like a cloud of vampire bats. I ducked, took an empty on the shoulder and noticed that my Eskimo had caught a full Old Vienna square in the side of the head and he dropped like he was pole-axed. I yelled at my partner to pick him up and run and Stinky was dragged along face down by his left arm. One brave beer-gut with acne so bad his face looked like a pizza stepped into my path and I smoked him with one of those really gratifying rights that made his nose disappear. We went right over him.

We crashed through the door and into the parking lot. My partner had the keys and threw the limp one onto the roof of the car while he got it unlocked. I had stopped by the back door and as the fifteen or so heroes bottle-necked into the door to get outside and after us, I parked the business end of my Python's six-inch tube on the end of the first guy's nose. There were no takers. I always said that Colt was a terrific argument squelcher.

I heard the Plymouth roar to life and I took off for it in my best sprinting form. The passenger door was open and our bad boys were stacked in the back and I dove in just as the crowd burst from the rear door of the bar. I had long suspected that my partner could always find a good time no matter what we were doing, and true to form, he cranked the wheel on the aging Plymouth and stood on the gas pedal. All three hundred and sixty cubic inches of engine responded and the effect in the gravel parking lot would have been an instant winner in Best Home Video of 1979. We broke every window for a block. Numerous bodies were strewn near the exit door having been strafed repeatedly by three quarter down crushed limestone. After about the eighth full-whirly, my partner became bored with his new distraction and he straightened it out and headed for the barn. The Eskimo kid woke up about ten minutes later, seemingly no worse for wear except that he had pissed his pants. We locked them both up.

Although looking for a good time was traditionally at the front of our very being in those years, we never had to look very hard because everything we did was a roller-coaster ride of hilarity and opportunity to make each other laugh. Pig Pen and Weird had been partnered for at least a couple of years before I came along, and were cornerstones in the Drug Squad. They were unquestionably the funniest pair of cops I ever encountered. Without exception, whenever I used to think back on virtually every member of that unit that I was associated with, one truly monumental stunt concerning that particular officer would stand out above all the rest. Pig Pen's greatest moment fell on a crisp fall evening in 1977.

Back in those days, a long-standing tradition in the Drug Squad was the occasional riverbank party. They always took place in the fall, as in the spring it was too muddy from the annual flooding of the Red River. Summer was out with the onset of Manitoba's famous man-eating mosquitoes and winter precluded any thought of it in that exposed flesh would usually freeze solid in something under twenty-five seconds. It was always on the last late shift of a week-long stint which fell on a Sunday night and the office closed at midnight. Eight to twelve of our guys was the usual with the occasional visitor from uniform or other plainclothes units dropping by for a few cocktails. In the 1970s, most of the city's downtown riverbanks were still in their natural state and in much the same way they had been for hundreds of years. The isolation of the well-treed riverbanks with lots of brushy undergrowth—backing onto the serenity of the big river—provided a perfect environment for a bunch of cops to blow off a little steam.

Over time, the gatherings became more and more popular and within a few years it was common for dozens of cops from all districts to be present with a large portion of them having come from the uniform ranks. One bonfire led to two and then six. Naturally, with the attraction of all the extra light and noise, it wasn't too long before something had to give. And it did. It was in the early 1990s when some of the city's finest were whooping it up in the wee hours. A couple of dirt bags from the surrounding area wandered into the party and started helping themselves from the assorted cases of beer that were piled near the fires. Cops are pretty quick, even when moderately lubricated, to spot a pair of interlopers within their ranks, and about forty of them took exception to the presence of their somewhat sticky-fingered and uninvited guests. The story went that a fairly lengthy verbal chastisement occurred followed by what was rumoured to have been a light spanking.

Most likely, the two sewer rats would never have caught on to the fact that all the beer owners were cops except for the fact that there were two or three uniform patrol cars parked nearby which belonged to the on-duty crews who had stopped by for a short visit and some camaraderie with their brothers and sisters. One of punks made a complaint and it hit the fan with never-before-known intensity. I'd estimate that somewhere around sixty-seven sergeants were assigned to the six-month long internal investigation wherein approximately ninety of the suspected party-goers were interviewed. ONE of them, who was most likely only at the party because he had a note from his Dad, decided it was in his best interests to come clean and he actually admitted to being at the party AND to consuming liquor. He was promptly rapped three days of Weekly Leave, but years later he went on to have a rewarding career as an Internal Investigation sergeant. They always took the smart ones.

The night that Pig Pen became famous, the usual group of about a dozen guys were being royally entertained over drinks by

Weird—who could perfectly imitate an orangutan, including all sexual postures and facial expressions. A huge, cheery bonfire was going which provided adequate light and a bit of warmth against the autumn chill. It might have been the ongoing primate theme, or the several cocktails he had already killed, but something prompted Pig Pen to do his Tarzan impersonation. He was wearing one of those black and red plaid lumberjack shirts—the ones known locally as a Transcona Dinner Jacket—and he had a sealed mickey of hundred proof rum in each of the top pockets. Despite his two hundred and sixty pounds, with amazing agility, he flew up a nearby maple tree and out onto an out-stretched limb some fourteen feet above the fire.

He did quite an extended rendition of the famous Ape Man's yell, while beating his chest and jumping up and down on the branch. The rest of the boys went wild and the shouts of encouragement and applause lasted several minutes. Pig Pen kept it up and then the branch broke. He plummeted straight down like a hairy B-52 with all the engines shot out—arms and legs flailing—and hit with a spectacular crash in the middle of the fire, sending sparks and burning logs sailing in all directions. Being tough as nails, he was up in a flash, but it became immediately evident that the fall had smashed both rum bottles in his pockets and he ignited with an impressive whooshing sound.

Quite obviously, it was apparent that Pig Pen had not been paying attention in his First Aid Refresher Course, as Stop, Drop and Roll never entered his mind. He was really starting to burn and looking a lot like a Buddhist monk with dual exhausts, when he sprinted for the river which was only thirty feet away. With absolutely no thought whatsoever regarding proper diving form, he belly-flopped into the mud and water at full speed. The light singeing and bruising that he suffered was insignificant in comparison to the real dilemma he was facing at that point. Not unlike a hairy mammoth mired in the LaBrea Tar Pits, the Red River gumbo held him fast and it was only after extended pleas for assistance that everyone else could stop laughing and get him out.

CHAPTER 5 Uniform — The Early Years

I learned from and worked with some of the best street cops that the times had to offer. Fearless, tough, brook-no-bullshit kinds of guys that shot and talked straight and kept my ass intact through some pretty wild nights and days. Probably consistent with The Law of Averages, I also had brief partnerships with a couple of less than desirable car partners—at least from a compatibility perspective.

One in particular really stood out—maybe because it was very early in my uniform patrol career and maybe because he was the outright most totally strange candidate to become a street cop I ever saw. His sobriquet was Elmer. Not only because he looked a lot like Elmer Fudd—he also talked a lot like him and seemed to be about as quick on the uptake. He had a few immediately noticeable drawbacks as a car partner.

He couldn't run (because he was a lard-ass), he couldn't shoot, and he couldn't drive. There was absolutely NO way he could make a right hand turn without pinching the right rear wheel rim into the curb. We had four flats in the right rear tire in two weeks. On top of that, most nine-year-old girls could beat him up. He wouldn't even piss in a back lane when he had to have a leak on night shift. You had to drive his ass all the way back to the station.

What really burned me was the fact that when it was about ninety degrees outside, he refused to roll down the window on his side of our non-air conditioned BLACK cruiser car. The reason was because he had the worst comb-over in the history of haircuts. The passing breeze from an open window caused the nine-inch hairs that he pulled over the top of his bald head to all fly straight out on the rooted side. Then, when we stopped, they stayed that way because of the goop he used to plaster them into place, and we went into our next call with him wearing half of a Bozo the Clown hairdo—which did little for our professional image. Then there was the little thing about his annoying habit of putting the shells into our shotgun's magazine BACKWARDS—usually about ten seconds before we really needed it. I was getting at the end of my patience with him.

The old Stock Exchange Hotel was a unique sort of a place in that the front entrance to the bar was right on the front sidewalk. You opened the door, took one step and you were in the toughest bar in the core area. It was a blue-collar battlefield in those days—railway workers, truckers and brassy working girls. It was about ten o'clock on a Friday night when we got the fight call. I was driving, so we managed to park at the front door without having a flat. I walked in first and I believe what caught my eye first was the seven or eight bodies with assorted injuries that were strewn on the floor. Also fairly attention-riveting was The Missing Link who was standing in the middle of them.

The guy was six foot seven in his socks and tipped the scale right at three hundred. He was about thirty, and dressed like Yukon Eric. He was very drunk. I came up to the top of his shoulder if I stood on my toes, and faced him from about three feet away. He looked down at me and I thought I detected that look of an errant schoolboy who hadn't done his homework. I casually said "So...you about done here, Big Guy?" He looked around and slowly nodded his head. The bartender walked over—but not TOO close—and told me the giant hadn't started it and that it had looked a lot like a grizzly bear slapping down a pack of retarded wolves when it happened. I stepped a bit closer and said "Well, why don't you just grab your coat and we'll head on out to the car." He finally spoke, and softly answered, "Okay, officer." So far, so good.

So he got his coat and was walking along nice and easy with me to the door when Elmer jumped in. He had been standing back and now that we were leaving he didn't want to miss out on a little grandstanding for the thirty or so honourable citizens in the bar that hadn't been body slammed. He ran up behind the big guy and grabbed one of his wrists and attempted to force the arm with the twenty-inch biceps up behind his back. In a flash, Elmer was flung off like a water drop and sailed over a nearby table without spilling a beer. Then Mr. Big and Tall was back into Murder Mode and I was the closest thing to him. He loosed a haymaker that would have derailed a train if it had landed. I jinked and it JUST missed. I tried to cajole him but he was all done with polite negotiation. I was exactly one and a half running steps from him—straight on—and he was winding up with another catcher's mitt-sized fist to rattle my brains with. So, I did the natural thing. I ran right at him and kicked him right in the nuts with every ounce of strength I could muster. And then I retreated. He blinked twice, gulped and then slowly sagged to his knees as he grabbed his privates and then fell on his face.

I sprinted back to him, and using BOTH of my arms I managed to reef ONE of his arms behind his back while screaming at Elmer to give me a hand. He did. He pulled out his cuffs and managed to actually close one—on the very last notch—around one of the oak four by fours that this guy had for wrists. I grabbed the other arm and got it twisted back behind him. Elmer deftly grabbed the remaining open cuff and promptly snapped it shut on MY wrist just as Lurch regained his feet.

I must have hit the end of that chain twelve times in the next ten seconds as the big fellow attempted to fling me away from him. Much to their credit and to my disappointment, the Smith and Wesson cuffs held firm. He used me to clean off tables, wipe out seated bar patrons and do a little light dusting in the general billiards area. Fortunately, three additional downtown units had pulled up and six more cops burst into the bar. The monster was still on his feet with seven cops hanging from him like rumpled Christmas ornaments. Finally by sheer volume he was tipped off balance and with the assistance of one of the working ladies he was pinned to the floor. Shirley liked cops and had jumped in right at the end to tip the scales in our favour, lending her hundred and eighty pounds in the nick of time. Her pendulous breasts had the Mad Lumberjack's head crushed firmly to the tile.

They finally unlocked me and my wrist looked like I'd deflected a chain saw attack. It took a month for the hide to grow back. We couldn't get the big drunk into a cruiser car so we called the wagon in anticipation of another rumble to get him loaded. The bristling giant was just warming up for it when one of the senior guys walked over to him and whispered into his ear. Then Big Boy smiled and walked calmly over to the back of the wagon and stepped up and in on his own. I was dumbfounded and just had to ask what could have possibly been said to this wild man to cause THAT reaction. The old cop said he had promised him that if he behaved Shirley would sit on his lap on the way to the Drunk Tank. She did. They may still be dating. I had secured a pool cue from the bar to beat Elmer to death with, but he had needed a pee and had already left for the station on his own.

Not a week later, still in the grips of a February deep freeze, we were sent to assist another unit with a gun call at a hotel in the southern part of Downtown. The Westminster was famous for punch-ups and for catering to the bottom five per cent of the city's gene pool. Some dope-head had popped off a few shots in the bar and missed everything but an overhead pool table light and then had fled on foot. Unit 3 was already on scene on the north side of the parking lot with the male suspect in custody. They had seized a loaded .32 belly gun off him. I wheeled in from the south side and noted that there was about forty onlookers from the bar crowded around the back door on the parking lot. It was the usual dregs of society—both male and female—and a couple somewhere in between.

I had to stop short of the other unit because of the concrete curbs used to regulate parking in the lot. They were about six inches high. Spotting the potential audience, Elmer leaped from our cruiser's passenger door, pulled his Smith and Wesson, and holding it barrel up at head height for maximum effect and exposure, he began to jog dramatically to the other unit which had the suspect. He made it about eight feet when he tripped over the nearest parking curb and hit the concrete face down. His gun skittered about twenty feet past him and into the snow on the edge of the lot. The crowd went WILD. The applause and jeers lasted a full two minutes with repeated shouts for an encore. I left the would-be hero where he lay and fished his piece out of the snow before one of the bar rats did. By the time I walked over to the other unit and ascertained that they had already finished eliciting a full confession from their suspect, Elmer was upright but woozy. He had some serious road rash on his right cheek and temple and about a tablespoonful of gravel and what might have been the corner off a condom wrapper ground into his right knee.

My final tour with Elmer came the following week. We were working 11:00 P.M. to 7:00 A.M. so the first half of the shift was the busiest as most people are still out and about. The passenger in the patrol unit was responsible for all police reports that occur in the first half of the shift. The first night I went down to our unit after the shift briefing and Elmer was sitting behind the wheel. I jumped in and away we went. We were flying from call to call until well after 4:00 A.M. when we broke for lunch and switched seats. The next night we were dispatched early—even before the briefing—for an emergency call and when I hit the floor of the garage, Elmer had it running and with the flashing lights on and I just jumped in and away we went again. The second night was worse than the first. I was up to my ass in paper and I knew I'd be typing for a week.

After the briefing on night number three, I went for a leak and headed out to the garage. Elmer was sitting behind the wheel. I walked over to the driver's door, opened it and told him to get out. He informed me quite indignantly that HE was senior and that it was HIS decision to drive or take reports as he saw fit. I lit a smoke, and reminded him that I had jumped first on both of the previous nights and I was NOT going to do it again on this particular occasion. Besides, I had been in court all day, I was tired, I'd had a fight with my girlfriend and my Winsday Ticket hadn't won shit. Again he refused to budge. I crushed out the smoke, and reached in and grabbed him in a headlock. He responded by wrapping both of his arms into the steering wheel so I couldn't reef him out of the car. That was IT! I let him go, stepped back and popped him with a short left in the side of the head. When he went limp I threw him onto the garage floor.

While verbal disagreements are quite common, actual fisticuffs between brother officers were rare. I had first seen it in my earliest Cadet service, most likely on my first nightshift. There was a twenty-four hour cafeteria that operated on the fifth floor of the Public Safety Building. Most the major food groups in the normal police diet of the day—salt, fat, sugar, grease, and caffeine were available. Only beer was missing. I was sitting in the semi-darkened lunch room at a full table of eight officers, including myself. Most of us were brown-bagging it, but a couple of the officers were choking down a soggy grilled cheese with some fries that were swimming in animal by-products. It was 4:00 A.M. and everyone was tired and pretty quiet. At the far end of the table, near the windows, I detected a just slightly elevated voice for a second or two. A cobra-quick meat hook sailed straight across the table and flush into the face of the officer who had been vocalizing his displeasure just a second before. He toppled over backwards and crashed to the floor. No one moved. Or looked. Or stopped eating. Except me—I did all three. The Sergeant sitting next to me folded up his lunch bag and announced it was time for his 4:03 pee and left. About a minute later, the obviously dazed recipient of the love-tap-to-the-lip struggled to his feet and headed out. And that was that. It ended right there.

It struck me much later on that in a profession where our powers of observation were really the keys to our success, how adept we had all become at seeing nothing when the matters at hand dictated it. Today, an Internal Investigation lasting over six months would have followed in the wake of that incident, no doubt with criminal charges resulting, suspensions from duty with or without pay, five transfers and a half a million bucks in investigators' salaries, union support expenses and legal fees.

Anyway, when Elmer came to a minute or so later, he got up and wobbled up the stairs towards the Sergeants office, holding the side of his head. Five minutes later, Big Earl sauntered down from his supervisory perch and walked up to driver's side of the parked police unit where I was now sitting behind the wheel. He looked at me in his fatherly way and asked me if I'd smacked Elmer and thrown him in the grease on the garage floor. Even the Sergeants called him Elmer. I confirmed that I had. He blew a perfect smoke ring and said, "You're Acting Patrol Sergeant in District Two for the rest of the night—they're running short."

That was it for me and Elmer. He spent a number of years in the department, later ratted out his platoon Sergeant to the Chief of the day for having a beer with the boys after shooting practice one hot summer day. The Chief told him to leave it with him—with his notes. That particular Chief is now deceased but I'm sure he assigned someone to continue with the investigation on his behalf. Although it has been over twenty-five years, I'm thinking we should be hearing the results any time now. Twice in my career, at least two of the Chiefs I worked for poured me a straight up whiskey as we discussed the matters at hand. He was one of them. I heard Elmer found Jesus later in life which was good for him, I suppose. I wonder if he knows how many of us were contemplating arranging the meeting much earlier in his career.

The only other car partner that I experienced a lack of compatibility with occurred after my first tour in the Drug Squad. I was sent back to uniform in The North End with Turk, who had also worked Drugs for a number of years with The Shadow. Turk and I got assigned on the old three-man rotation with a junior kid who didn't appear to have both of his oars in the water. He pulled a lot of stunts that most guys with a little experience wouldn't even consider, one of them being his continual tearing around on glare ice at sixty miles an hour going to unconfirmed holdup alarms that didn't warrant the danger involved. I tried to diplomatically explain to him that it might be in everyone's best interest that we arrived ALIVE at those calls as we might be less effective if we were killed en route. He didn't get it.

Back in those days, it wasn't at all unusual—even in the busier districts—for the patrol units to actually have some free patrol time. On the late shifts, it was a common practice to prowl around out in the boonies just to see what was happening. Naturally, a lot of what was encountered—besides dumped stolen cars, dead bodies, or idiots trying to pound open stolen safes—came in the form of couples parked out in the middle of nowhere looking for a little privacy. Cops are amongst the last people in the world who would purposely interrupt anyone's intimate evening, most likely because we spent a lot of ours driving around in police cars. After a quick check to make sure the guy wasn't twenty-five and the girl wasn't fourteen, we'd leave them with their dignity and a couple of more hours to fool around. Most often we'd ask the standard, "What are you kids doing out here?" And, even if they were naked, they'd always answer, "Oh, just talking." Then we'd say, "Okay. Have a nice evening." Even the odd open beer or bottle of wine would be overlooked as long as everyone was happy and approximated the age of consent. It was different with this junior officer.

I caught onto this one late winter night as we were cruising the back roads just after midnight. The moon was full and with the snow we didn't even need the headlights to see for miles. We spotted a Mustang parked about a quarter of a mile ahead of us, and the exhaust in the cold air told us it was running. We pulled up, quietly got out of the patrol unit and walked up on both sides of the coupe. Both backs of the front bucket seats were folded forward, and in the back was a couple, naked as the day they were born, heavily engrossed in some serious fornication. I whacked the top of the car with my flashlight which set off the usual mad flurry of grabbing at discarded clothing and then I stepped back to give them a minute. About five seconds later, I noticed that the moron dressed in the police uniform on the other side of the car had the girl standing outside the car in her birthday suit—in the snow—while he was shining her up and down with his flashlight. I walked around the back of the Mustang, opened the door and told the young lady to get back in. Then I shoved Stupid towards our police car and told him to smarten up.

My buddy Turk landed Stupid for a few shifts. I asked him how it was working out with him and the kid. With his usual tact, he said, "What an ASSHOLE. He spends more time looking for poon-tangers than crooks!" Enough was enough. Turk and I went in and had a little chat with our boss and suggested that it might be beneficial for all concerned if we got a third partner with a bit more maturity on our unit. He didn't even ask why and it happened that day. I heard later on that the kid kept it up once too often with his "coitus interruptus" and that he had flung the door open on a scantily-clad lady who was entertaining her off-duty Detective friend. I also heard that he got his attitude adjusted on the spot.

I worked with a lot of the older characters of the era on a relief basis when I was walking the beat and I found them to be tremendous sources of entertainment besides being tremendous sources of wisdom and knowledge. One of them, B.G. was the quietest human being—outside of dead people—that I had ever encountered. In an eight-hour day with him in a patrol unit, the entirety of his conversation consisted of a handful of one word responses. "Coffee?", "Yes", "No", and "Okay" were about it. He was approaching his thirty years of service and was one of those solid guys who were always there. It was his driving, however, that really caught my attention. He drove ALL the time, because I was junior and likely at the time wasn't approved to operate a department vehicle, so I got to observe him and appreciate the humor value in it quite a bit. B.G. went everywhere at twenty-five miles an hour. He was a model driver—careful, courteous and signaled every turn and lane change. The problem was, in rush hour traffic on the major thoroughfares, he still went twenty-five miles an hour, even if the speed limit was forty. The road would be wide open in front of us for two miles at 5:00 P.M. and there'd be four thousand cars jammed right up tight behind us because everyone was afraid to pass a police car.

When the occasional hold-up alarm call came in, B.G. would snap rigidly upright in the seat and firmly grasp the steering wheel at ten and two o'clock with both hands in a death grip. I'd hit the lights and he'd punch that gas pedal until we hit THIRTY miles an hour and were almost keeping up with the other traffic. Most bank robbers would die of old age before we got there, but we always got there safely.

The funniest thing he did though, was about his candies. Without exception, on every shift, B.G. had a stash of those little hard candies in plastic wrappers in his LEFT front trouser pocket. Usually at night, under the cover of darkness, he'd make his move. One could hear the faintest rustling sound of candy wrappers on B.G's left side—the opposite side of where his partner sat. I'd pretend I didn't hear it, and then, a few moments later, B.G. would feign a small cough and pretend to cover his mouth his left hand—the one he had just unwrapped a candy with—and pop the candy into his mouth. He was famous for it. At that point, whomever he was riding with would shriek at him, "Goddamn it B.G.!!! Are you eating candies again??" Caught red-handed and struck with panic, he did the natural thing. He lied. A stuttered "N-N-No" was the usual form of denial and life went on with all concerned knowing he would have never given up one of his candies.

CHAPTER 6 R.J. and Red

It was in the period of late 1974 to the fall of 1976 that I was assigned on a downtown patrol unit with two of the finest street cops I have ever known—R.J. and Red. It was on the old three-man rotation where one of us was off duty while the other two ground it out in one of the tougher cruiser car districts in the entire city. Both of these guys were smart, accomplished street fighters, superlative pursuit drivers and tremendous shots with any kind of ordnance that happened to be in their hands at the time. I could out-run both of them and out-eat R.J. but that was about it. We will always be brothers.

R.J. had been one of the city's very first police dog handlers. He and his dog were awarded with the Canadian Bankers Medal as the result of a fatal encounter with a bank robber following a stake-out a few years previously. The well-known armed robber had fled on foot from the Logan Avenue bank with an assortment of Detectives and other officers in hot pursuit. R.J. and his German Shepherd were out in front and closing fast on the suspect who was running down a back lane in an adjacent residential area. He had actually hidden behind a garage and was waiting for R.J. to run right up to him before he ambushed him and opened up with his .32 automatic.

However, the dog tracked straight to him a few seconds ahead of R.J. and took him down hard—as in REAL hard. I got to know that old dog very well in his retirement years, and he could bite like a Nile crocodile. I'd scratch his belly and he'd moan happily with both of us knowing that he'd tear my throat out five seconds later if R.J. had told him to. The dog and the suspect were rolling around on the ground with the dog firmly latched onto the suspect's gun arm and shaking him like the rat he was. Despite popping off several shots in an attempt to kill the dog, he missed with everything except the last one with which he drilled himself an extra orifice in his head. Today, a year-long Internal Investigation would have followed in the wake of that incident, and most likely would have culminated with the dog being charged with Murder.

R.J. was always on top of his game, was tireless almost to a super-human level and may have originated the term 'No Fear'. A few guys would hang onto calls as a shift wore on, if for no other reason just to catch their breath for a few minutes or grab a fast coffee somewhere. Not R.J.—he cleared every call at exactly the same second he finished with it and volunteered for everything that needed two cops in a hurry even if it was halfway across the city. If another unit was sent to a bar fight or anything else that had the slightest possibility of turning to violence, R.J. went—even if we had a couple of prisoners in tow. He lived for action and cared nothing about paychecks, promotions or politics, being focused only on doing his job.

He and I were out of our usual patrol area late one fall evening and were heading back into the downtown station with a prisoner we had taken in a rooming house south of Broadway. A call was broadcast to several units that the St. Charles Hotel had just been robbed by a male with a handgun. We weren't exactly close, and about five other units responded but R.J. punched the gas pedal and we were off. The description was about as poor as they come—the standard dark-skinned male with long dark hair wearing dark clothes and maybe twenty-five years old. We spotted about thirty potential suspects in the next three blocks.

R.J. booted our aging cruiser east on Broadway and then swung north on Smith Street which still left us over half a mile south of the hotel. If the suspect had a vehicle, we knew he was gone, but

R.J. was gambling that he didn't and was thinking about how far the guy could have in the head-start that he had. About a block ahead, a cab was northbound and suddenly stopped in the middle of the street as it was hailed by a male running out of the front lobby of the St. Regis Hotel. A dark-skinned male with long dark hair and wearing dark clothing. R.J. said only "That's the prick." The perp didn't see us as we were still a block or so away in traffic, and he jumped into the back seat of the cab. I wasn't so sure, but when the cab stopped for the red light at Portage Avenue we were out and R.J. had the back door of the cab open on the suspect's side and was going for him.

Being fairly street-wise, R.J. had his revolver in his right hand as he opened the right back door of the cab, and I shouted to the driver to stay put. The suspect's hand flew inside his jacket to the waistband area of his jeans about a quarter of a second before the barrel of R.J.'s revolver caught him square on his forehead. R.J. dragged him out and flopped the unconscious human rodent on his back. The seven hundred dollars from the St. Charles robbery was in his jacket pocket. After we got the suspect under the bright lights in the station, and before the body snatchers from the Detective Division took him off our hands, we could see that he had the most interesting indentation in his forehead which I'm sure faded over time. It looked like a rather dyslexic stamping of "Colt's Manufacturing Co. Hartford CT. USA."

On a snappy January nightshift, R.J. was cruising down Ellice Avenue near Arlington Street. A radio message was broadcast to all units that a red Mustang had just been stolen in the previous minute from the 7-11 right on that corner. I had hardly written the license plate number down when it passed us heading east. R.J. could wheel a cruiser car with the best of them, and we went from forty miles an hour westbound to seventy miles an hour eastbound in about a second and a half. I only hit my head on the side window three times during the manoeuvre. The roads were glare ice and it had been one of those winters with abnormally heavy snowfalls, so the sides of every road were piled with five-foot snow banks from the snowplows. We were up on the Mustang a second or two later and R.J. hit the lights. In a split second, the weasel behind the wheel downshifted and did a right hand turn south on Home Street and tried to open that 390 four-barrel up. There were so many horses crammed under the hood that none of them could get any traction on the ice and with wildly spinning tires and a violently swaying rear end the Mustang finally got up to about sixty miles an hour before the ruts in the ice flipped the coupe sideways in a long slide.

Those were the moments that R.J. lived for. Nobody had yet invented a Pursuit Policy back then and I caught that look of glee on R.J. who had managed to maintain straightforward progress with our unit at around sixty miles an hour. He sped up as he closed on the skidding Mustang. We nailed it straight in the driver's door and launched it up and over the snow bank on the east curb. We lost sight of the stolen wheels for a few seconds as R.J. fought what was left of our unit to a stop and we ran back to the now upside-down Mustang that was in somebody's front yard. The first thing I noticed that there was NO driver. However, his widely spaced footprints in the three feet of snow quickly let us know he was heading east through the houses and that he was RUNNING. He made it about fifty yards on what we figured was pure adrenaline before he nose-dived. He had a seriously dislocated shoulder which he hadn't yet noticed when I found him. He was laughing and smiling about being sprawled out on the snow and told us we were way too serious. By the time we got him on his feet, the shoulder was starting to get his attention a little bit and he wasn't hee-hawing quite as much, but we cuffed him anyway. He got a year for swiping the car in Provincial Judges Court and a short time later another six months consecutive from the Federal Court judge for the four pocketfuls of weed he had on him. We saw him in court the day he was sentenced for the dope. He wasn't laughing at all. R.J. told him he was way too serious.

R.J. always had a great comeback line. Late one evening he and I were cruising around and a fairly new Buick caught our attention as it headed south on Balmoral just off Notre Dame Avenue.

It was rolling along at thirty-five miles an hour on the right front rim as the tire was long gone. It became abundantly obvious that the driver hadn't noticed. The guy behind the wheel was so drunk he didn't see or hear us behind him—and then beside him—with all the emergency lights and the siren on as we tried to pull him over. He turned right onto Sargent Avenue and then drove over the curb and into the 7-11 store's parking lot. We pulled him out of the car right there.

The first two things that we picked up on were the fact that he could barely stand and that he had pissed his pants. R.J. told him he was under arrest and started to charge and caution him for Driving While Impaired and the guy started to sob. We stuffed him into our back seat and quickly ascertained that it was his third Driving While Impaired in six months and that he had no driver's license. Drunk or not, he knew he was going to be doing a stretch in jail and he began to sob even louder and pleaded for us to let him go. R.J. looked at him for several seconds as the guy was waiting for an answer to his pleas and then he said "Okay. If you can name The Four Horsemen of the Apocalypse in alphabetical order we'll let you go." The drunk opened his mouth a couple of times to likely venture a guess, but then he just held out his wrists for the handcuffs.

Red was a whole different matter. He and I had actually started on the street as probationary constables the same night—May 22nd. By eerie coincidence, that was the same day of the year that a handful of my ancestors had dug in with thirteen thousand other Confederate regulars in their attempt to prevent Vicksburg and the subsequent control of the Mississippi River from falling to the Union Army—in the form of General Grant's thirty-five thousand Federals. Even more eerily, after driving back every frontal assault the Yanks could muster in six weeks of fighting they were finally starved out and surrendered on July 4th—my birthday. Any Southerner will insist that they never gave up—they just gave out. It was such nasty little coincidences like this that always made me wonder if there was a message in there somewhere about getting involved in lost causes, and if police work was really going to be for me. It turned out that it was, but I too surrendered in the end. Bad politics caused by my refusal to pay homage to any particular Godfather and my inability to keep my mouth shut in supporting horseshit initiatives that couldn't possibly work seemed to make for swimming upstream most of the way. But it was a hell of a party, and it lasted thirty-three years. Red made it twenty-five.

Since Red and I were still just getting our feet wet, we hoofed it a lot our first summer—mostly on Main Street. I found him to be solid and unshakable and one of the very best toe-to-toe standup punchers I ever knew. At just under six feet and usually around two hundred and thirty pounds, his formidable size and the fact that his normal gaze was as unsettling as a Gaboon viper's, caused most people who wanted to beat up a police officer to naturally re-focus their hostility on me whenever he and I were together.

I had grown up in the suburbs and Red hadn't lived in the city until he went to high school, so we were both more than a little unfamiliar with the core area. Coupled with the fact that we had about two months of police experience between us we found ourselves winging it a fair bit. This became quite evident one summer night when a shortage of manpower had pressed us both into service together as a makeup cruiser crew. We were assigned a radio call to an address on Agnes Street regarding a number of shots having just been fired into the front of the house. We lit up all the emergency equipment and took off west down Ellice Avenue. And then back east on Sargent Avenue. And then west on Wellington Avenue. And then around and around for a number of minutes until we both confessed that neither of us had any idea exactly where Agnes Street really was, but we knew we were close. Fortunately, we spotted a backup unit heading right to it, and we swung in right behind it. The steely-eyed Patrol Sergeant who was waiting out front when we finally arrived enquired if we had stopped to bake a cake along the way, but we assured him that we had opted for a simultaneous arrival of units in the interest of officer safety. I didn't get the exact wording of his response as he was walking away when he said it, but it did sound a lot like "Bullshit"—which is what the call turned out to be in that a Volkswagon van backfiring was found to be the source of the "gunshots."

With the passage of not a lot of time, Red and I were assigned to a core area patrol unit. I learned right at the outset in our partnership that Red's personality did not allow for any form of retreat, backup, tolerance of disrespect to himself personally or to the uniform he was wearing. This was best borne out on a crisp fall night when we had just hit the road on midnight shift and immediately took a call for a loud stereo in the short block of Stanley Street. We pulled up in front, and Jimi Hendrix was being broadcast to the Western Hemisphere. The place was a hovel with shingles on the sides of the house and it sported two rooms. We strolled right in as knocking would have been pointless with the noise level being what it was, and we were met by a really big Indian who was less than enamoured to turn around and find us messing with his stereo. Red hit the master power switch and it was quiet—for about two seconds. The guy was six four and two hundred and seventy pounds with not much beer gut and I immediately found him not to be much of a people person. He started it all rolling with, "What the fuck do you PIGS want?"

Red looked at him like he was from Mars, and off-handedly answered, "Hey, Geronimo. Can you play a fucking harp?" I started to laugh and I remember thinking at the time that we still held the upper hand in that I was sure that between the two of us we could handle the music man if we had to. It was just at that precise moment that the biggest and meanest-looking Indian I had ever seen loomed into the doorway from the back room. He was close to his little brother in age, but he was six foot eight if he was an inch and three hundred and twenty pounds of scowling cop-hater. He could have played the front four for the Washington Redskins by himself. He too, appeared not to be a big advocate of Caucasian police officers. His American Indian Movement T-shirt with the sleeves torn off seemed to bear that out with the six-inch neon AIM letters on the front superimposed on an artist's rendition of a mounted brave piercing a cavalry officer with a fourteen-foot buffalo lance. He glared at us for an eternity and then quite articulately suggested, "Why don't you two fucking PIGGIES just FUCK OFF before I cave in your fucking PIGGIE heads?" And then he made a number of those really aggravating wee-wee-wee noises. It worked for me, but Red threw out, "Why don't you come over here and try it you big, ugly son of a bitch?" and he actually took a couple of steps towards him. My brain was silently screaming "NO! NO! WRONG ANSWER!! OH SHIT!!" but it was too late. It was at that point that I permanently disabused myself of the idea that Indians never attack at night as it had been stated in the numerous old Western movies that I had watched. The monster glared a hole in us for a full thirty seconds and then he seemed to change his mind. He smirked, "Not today. We'll keep it down. So fuck off." So we did, but on his way out, Red turned and offhandedly asked, "What's that AIM on your shirt stand for? Assholes In Moccasins?" They were still yelling as we drove away.

It wasn't that Red was prejudiced against Aboriginals—or anyone else. I learned in time that he hated most everyone equally and didn't differentiate in his opinions of people by their colour or creed—especially when he was giving them a hand-to-hand combat lesson. He had grown up fatherless and that triggered something in him which came out whenever neglected or abused children were in the mix at one of our calls. This was never more obvious than on one bitter January nightshift when we took another noise complaint just off Logan Avenue. The place looked like it had been an old stable at one time and had been poorly converted for human use. It was snapping at twenty below and the building had but one room with a sort of lean-to built onto the rear with a sloping flat roof. A wood stove was chugging all out in one corner and the temperature might have struggled up to forty above inside. There were eight or nine adults in the place—male and female—who were well into the beer. Dinner appeared to have been four or five boxes of Old Dutch potato chips.

There was a portable record player screeching out some Ferlin Husky on the table and Red yelled over the din for someone to turn it off. His request met with the usual lack of response from seriously intoxicated persons and about three seconds later he silenced it by drilling it about center with his three-cell Maglite. I began to impart some information to the effect that if we had to come back it would be with the Patrol Wagon at about the same time Red starting poking around in the back of the room. There was a blanket of sorts hanging from the ceiling that was being utilized as a divider between the main room and the add-on and I saw Red lift one end of the blanket and shine his light into the back area. About two seconds later he tore the blanket down and I saw what had caught his attention. Two little kids—a toddler about two years old clad only in a diaper and a little girl about three wearing only a T-shirt and her underpants—were scraping away with spoons on the frozen remains in a pot of the most God-awful looking stuff in all of Creation.

The tyke's diaper hadn't been changed in at least two days and both of them were obviously very hungry as they kept working away on the pot, ignoring their runny noses, us and the cold. Finally, the little girl looked up at Red as he bent over to take the spoons from them and smiled. I knew it was coming. Red bellowed out, "Whose kids are these?" and when the more drunk of the two females present stumbled up to him yelling, "Fuck off you cop! Those are my fuckin' kids!" He dropped her like a rock with a short jab to the side of her head. And then, in less time than it took to tell about it, he was around the room like The White Tornado and gave the rest of them the same treatment—one per customer—save one fat boy who fancied himself to be a boxer of sorts and he got three.

I went out to the cruiser and retrieved the two wool blankets that are kept in each unit for such eventualities and we bundled up the kids and headed out, leaving the swath of fallen revellers on the floor. We put the call in for the Children's Aid worker to attend and take charge of the tykes and before she arrived the Matron on duty in the women's lockup up on the third floor had them bathed, fed and working on their third hot chocolate. Red and I walked down with her and helped her load the city's newest foster children into her agency van after learning it was their mother's third strike for neglecting her children. I saw Red slip the worker a twenty. He was quiet for a long time when we went back on the road. I razzed him about giving the worker twenty dollars to buy candy bars for all the kids at the foster home. He told me to fuck off and to mind my own business.

Red wasn't a whole lot different when the victims were grown up, either. He just had this thing about people who brutalized the helpless—along with the things he had for rude people, criminally-motivated people and others too numerous to list. Just a month or two later, spring was in its early stages and the city was its usual half ice and half water. It was late on our evening shift and we took a priority call out of our own patrol district down at the south end of Furby Street regarding an assault on a woman. The place was a three-story walk-up and we had to park about a hundred feet down the street as the water was backed up right in front. We managed to get out of the car and over the ice ridge on the curb to the sidewalk.

The suite was at the top and after knocking, the door was slowly opened by a young black woman with a still oozing broken nose. Her left eye was swollen shut and there was no doubt in either of our minds that in the previous half hour she had been beaten quite severely. She was Nigerian and in the country as a visitor. In her heavily accented responses we learned that she had not called the police and in fact did not have a telephone. We had no way of knowing who our witness might have been and what that person had heard. We weren't making much progress in the area of how she had become injured—and by whom—and she was guarded in her responses. About a minute later, we found out why.

He strolled out of the small living room to the doorway where we stood wearing only trousers and a very bad attitude. The man—who turned out to be our victim's husband—had been in the rum a fair bit but I suspected he wasn't a nice person even when he hadn't been drinking. He was about six three and couldn't have weighed any more than a hundred and forty with his pockets full of rocks. There wasn't an ounce of fat on him. Before the conversation went downhill, we did ascertain that he had also come to Canada from Nigeria, had already become a Canadian citizen and had just recently brought his wife over.

It was at that point that Red got around to asking him about the woman's injuries as she was still saying nothing and was obviously extremely fearful of her husband. The man immediately stepped right up into Red's face and informed Red that it was his RIGHT to treat his wife as he wished and he could discipline her as he saw fit. And he DEMANDED respect from us. He emphasized his point by poking Red on the chest with his finger. I saw it coming. Red had the offending finger in his mitt in a heartbeat and bent backwards with some serious upwards pressure on it about another heartbeat later. In a calmly delivered fashion, Red informed the husband that in THIS country, NO ONE could beat a helpless woman and any-one that did was HUMAN DOG SHIT. To emphasize his point, Red shoved the husband back against the wall and out of his face.

Screaming, "I DEMAND RESPECT!," Hubby flew at Red with his arms outstretched like he was going to grab him in a giant bear hug and at the last second made a feint to try and grab Red's gun. Red nailed him with a straight shot to the ribs that I felt standing six feet away. The husband shrieked, "HOOOOOOOOO BOY!" as he crashed to the floor which I assumed was a form of Nigerian col-loquialism for "SHIT! THAT HURT!" We were both on him before he could get his breath back and cuffed him with his hands behind his back. In those days, before the rigid zero tolerance guidelines of the Domestic Violence Policy, if there was no complaint made we didn't usually arrest the suspect. However, we employed The Ways and Means Act and Hubby was coming with us. He started to spit on us and kept up with the "I DEMAND RESPECT!" while kicking like a wild man, so Red stair-surfed him down to the main floor and out the front door.

It was going to be a long drag down the sidewalk to our some-what distant cruiser car with the violent antics of the husband, so Red took hold of the cuffs and dragged him over the ice ridge on the curb. Then he pushed him face first into the two feet of ice-cold water with the mini icebergs in it. Hubby again shrieked "HOOOOOOOOO BOY!" which I assumed was also Nigerian for "SHIT! THAT'S COLD!" Red began dragging him in the knee-deep frigid water towards the parked cruiser. Whenever Hubby started to spit or kick or generally act up Red just dropped him face down and he sank. He had settled right down by the time we locked him up in the Drunk Tank and we went back and took his wife to the hospital. It was the best we could do for her.

Red's ability to turn any kind of physical alteration around to our favour never ceased to amaze me. More than a few times, someone who was too stupid to be afraid of him or had just enough of a buzz on to believe they were some kind of street fighter got to check out their own shoe size from the prone position in the second or two that followed.

On a cold Halloween evening Red and I were sent to a fairly serious motor vehicle accident in the westbound lanes of Portage Avenue right at Maryland Street. A family of six had been stopped in their Dodge station wagon at the red light about 8:00 P.M. when a '63 Ford Galaxy XL had nailed them straight on the back bumper at about forty miles an hour. The drunk behind the wheel was already suspended from driving—for life—and had opted to leave his very dazed girlfriend slumped over in the front seat of the borrowed car and had fled the scene on rubbery legs heading west. A Traffic unit came to help us out, and Red and I immediately took up the search for Crash. We caught up to him about five blocks down the road and he was gum-booting it as fast as his drunken legs could carry him. If he could have managed to run in a straight line he most likely would have been twice as far from the scene and might have made good his escape. However, with the several fresh gashes in his scalp and face and the fact that he was totally shit-faced led us to believe we had found our man.

He was moderately belligerent, but had been around enough to know when the jig was up. He wasn't a big guy, about five-nine and a hundred and sixty, and had the worst prison tattoos in the world. They looked like they had been done by some cross-eyed con after lights out by the pale glow of a flickering candle. We loaded him into our cruiser and headed for the Misericordia Hospital to get him sewn up. He refused a breath sample when we charged and cautioned him for Drive Impaired, Leave the Scene, Drive Suspended, Drive Carelessly and a few others we dreamed up, so it appeared it was going to be a relatively straight forward sew up and lock up. We got him into the Police Room adjacent to the Emergency Ward and were awaiting the pleasure of a doctor when the suspect started to act up. I had already un-cuffed him so he could hold a wad of paper towels on the numerous leaks in his head and I was standing about three feet from the chair we had parked him on. Red was sitting on the edge of a table on the other side of him. I got tired of his running his mouth fairly quickly and told him to shut up because there was nothing we could do to make the hospital folks move any faster on his behalf. He jumped up and started yelling and as I turned to face him square on he threw his best roundhouse right. It was the only punch in thirty-three years that actually connected on me, and I saw it coming, but just a half second too late. I managed to get about ninety per cent of my face out of the way, but he caught me with the very end of it on the chin and it rocked me back for a quarter of a second.

That quarter of a second was all the time Red needed. He was wearing a pair of those black issue ankle boots—the ones universally known as North End Dancing Shoes—and he sunk the toe of the right one clear up to the third lace eyelet dead center in the pressure point on Crash's left thigh. It was one of those spectacular kicks that launch game-winning field goals from sixty yards out. A scalded spider never folded up as fast and just as he hit the floor—howling in some special kind of agony—I was on him. I hammered him about six or seven of my best ones as fast as I could throw them. Red pulled me off him and matter-of-factly said, "You don't have to stick a fork in his ass to tell he's done." The first punch had split the left end of his upper lip for over an inch but it was lost in the road map of gashes he already had. I really didn't care anyway. If one was stupid enough to take on someone else two weight classes up and sober, one best be prepared to swallow what they bit off.

Crash was no longer ambulatory and I doubted at the time if he could have walked on that left leg for at least a week. We dragged him back out to the cruiser car while he was still somewhat groggy, but true to form, he started to come out of it and was back to being a complete asshole in a couple of minutes. It was pointless to try and get him detained in the lockup without getting him some medical attention, so Red headed for the Health Sciences Centre. I went in and explained that we had a fairly exuberant drunk driver who was in the market for a serious bout of stitching up and that we'd likely have to stand by for the medical staff's safety. Triage was skipped and we got the green light to wheel him straight into the back treatment area. The doctor was a black fellow from former Rhodesia and was built like a fullback. He was a class guy in every dealing we'd ever had with him and you could tell that his entire life was dedicated to helping the sick and injured.

Red and I had plunked Crash down on his back on a gurney and un-cuffed him as it was most likely that he'd have to get at least partially undressed to be treated. Both of us had one of his arms pinned down and we weren't too worried about him moving his legs. The big doctor strolled in and leaned over for a look. Crash spat straight into his face and yelled, "FUCK OFF SAMBO! NO FUCKING NIGGER IS GOING TO TOUCH ME!! The doctor's easy smile was gone and with amazing calm he requested that we assist in restraining the patient while he administered a series of local anesthetic injections. We were only too happy to help out. The good doctor leaned in again with a hypodermic loaded up and Crash spat in his face again and screamed, "YOU FUCKING NIGGER!" about thirty times. Red suggested that perhaps the patient was declining the anesthetic and winked at Crash. The doctor put the unused syringe down and picked up a suturing needle about the size of a railroad spike, threaded it with four feet of catgut and his easy smile was back. He looked at Red and I and said, "You gentlemen will be good enough to hold him down?"

Red clamped him in a choke-hold. We had re-cuffed each arm to the gurney and I was sitting on his legs so there was no way he could injure the doctor. Whistling softly as he worked, and using a very inventive version of the pathologist's loop stitch, the doctor got all the leaks stopped and the gashes closed up. Crash didn't seem to be enjoying it very much without the benefit of any deep tissue freezing. I could tell because he screamed every time the needle went in and again when every knot in every stitch was snugged up. The liberal dousings of antiseptic poured directly into the deep cuts seemed to cause him some additional discomfort as well. Personally, I always thought that cuts and gashes were sutured with shallow, closely spaced stitches of fine thread diameter and applied with a smaller needle, but what did I know. When it was over, Crash was pretty much reduced to a sobbing shell of his former bluster. He didn't even get an aspirin and we dumped him into the lockup.

Crash got a Legal Aid lawyer who attempted to launch a police brutality defence. I already had stated in my direct evidence elicited by the prosecution that I had punched Crash in the face a number of times in order to overpower him after he assaulted me. The cross-examination fizzled and was put out of its misery when the judge stopped it and tore the Legal Aid boy a new one for wasting the court's time in the face of such compelling evidence of his client's guilt. Crash was convicted on all counts and got rapped hard for the Assault Peace Officer business on top of everything else.

Very strangely, twenty-two years later, I was working an evening shift in the Duty Office on an overlap, and when the night-shift Inspector came in, I decided to head out onto the street and take in a few calls. It was a fairly quiet evening in the city and I was heading south on Main Street from the North End—approaching Higgins Avenue. The extreme right hand lane traffic is compelled by a number of traffic signs to make a right turn onto Higgins Avenue. For some reason, the compact car in the right hand lane ahead of me barrelled on through without making the mandatory right turn, and I stopped it a block farther south. The driver was a bespectacled, middle-aged fellow who weighed close to three hundred pounds. He was polite and readily produced his driver's license and registration. I was just going to point out his error and let him skate on it. While he was digging them out of his wallet I kept thinking the guy was somehow familiar but I couldn't place him—until I saw the name on the license. It was Crash.

I said, "Put on a few pounds haven't you?" He looked at me long and hard and finally answered, "Do I know you?" I offered up that I had given him that white, one-inch scar on the left corner of his upper lip. In the next ten minutes, I learned that he had never been in trouble with the law since that day in court. He'd quit drinking and swore off drugs and got himself a full-time job and a good woman. He finally managed to get his driver's license back over time and had really turned his life around. He stuck out his hand and we shook. He said he deserved everything he got that night way back then and I said, "Yes, you did."

Red always got the job done, but in all fairness he gave the people we were dealing with the opportunity to shape up on their own before he expedited matters. On another evening shift tour, we got a noise complaint from a small house on Ellen Street not too far from the downtown station. We knew we had the right place, because when we pulled up out front, a full beer came sailing out through the single pane window beside the front door. Even before we got inside, it was apparent that there were at least twelve or fifteen people inside and the place was rocking.

We hammered on the door loud enough to be heard over the racket coming from within, and the door was answered by a woman in her thirties who could have been the poster child for Genital Warts. She was wearing filthy black Spandex pants with some of those wool lumberjack socks with the white band and red stripe at the top—known everywhere in the police world as Nipigon Nylons. Her teeth were gone, save one blackened snag on the bottom which caught her upper lip not unlike a crocodile's. She yelled a "WHADDAYAFUCKINWANT???" and then stumbled drunkenly back into the place with us close behind. The floor was covered with broken bottles and beer and everyone inside was so drunk they didn't even notice us.

A middle-aged guy was flailing on a cheap acoustic guitar in the corner with accelerated enthusiasm which I suspected was intended to make up for his lack of singing prowess. Red bellowed for everyone to can it and there was about a three second lull before the musician took up where he had left off. Red stomped over and clamped a hand over the guitar neck and strings and stifled the audible onslaught while I began to point out that the party was over. I had barely caught the crowd's attention when Mr. Music's chanting and strumming started up again with increased volume. I saw it coming. Red was only a step away when the drunk ignored our second request for a little break in the entertainment and in a flash, Red had snatched the flat-top out of his hands and swung it using both arms in a full over head arc. It crashed down on the musician's head—which immediately popped right through the hollow body and the instrument exploded into about a dozen assorted pieces. The drunk shook his head and looked up at Red and whined "You didn't have to get MAD, eh!" Red asked if anyone else wanted a guitar lesson but they were all too busy leaving.

It was Red's way. Even in tense situations his demeanour was always calm and he had the knack of using his calm and polite professionalism to further aggravate people who were annoying him. One fall evening a smaller vehicle blew the red light at Ellice and Balmoral going west. It wasn't even close and fortunately, nothing had been going north or south when the vehicle sped through. We got the fellow stopped several blocks further down Ellice, and as he was fumbling with a number of expired drivers licenses and registration papers, I asked him to accompany me back to the cruiser car and I had him sit in our back seat as Red wrote out the ticket. The driver was pretty upset that we had stopped him and continually denied running the light. We finally got the current license and registration and the fellow's surname was found to be "NG". Red pronounced it as it appeared to him when he was filling out the tag and referred to the man as "Mr. Nug" while explaining the offence and section under The Highway Traffic Act. The fellow immediately countered by loudly responding "Eng." Red continued with the ticket and when explaining the voluntary court dates to the offender he again referred to him as "Mr. Nug." Quite tersely, the driver responded "ENG! ENG!" Red wrapped it up by presenting the ticket to the man and wrapped it up with a pleasant "Have a nice evening, Mr. Nug." The little guy was jabbering "ENG! ENG! ENG!" all the way back to his car and gesturing with his arms as he went. Red looked at me and said "What's with that ENG thing with him every time you say something to him? What a nasty quirk." I said I thought it was Vietnamese for "Fuck you." Actually, it wasn't. Red was a smart street cop, but was obviously a "I'm Stuck On Phonics" graduate and how it sounded was everything about how it looked — or vice versa.

This was never more apparent than one evening later in Red's career when he was about halfway through a stint as a Fraud Squad investigator. He was teamed up with a more senior officer who used a lot of words that no one could understand. They had attended to a very sophisticated lady's penthouse apartment to speak with her about the events leading up to her stolen credit card having been used in rapid succession by a numbers of suspects. The boys were served tea and imported cookies in the sitting room, and it was quite obvious from the books and displays that contributed heavily to the theme of the room, that the woman was an avid and renowned stamp collector. Red's partner, precisely at the moment when Red was taking a generous sip of his Darjeeling blend, casually stated to the gracious hostess "Well, I see you are a philatelist." Red spewed his mouthful of tea all over the serving table in the next quarter-second in which he had already decided that "philatelist" was the word for a person who practised "fellatio." To his further bewilderment, the lady smiled appreciatively and cooed "Why yes! I am! How DID you know?"

On another sweltering summer midnight shift, we had been running from call to call chasing fight, noise and drunk calls, but around three in the morning we were sent to an apartment on Elgin Avenue about three blocks from the station. The call was "a stabbing — no further information" so we were cautious when we wheeled up. The place was an all too familiar multi-suite dump we had been to several times before, and we knew right where suite three was. The door was ajar and we eased it open for a look around before we strolled in.

The sum and total of the furniture in the place consisted of an old chesterfield with all the legs broken off and a cheap record player sitting right on the floor in a corner by the wall plug. That was it. On the chesterfield sat a man and a woman—both well into advanced intoxication—and on the floor adjacent to the record player a second male lay moaning on his back. I suspected his discomfort may have had something to do with the paring knife that was stuck in the middle of his stomach—right to the handle. There wasn't much blood and the guy was conscious but you could never tell with those kinds of wounds. We radioed for an ambulance and told them not to dawdle. It turned out to be a good call, as his liver was lacerated and the doctor later said he'd have been dead in another half hour.

We got around to speaking to the pair on the couch, and ascertained that the woman was the wife of the male who was lying on the floor. The other male, who was really past providing any insights into what his name was or what had taken place there or what planet he was on, turned out to be her boyfriend. The three had been enjoying a few beers—about forty-eight to be exact—and some music over the course of the evening. I had to ask the lady how her husband had come to be lying on the floor with a knife stuck in his gut. Matter-of-factly, she responded: "Well, he wouldn't change the Johnny Cash record so I gave him a stab." Any statements were out of the question until they all sobered up, so we parked the couch couple in the Drunk Tank with a hold on them. When we were wrapping it up that night, Red said "I can't really blame her. I hate that country-western shit, too."

Despite his no-nonsense aura, Red had a terrific sense of humour. And, it came out at the strangest times. Red had been sent to downtown Ellice Avenue right near the University of Winnipeg one hot summer afternoon regarding an industrial accident. The entire Westbound roadway was torn up and a trenching machine was being utilized by the repair crew to dig expeditiously down into the earth eight or ten feet after the old road surface was broken up and bulldozed back. The exercise was to facilitate the installation of more modern storm sewer lines in that part of downtown.

The trenching machine itself was a huge apparatus consisting of a three foot wide belt conveyor about fifteen feet long which had off-set steel scoops intermittently spaced over its surface. The whole works was turned on, and then angled down into the earth and a trench was dug the length and width of the belt in short order by the scoops and the earth was piled automatically at the rear of the rig. The trencher operator had been working alone on the rig while the rest of the crew was busy elsewhere, and several minutes had passed before someone realized that the worker had somehow become caught up on one of the scoops. It had pulled him effortlessly into the trenching process and he had been cycled around and around on the belt dozens of times before someone managed to shut the whole works down. What was left of the worker was pinned at the bottom, under the belt when Red and his partner arrived. After they disconnected the power cable to the unit, both officers jumped down into the trench to check for any signs of life from the worker.

It took about two seconds to see that virtually every bone in the man's body was broken in multiple places and that he was nine kinds of dead. Red told me later the poor guy looked like Hamburger Helper with pieces of yellow hard hat and dirt in it. They shouted up to cancel the ambulance and requested the backup crew call the Medical Examiner. While crouching in the trench and taking in a more complete visual examination of the scene, Red's partner for the day—who was filling in for me as I was on leave—was straining to keep his lunch down while Red, unfazed as usual, had his nose inches from the body parts. Suddenly, Red hissed to him "LOOK AT THIS!!!" The greenish partner moved ahead enough to allow a better view and thinking Red had uncovered some secret into the tragedy asked "What???" Red pointed out a section of barely recognizable arm and exclaimed, "His fucking watch is still ticking! And it's a TIMEX!"

Red was always a man of few words and made it plain from the outset of every situation that he had no time to argue with drunks or idiots. And, once he made up his mind on something—that was it—the negotiating was over. Some years later, he became our department's Outlaw Motorcycle Gang co-ordinator which was attached to the Vice Division. He was a perfect guy for the job in that he knew more about motorcycles than anyone in the entire place and could spot an odd-ball part or an altered serial number from two blocks away. He was also tough as nails and took no crap from anyone. In those days, our biker officer was always teamed up with one from the RCMP's "D" Division Headquarters which put the work into the national network of police agencies and made for some good intelligence sharing on the activities of the numerous gangs that existed in that era.

The Mountie that worked with Red was a good sort and very dedicated to his duties as well. He was also a huge individual, and some kind of master in Gung-Fu. They were doing some high quality in-your-face policing on our local Los Bravos outfit. Red always called them the Lost Bozos—usually to their faces—which I suspected somewhat added to the gang's total lack of hospitable behaviour when they saw the two officers wherever they went. As luck would have it, one of the bikers decided he'd had enough police harassment for one day and he swaggered over and got up and into the big Mountie's face and made the very fatal error of poking him on his size fifty-four chest with a finger. He was immediately fed a "cat's paw"—a short jab with the first joint of the fingers remaining rigid and in line with the palm with the second and third joints curled back—straight into his windpipe which seriously effected the lad's ability to suck in fresh air for the following two or three weeks.

A complaint of police brutality was made and since it had been the RCMP officer that was identified as the alleged assailant the matter was directed to the federal police force's Internal Affairs Division to be investigated. Strangely, in those days, RCMP members had NO rights and were compelled to cooperate with all such investigations from within their agency under the provisions of the RCMP Act or some other existing legislation in existence at that time. In other words, they HAD to make some form of statement to their investigators concerning their actions or observations regarding the incident under scrutiny. The Internal Affairs lead investigator was an RCMP Staff Sergeant and they had extracted a written statement—under charge and caution—from their officer. They then decided that they would interview Red as a "witness officer" and also take a written statement from him.

Red was notified by our Staff Inspector to head on over to RCMP headquarters for the appointment and he attended as required. However, that ended his participation in the witch hunt. The RCMP Staff Sergeant obviously didn't have a full understanding of the concept that W.P.S. officers DID have rights and after reading Red a very long and boring preamble DEMANDED that Red provide them with a written statement concerning his observations of or participation in the alleged assault on the biker. Red simply responded "I have nothing to say."

The Staff Sergeant was notably irritated by Red's impudence and leaned right into his face and repeated his demand for cooperation. Red was starting to get a little aggravated himself but repeated "I have nothing to say." Not at all used to getting "No" for an answer the Mountie lost it. He began yelling at Red "You WILL cooperate and you WILL make a statement." Managing to quell his desire to jump up and knee-drop the source of his annoyance, Red said nothing and remained seated. This appeared to only enrage the Staff Sergeant even more and he screamed at Red "You WILL say something to me right NOW!" Red smiled and calmly answered him with: "Okay. How does FUCK OFF work for you?" and then he got up and walked out. The Mountie was wild with rage and was smoking the dial off the phone before Red was probably out of their building. He called up our Staff Inspector and in barely controlled bursts of emotion he indignantly relayed the story—leaving nothing out. There was a long pause as he anticipated our boss's grovelling apology and promise of disciplinary action against Red. Instead, he received the standard "Leave it with me" which meant he was in for a bit of a wait for any results.

As funny as Red was when someone really infuriated him and he COULD do something about it, he was even more hilarious when circumstances prevented him from even saying anything. A classic moment of this occurred one morning when he and I had been in the station all morning typing reports. We were on the old manual typewriters and you really had to pound the keys to get through the four or five layers of carbon paper so your last copy was legible. It was more like engraving than typing. To make matters worse, Red typed with the natural ability of a double arm amputee so it took him three times longer than most officers to crank out a report. He had inherited some kind of obscure investigation that involved The Public Trustee and about six other social agencies and he had no idea how to write the report and what information was required in it. So, he sought out the expertise of the Sergeant Reader of the day whose office read and signed off all written reports from our division and disseminated them for follow-up as required. The problem on that morning was that there was a whining old bastard of a Patrol Sergeant that everyone hated in there for the shift and who wasn't noted for his quality of advice.

Red listened to his instructions on how to write the report and what forms were required for about five minutes. He then secluded himself in a back corner of the typing area where he would be free of distractions and he commenced the report. Three and a half hours later, I had just finished my fifteenth or sixteenth report and was finally caught up on my paperwork. I walked to the back to see how Red was making out and he was just signing his name on the impressive stack of papers in a report that appeared to be somewhat longer than The Complete Works of William Shakespeare. It was right at shift change and there was another Sergeant from the next shift in the Reader's Office talking to the one Red had received his instructions from. We dumped all of our reports—with Red's life work on top—and were standing in the hallway talking to a few guys when it happened. The later shift Sergeant came out of the Reader's office with Red's report spread out in both hands and waved him in. I tagged along and the Sergeant looked at Red like he was a retard and asked him "Who told you to write this report like this? It's all wrong." Red looked over at the Sergeant from our shift who was standing right there and said "He did." With a theatrical sense of outrage the old bastard stomped over and had a three second look at the report and announced, "I NEVER told him to write it like THAT." Red went RED, and then purple and then back to red so I grabbed his report and tugged him out of there before he lost a couple of day's pay — or worse. I took him down to the garage to cool off and he booted a garbage can about forty yards and growled "That LYING son-of-a BITCH! That PRICK!" About three garbage cans later he started to wind down and I was howling with laughter. I typed the report for him the next day. It took forty minutes. He bought the pizza.

CHAPTER 7 Boots

My very first Drug Squad partner was a forty-two-year-old former suburban force Detective that the Vice Division had inherited when the municipal police forces amalgamated three years earlier. At the time he had a fourteen-year-old kid who later became a Sergeant in the force and was a good guy just like his Dad.

I'm not exactly positive how the Boots handle stuck to my partner. He had an array of other handles, Chopper, Mr. Tomato Plant (he'd actually gotten a search warrant and raided a greenhouse with three hundred tomato plants and never lived it down) and others. I suspect "Boots" resulted from the frequent application of his footwear to the posteriors of a few of the local punks from his former municipal policing duties. He was absolutely the most dedicated police officer I ever knew and I learned most of what I ever knew about street drugs from him.

The very first day I worked with him was in the spring of 1977 and he had a search warrant ready to go for some acid dealer in a downtown apartment block. He stressed that it was important to get in fast and make sure they couldn't make it to the bathroom to flush any dope they had. We knocked, ready to hit it fast and hard. No answer.

He said we'd have to go in anyway because his warrant would expire that day. So we did—with a little help from an earlier version of a Slim Jim that Boots had in his sleeve. The place was fairly livable and we had a good look around. We found six hundred hits of Mickey Mouse blotter with another hundred and thirty purple micro-dots and about two grand in cash. It was all stashed in a light bulb box and stuffed way up the cold air return in the living room. Even with the cover plate off you still couldn't see it and you had to feel for it in the duct. It was just a fluke we found it. So we waited…and waited…six hours later Boots announced that he just HAD to have a dump. He had hardly got settled in there with the fan roaring when I heard a key in the door. A really racy looking redhead in a jumpsuit strolled into the foyer and then stopped and stared at her closed bathroom door. The fan WAS loud. I stepped out, badge in hand and announced myself and presented her with the search warrant. After a quick look at the paperwork, she enquired about who might be in her bathroom. I explained that it was normal procedure when executing drug search warrants that we secure the bathroom area in the interests of evidence preservation. She had no idea what I had just said, and I escorted her to the living room. Three flushes later, Boots emerged and we got on with the business of the acid.

I charged and cautioned her with Possession of a Restricted Drug for the Purpose of Trafficking. This was still fairly serious in the 1970's as anything more than a simple possession rap with LSD meant jail. She had no idea what we were talking about. We showed her the dope and the roll of cash we had found stashed in the air duct. Nothing doing—it wasn't hers and she had never seen any of it before. We enquired if she lived alone. Yup. Good job… nice car…no record.

Boots went at her. "Who the FUCK are you trying to shit here, Honey? Did the fucking Dope Fairy fly in here when you weren't home and plant this fucking shit just to get YOUR ass busted? Unless you start developing a fucking memory right NOW your ass is in the Lesbo-Lockup for the next forty fucking YEARS!" She started to cry. I'm not sure if it was from Boots yelling at her or the acrid, eye-burning vapours that had been emitting from the bathroom.

We left her sitting on the couch and did a hurry-up meeting in the bedroom. His snitch had only told him acid was being dealt out of the suite. He'd had no idea by whom. It didn't add up or she was Liar of the Month. The light went on in both our heads at about the same second. The Caretaker. Who was the caretaker? It had to be. No one else had a key. She pulled out a rent receipt and it matched the name she knew him by. She said he gave her the creeps. We ran him. Four convictions for drug trafficking down east. The smart prick was using her suite to stash and do business in when she wasn't home. He knew her hours, too.

I alluded to the fact that it might be a little tough proving our theory and that even if we got his prints in her suite it meant nothing because he was in and out of there in the usual course of his caretaking duties. Our only hope was that the cash we seized might cough up a finger-print that matched his if the Identification Unit could give it a once over with silver-nitrate. Boots said it was still pretty thin because any bottom feeder that represented him would say he touched the cash while he was in there on regular caretaking business and a judge may deem it to be reasonable doubt. And, of course, the usual bullshit about some previous tenant leaving it there would be the first thing the defence would throw out for sure. It was all too obvious that HER prints weren't going to be on anything inside the air duct.

Boots was moving. I followed. We rode down to the main floor and he pounded on the caretaker's door. From the description the redhead gave us, it was our guy that answered. Boots never said a word, but planted a spectacular kick in the nuts on him, followed by a flurry of four or five more in the ribs after he fell. I wish he had told me that he was going to do that ahead of time. I was positive he had seen a knife or a gun and I reflexively yanked my big Colt and stuck it on the scumbag's eyebrow. Boots later recorded in the report that he too had been in error when he had commenced a series of immediate defensive manoeuvres as he had mistakenly construed the television remote in the suspect's hand to be some kind of weapon.

After we enlightened him about who we were and the nature of our business with him, we found him to be extremely co-operative—even relieved to learn that we were police officers—and he told us exactly how many hits of acid there were, what kinds, how much cash there was to the dollar, where it was hidden and in what kind of box. He was remanded for one court day and then copped out without counsel. He got four years. The redhead bought me dinner and drinks a week later. I told her Boots couldn't make it.

Despite his many strengths and high level of expertise as a drug investigator, Boots had one GLARING flaw. He had the weakest stomach in the Western Hemisphere and as the result, quite often fell prey to the cruel and unusual pranks of his co-workers. I'd heard about it, and also quite a few of the different versions of who made him throw up and how. One of the office favourites was for guys to slip out the back door of the Vice Division into the second floor hallway by the rear elevators where there was a "fully equipped" female staff washroom. One prankster from the team of Drug Squad officers would have a straightened out coat-hanger with a little hook fashioned on one end. He would insure that no ladies were present, slip in and then use the coat-hanger to fish out the latest deposit which had been made into the used feminine hygiene products disposal bin. In the meantime, back in the office, that officer's partner would have successfully picked the lock on Boot's locking drawer. The deposit into the drawer was made—right into Boots' coveted coffee cup—the lock re-secured, and then the word was passed quietly throughout the Division announcing when Boots was next reporting for duty.

Perhaps the fifteen or twenty extra officers in the office should have alerted him to the fact that something MIGHT be up, but that was not the case. Being a stickler for punctuality, he always hit the door right on time and almost immediately opened his drawer to grab his gun, handcuffs and coffee cup. The last time, he had apparently vomited directly into the internal workings of a typewriter and it had cost forty dollars to have it cleaned. So, word had come down from high places—in the form of and I quote "Which one of you fucking degenerates put the Transylvania Tea Bag into Boots' cup?" with strict orders that there would be no more trips to the ladies' room. Apparently no one confessed.

There was one slight variation of this modus operandi which had reaped spectacular results. At one of the regular "board meetings" of the entirety of the twenty- odd man Drug Squad which took place every month or two, it was decided that a vast array of Chinese food specialties would be served. In fact, Boots himself had actually scrounged the chow from a buddy of his over in Chinatown. We were all tying into paper plates heaping with some really fine Asian cuisine when Boots put his down to go pour himself another double. In the thirty seconds he wasn't looking, Weird had the NEW Tampax out of his pocket, unwrapped and entombed under Boot's beef and greens. Naturally, everyone was in on it—except Boots. He took a long hit off his cocktail and dove back into his food, laughing and jiving with the rest of us. It was really amazing he didn't see it before he actually did, but the lights were low and he'd had a few. Then he DID see it and actually poked it with his plastic fork in some kind of stunned disbelief. The plate and fork slid from his grasp and he fell forward emitting a powerful "HHHHHUUUNNNNNNGGGGHHHHHH!!!" noise as his stomach walls collapsed and his super-human gag reflex kicked in. He had barely stabilized on his hands and knees when the by then well underway first heave propelled a gastronomical train wreck of chicken fried rice and dry ribs at least six or seven feet. The boys already had the score cards made up well in advance and they were gleefully displayed between the second and third bouts of projectile vomiting. I gave him an eight point five.

Summer was wearing on and we were wearing out. It seemed like it was eighty-five degrees every day. I had caught a tidbit of information that lead us over to a dump adjacent to the University of Winnipeg. There were a bunch of hippie leftovers that hadn't seen soap and water in about six months crashed in a place with no utilities as everything had been cut off for non-payment of bills and the place was awaiting the wrecking ball.

I moped into the joint with my best slouch and dirtiest jeans looking for Ernie. The reception was noticeably cool and without much real enthusiasm for disclosing his possible whereabouts. The fact that I had cash and nearly a full deck of smokes escalated their interest considerably. About five minutes later, Ernie magically appeared and full of caution he enquired about my reason for attending. I told him my buddy Kenny from the Dynamite Arcade told me I could score some weed here. Kenny was really a first rate street rat whose ass got kicked by every cop in town. After cursing Kenny for being a blabbermouth and a retard, Ernie whipped out a half dozen O-Z's of pale looking grass that looked like it was mostly lumber and I selected one and flipped him a marked twenty. We yukked it up for a few minutes and then I took off.

The troops crashed in and tossed the place and we all headed for the office with four lethargic and quite aromatic pot-heads in tow. Boots LOVED this shit. He was slapping on handcuffs and yapping out of the side of his mouth and telling all of the rodents that he would give them Heat For Life. Ernie was looking at Trafficking—his third—and a bonus Possess for the Purpose and wouldn't have to be worrying about paying those exorbitant Unemployment Insurance premiums for a while.

We hit the back office and started parking the bodies in different interview rooms. Boots had one of the younger ones who looked like he hadn't been out of his clothes in three months. He had on a pair of worn out black leather side zip slip-ons—the ones every-one called Fruit Boots back then. Boots uncuffed him in Interview #1 and starting skinning him down to check for any weapons or hidden dope. After the pockets were done, the suspect was plunked down on a chair and Boots told him to shuck the shoes.

When the first one came off, a number of things became dis-cernable very quickly. First of all, the suspect was not wearing any socks, AND he had the probably most advanced case of black toe jam in recorded history. His greenish, opaque toe-nails were pro-truding a good half inch past the end of his toes and the crud was heavily packed between each digit. It seemed to grow right up past his ankle. Even before the debilitating stench hit Boots's nostrils, he was done. Too late, he desperately tried to choke off the first invol-untary spasm as the exposed foot's visual impact staggered him.

It started off as his usual "HHHUUUNNNNNNNGGGGHH!!!" but right at the outset he clamped his right hand tightly over his mouth as he spun out the door and into the general rear office area. Nine of us, including the other prisoners, stared in disbelief. It was about thirty-five feet from Interview Room #1 to the rear door which lead out into the back elevator hallway and the washrooms. He went for it. It was apparent that the BIG problem for him was the fact that the back door to our office LOCKED when it shut, and you had to use a big brass key to open it again. As he staggered across the room, the pressure was obviously building and little rivulets of vomit began to shoot out between his fingers. It became necessary for him to reinforce his right hand with his left as the pounds-per-square-inch were mounting to terrifying proportions, but he was doing pretty good at holding it back until he hit the door.

Wild-eyed with desperation, and now helpless to extract the much-needed key from his pocket he was deadlocked with destiny. If any of us could have willed ourselves to move and help him out we most certainly would have, but once again we were jointly struck down with the sheer hilarity of Boots's antics. He spewed an impressive amount on the office floor, the back door and some of the adjoining wall.

Ernie turned out to be a Mountie snitch and he wasn't in the lockup a full day when I got the call from a guy I knew over at D Division. I had no problem with our charges being stayed as the Queen's Cowboys had made an impressive seizure overnight from some information Ernie dropped on them from the lockup to get his balls out of the wringer. I called the federal prosecutor and made it happen as I was under the impression that all of law enforcement was on the same side.

My stogie-eating Divisional Commander became aware of it when reviewing our Divisional charges and dispositions a while later and he freaked. He was well underway with tearing me a new one when I interjected and told him if I was given the autonomy to go out, find drug dealers, buy dope off them and create these charges, I thought I should have the same autonomy to deal them off in the best interests of law enforcement. Today, there exists a pretty workable Informant Policy which covers everyone's butt right down the line. I also told him I was really sick and tired of going to get some money to make a drug buy and finding there was a grand total of twenty-six dollars in the Divisional fund to last a whole weekend. Finally, I wrapped it up by adding that perhaps it might be most beneficial to our Drug Squad if the business of conducting our business was left to those of us that knew something about it. We were really getting pissed off with him looking at a gram of hash after one of us made a buy and saying "You paid TEN DOLLARS for THAT little bit of shit?" We always gave about the same answer: "Yes, Inspector...that IS the going rate on the street and none of these dealers seem to want our Canadian Tire money."

There was a long pause and I figured I had just guaranteed myself a permanent night shift beat on the moon. I was due for a haircut, anyway...it had been three years. He got up, walked out to the Sergeant and instructed him to have every member of the Drug Squad at The Peace Officers Club at 8:00 P.M. sharp. We were there and he bought the drinks. He heard our complaints and we heard his—not that we really gave a shit—but it turned things around and we got as big-city as we could. He retired right in there somewhere, but he always shook my hand or punched me (a little TOO hard) on the shoulder whenever I saw him afterwards.

Most of the rotten things we did to Boots to get him to throw up were confined to the back of the Vice Office or a private club room where we held our unit get-togethers. However, his most spectacular performance was moved—quite by accident—into the public view where he attained true legendary status.

At least half of the Drug Squad has historically consisted of Detectives while the other half was made up from Constables who rotated through as Acting Detectives (later Plain Clothes Constables) in tours of one to three years, depending on ability, politics and the longevity of some projects. Except for a little difference in salary in the first year there wasn't much distinction made between the members in the division, except that as Constables it was incumbent on us to keep up with our regular refreshers.

The most dreaded was a three-day classroom ordeal known as The Senior Constables' Refresher Course and it was about as titillating as deciphering the Dead Sea Scrolls. Besides changes in statutes, new procedures and updates on The Rules and Regulations, it also included "Blowing the Dummy" which was some hands-on C.P.R. training that had started off using a plastic woman but was later replaced with plastic child of indiscernible sex. I suspect the reason for the change was that in every class previously, some class clown ALWAYS attempted to resuscitate the plastic woman by lifting her chin to clear the airway, pinching off her nostrils and then blowing on her breasts in an attempt to force air into her inflatable lungs. This disrupted the class for about an hour as several variations of increasingly perverse nature were demonstrated. The courses rolled around about twice a year and whenever one of us potential attendees received a notification from Training that we were due to go, we promptly fed it into the paper shredder and denied ever having seen it. In retaliation, some more creative Drug Squad members even produced and distributed a fairly passable Police Notice indicating that a number of Training Division members would have to attend Special High Intensity Training (S.H.I.T.) Course # 22 and designated a date and location for it.

It was working out pretty good until one day some efficient clerk in Training sent all thirteen or so notifications for those of us who were now long overdue to the Inspector instead of to each of us directly. It was a beautiful, sunny and warm late spring day when half of the Drug Squad hit the old Training Building out near City Park. We languished in our seats, dozed or just generally disrupted the first morning's class which was conducted by a couple of very junior instructors who were scared of us.

At noon we bailed en masse and headed to the Charleswood Hotel which was just a few blocks away to check out the shakers while we had the lunch special and a few hits. We figured the afternoon would go by a little faster if we were half lit. Boots hated beer. He always drank rye and coke with lots of ice. It never changed. Just as we were filing through the pub door, one of the guys spotted a gargantuan grasshopper that was the colour of cement. He obviously had been struck with an idea so he caught it and held it alive in his hand.

The dancer was already down to her white cowboy boots by the time we grabbed a huge table right at the bottom of the stage and the boys manoeuvred Boots into position as the drinks got ordered. Service was lightning fast as the lunch rush was short and the place was counting on second and third rounds. Boots was right under the peeler and he spent most of her three-song repertoire bent over backwards in his chair, gawking up at her with his mouth open. He'd had one good pull on his whiskey but now sat totally mesmerized by her grinding pelvis and baloney-shaped breasts that she could get going in opposite directions at the same time. She must have been a regular as the place was packed. Boots ate his roast beef sandwich with the side dill pickle and the show wound down.

The bug went into his drink so quick I almost missed it. Some of the guys really had a talent for the subversive stuff. It had been shoved well down into the glass, and as Boots took successive slurps off the top he kept missing it as he never took his eyes off the dancer who was by then backing up in the middle of an ankle-grab about three inches from his face. Just before he was awarded with The Kiss of The Brown Star on his forehead, she vaulted upright and whirled around. Boots went for another power-hit off his double. He dropped his eyes for just a second—which was long enough for him to see the grasshopper gung-fu'ing the inside of the glass in its last throes from drowning. We were ready for it but the stripper wasn't.

Boots shuddered like he'd been electrocuted and the glass slid from his grasp as he rocked forcefully back in his seat. And then it was there…HHHHHHHUUUUUUUUNNNNNNNGGGGGHHHHH!! He actually barfed UPHILL. He hit it all, including the dancer, the stage, his end of the table, the carpet and his pants. We told the waitress he had choked on his sandwich and they didn't charge him for it, which was pretty nice of them considering half their paying customers left within seconds.

CHAPTER 8 The Pig Pen Years

S earch warrants were always a lot of fun and usually called for the deployment of somewhere between four and ten officers depending on a number of factors. Anticipated resistance, suspects' known access to weapons or propensity for violence, numbers of suspects on the premises, and the physical size of the place that was to be hit were just a few of the considerations in the planning stage. Planning rarely took more than three minutes.

I had a special snitch who called once or twice a week and if he told you something was about to go down, you could take it to the bank. He was a master at wiping out the competition. Pig Pen and I met up with him and he fingered a smaller bungalow on a short side street in the Norwood Flats. Word around the camp-fire was that there was supposed to be a couple of shitheads liv-ing there—both drawing Unemployment Insurance between their dishwashing careers—who were supplementing their pogey with a fairly lucrative hashish business. A large supply of blond Lebanese was going to be delivered at 7:00 P.M. by an unknown male and the boys were going to spend the evening whacking it up into grams and wrapping them in foil. The Shadow and Space worked Drugs on the same shift and were both heads-up cops and good boys to have along, be it business or pleasure. It was the dead of winter, the snow was a mile deep and it had been hovering around thirty be-low for weeks.

In hindsight, the smartest thing we did was stash both sets of our wheels on the next street over. We had decided ahead of time that Pig Pen and I would thunder in the front and our support team would hit the back at the exact same moment. The front had a small screened-in veranda with a flimsy door on it but we didn't know much else about the layout from the one pass by we had taken before we got the warrant.

The lights were on and someone walked into the living room out of the back and sat down by a television that came on a second or two later. It was 8:30 P.M. by my watch when Space whispered into the radio that they were in position and I whispered back to go. We had waited long enough for them to get well into the packaging so any defence motion that the dope was "for personal use" would be dismissed forthwith and the Crown would have one less hurtle in getting these two settled into the Crowbar Hilton for a couple of years.

Pig Pen peeled the screen door off the veranda in one jerk and flung it aside. We rushed the dark door across eight feet of veranda and simultaneously hammered it as only a combined weight of four hundred and forty pounds of narcs on the dead run could hammer it. It didn't budge and we slid straight down onto the veranda floor. Not to be deterred, we were up in a flash and loosed a frontal assault on the unyielding door that lasted a full two minutes. In between full-charge shoulder rams, front kicks, side kicks, combined body impacts and shouts of encouragement to each other we finally noticed it was starting to give. With renewed hope and despite the fact that we were tiring fast we kept at it. I lost the heel off one boot. Pig Pen's nose was bleeding. The door had probably been a drawbridge in its former residence as it was a full three inches thick and appeared to be solid oak. The frame that held it fast was cobbled up from cross-timbers and the hinges were quarter inch steel plate fastened with lag bolts. Gasping for breath in the frigid air and cursing every cigarette we had ever smoked, we threw ourselves against the structure time and time again and it finally started to move. The top came loose first and in a final combined rush it toppled inward with both of us surf-boarding the door to the floor of the living room.

It took us a full thirty seconds to recover enough oxygen to detect light or colours and in about a minute things started to take on recognizable shapes. I sat up and noticed that Space and The Shadow were seated comfortably on living room chairs having a smoke, and that there were two handcuffed and very quiet figures prone on the floor beside us. They had made it into the back kitchen through an unlocked door in under two seconds and had both rodents cuffed and on the floor in less than ten. Pig Pen and I were making so much noise in our prolonged assault on the front door that we hadn't heard them yelling at us to stop so they just sat down and watched the show. A closer examination of the crash scene revealed that the door had proven to be a might sticky as it had been nailed shut with about a dozen ten inch spikes and hadn't been used in over twenty years. To add a bit more resistance to our endeavours to gain entry, the hash dealers had stacked their four thousand dollar stereo system on a multi-tiered shelving unit right across the living room side of the door. It was apparent that the stereo system was now under the door and didn't appear to be in operable condition at that time.

Drenched with sweat, Pig Pen and I, assisted by The Shadow, commenced a search of the place while Space babysat. In twenty minutes we hadn't found a thing. Nothing. Not a seed or a rolling paper. These two had been reported to be a bit brighter than most and were probably very cautious about where they stashed so we kept looking. After an hour and a couple of short whispered conferences the two residents, picking up on our lack of success, were starting to get yappy and we were starting to wonder how we were going to get out from under this slight social faux pas unscathed.

Pig Pen and The Shadow went back down into the dingy confines of the basement to have another look around as they said there was a lot of junk piled everywhere and they might have missed something but not likely. They had just moved out of view and I went into the kitchen to get my fourth drink of water in my attempts at personal re-hydration when I heard a soft knock at the back door. I looked out and a furtive looking individual was looking around on the step. I waved him in. Bold as brass, he threw a paper bag on the kitchen counter and apologized for being late. I had a quick look in the bag and it contained what later weighed in to be to be a full kilo brick of hashish wrapped in white paper. I smiled gratefully and the congenial delivery boy smiled back. I pulled out my badge. He stopped smiling.

It was quite a little party after we got the dope tagged and bagged and all three of our new friends appropriately registered in the court system. It convinced me there is a God and that he loved cops. We had NEVER parked that far away from a place before. If the rodent with the dope had come a moment earlier he would have seen what was going down and took off without us ever knowing he was outside. And, if the same goof had been at the place even one time before he would have known I wasn't one of the players and again would have vanished like smoke without ever knocking on the door. It was all plain horseshit luck. It probably saved my informant's life or at least from a light cattle-prodding. Naturally, our reports reflected a slightly moderated twist on the events of that evening. The precision, perfectly timed strike we had made culminated an intense investigation of extraordinary duration. It just made for better reading.

Door surfing seemed to be a trend in that grimmest of winters in late 1978. Not two blocks from the city's south-end police station a nice working couple had been ensconced in their tidy bungalow for several years. They had worked hard, paid it all off, and were just starting to enjoy the kind of lifestyle that they had toiled all those years to achieve. The only problem was that their low-life piece of shit nineteen-year-old was using their home as a command post for his entire drug-dealing network. I talked to his folks afterwards. They were nice people but their son had so many issues. He hadn't found himself yet and wasn't ready for college and his acne had made him crazy … and on and on … I was going to recommend that they take him ice fishing and provide them with the name of the business that rented thirty-six-inch-wide ice augers.

Our informant had called and announced that the folks were away and Junior's one-man operation was in full swing. We did it right. Six of us went down in three separate units and set up on the place. In five minutes we realized the place had more drive up business than A&W. Like clockwork, a car would pull up, one body would bail out and be admitted to the back door, and two minutes later the body was back and they were gone.

We took down three in a row, got the three bags of weed they had individually bought for twenty dollars a pop and elicited signed statements from all the busy shoppers regarding where and from whom they had bought their dope. It was a real improvement on what had sometimes passed for our Reasonable and Probable Grounds. We had to park them all for the time being at the nearby police station to keep them from calling and tipping off our dealer. The uniform Sergeant on evening shift over there was starting to whine about all the extra work we were causing him keeping them all guarded which really meant that we were making him miss his crib game, so it was time to move. We had sent a team for the search warrant after buyer Number One was in the bag and we were set. As sort of a last minute idea, we thought it wouldn't hurt if we made a buy off Junior ourselves and Space was elected to drive up in a beater car we had borrowed from one of the cops at the station.

Now Space wasn't exactly undercover material, but he had a lot of style. He was six foot four so he just didn't blend in well at the bars, but he had done a masterful job with his general appearance. He looked and talked like a shabby version of Ichabod Crane on Prozac. And he was crazy as a pet coon. One day, he had found a penny book of paper matches—the ones with the mail-order courses for career training on the inside cover. For weeks afterwards, all he talked about was training at home to become a drawbridge oiler when he retired from being a cop. In any case, Space wheeled up into the driveway, left it running and tapped on the back door. He never got in. Junior wasn't buying it or Space scared the shit out of him. He left and we did a two minute debriefing out of sight of the house while a couple of the guys watched it to make sure Junior didn't bail out himself with the dope.

The back door of the place opened onto a small landing and there were three stairs up to the left that hit a hallway and about twenty stairs straight in and down to the basement. We went at it three to a door, front and back. I pounded on the rear inside door after we broke the aluminum storm door and Junior looked at us through the window. I held up my badge and announced in my best radio voice that we were cops and that we had a search warrant. Junior wheeled like a scalded cat and vaulted upstairs with his long hair flowing behind him. In about three seconds, he dove back into the landing and on down the basement stairs. The door was double locked so I stepped back and in a hard rush kicked it right under the door knob. Much to my amazement, my right boot went clean through the door up to my knee and then I was hopping up and down on my left foot, attempting to maintain my balance and extract my now firmly imbedded leg from the hollow-core door. I didn't know they had a German Shepherd. Fluffy didn't know we were cops. Much to his credit as the family pet and protector, he latched onto my right boot with every bit of the six hundred pounds of bite pressure that evolution had given him. I was just starting to notice how hard it was to pull a hundred and ten pound buzz-saw through an irregularly shaped nine inch opening when I heard the front doors go down. Fluffy heard it too, and was off to seek something a bit easier to eviscerate.

I felt the bus-crash impact of my two rather beefy associates between my shoulder blades just a split-second before I was knocked senseless. The hollow-core door sagged in just enough to prevent my skull from exploding from the whack it took when it was driven into the wood at just over two hundred miles per hour. The door caved in and the three of us rode it right to the bottom of the basement stairs. NFL pile-ups had nothing on this one and it took a few seconds for me to regain my full faculties. When I did, Junior was chewing the basement carpet in his cuffed and prone repose and Fluffy was humping Pig Pen's leg—much to their joint amusement.

It was pushing forty below and I've always found it amazing how quickly potted plants will keel over from those continued blasts of Arctic air. There were now NO doors on the house so we propped the best parts of the ones we had wrecked into place and cranked up the furnace to around ninety. True to form, in thirty minutes we hadn't found a thing. We weren't in too much of a sweat over it, as we already had little Junior by the short and curlies with three counts of Trafficking but we knew there was more someplace in that house. And we needed to get it wrapped up before Mommy and Daddy got home.

Another once over netted nothing so we began to get analytical about it. I pointed out that the kid had run up and then down so I was betting that he had grabbed whatever he had from the "up" and took it "down" just before we got in. We fine combed the basement again. Zilch. Space had been unusually quiet throughout the search, but we figured he was just moping because he had gotten shot down when he was trying to make the buy. He stood at the very bottom of the basement stairs and looked up at the nicely appointed and perfectly installed suspended basement ceiling for about two full minutes. The wheels probably had been turning in there somewhere but we all looked at him like he was nuts. And then he spoke with his usual slow-motion rasp: "Youuuu knoww, whennnn I wasss a kiddd I useddd tooo hiddde mmmyyyy ssskinnnn booookss uppp therrre...."

The ceiling tiles were solid except for one right at the bottom of the stairs. Space pushed it up with his head as he stood on a chair and he shined the flashlight into the long dead space between the tiles and the floor joists. He stepped off the chair, clicked off his light and moved the chair out of the way. Then, he casually reached up and firmly took hold of the T-bar ceiling supports with both hands, and ripped down, what I believe was later quoted by the family lawyer as thirty-two feet of ceiling. In the cavalcading swath of destruction tumbling from Space's smoothest of moves lay a black duffle bag containing thirty ounce bags of wacky-tabaccy and a wad of cash that would have choked a horse. Junior went to court and got two years. His folks went to City Claims and got nothing. We went to the Deputy Chief's office and had our very sanity and the legitimacy of our births questioned in loud tones. It was business as usual.

The incident planted a little seed in my mind that grew over the years until I recognized it for what it was. It occurred to me that anyone with even minimal skills could be a good leader, or a good manager or a good administrator—as long as things were going right. Supporting your people under those conditions required nothing in the Guts Department. It was when things went wrong that the true leaders stepped up to the plate—often taking some of the hit themselves without any consideration of what such action might do to their careers. They didn't cover things up and hope they went away. They made intelligent critiques of any perceived reasons for concern or problems with how we did business and made changes on their own and not as the result of bad publicity.

More recently, in the wake of any systemic failure, the priority has appeared to be a deflection of total culpability from anywhere near the top and the driving need to BLAME somebody for it— usually some poor bastard who was just doing his job with a minimum of training and who had acted in good faith. I had only a couple of so-called leaders over the years that exhibited the balls of a hamster and always ran for cover when The Shit Storm rolled in. You could always tell when it was coming because they were gone and the troops involved—more than occasionally myself—had Ten Foot Pole marks on them. It stood to reason that the same leaders always seemed to be in the group photo when their troops stood swords in hand with a foot on the metaphorical slain dragon. The really GREAT ones seemed to always be in the background until there was trouble and then they were in the front row—the row ahead of the rest of us. I don't have the words to describe the level of respect that we had for them.

Someone—and I could never remember who—once wrote about power and using the power of one's office to the best ends possible. The wisdom of their words played out regularly in my observations of my superiors. There truly was a delicate balance. Lightly and deliberately applied with the grace and economy of motion of a fencing foil gained dividends far beyond those achieved through the methods of others who wielded power like a club and ran full speed with it bashing everything in their path. It made sense, just as it made sense never to belittle one's subordinates no matter how badly they screwed up or to raise your voice at them for any reason. I went with that.

I supposed we all had personal traits or funny little quirks that stood out in the way that we did things as individuals. Pig Pen's most notable was about guitars. Every time a group of us would execute a search warrant he'd snatch up every guitar that he saw and began to sing a love ballad with a borrowed title that he'd composed. If memory serves me correctly, I believe it was called "I Love You So Much I Can't Shit." He knew jack about playing a guitar, but he would then strum the instrument ONCE with a very rigorous stroke which would cause all six strings—steel or nylon—to snap simultaneously with a loud SPRONG! Additionally, most of the tuning pegs would pop loose. Most of the time the dopers had only a twenty dollar pawn shop piece of junk that they were playing, but occasionally they didn't. The odd time, we'd be tossing some dump and Pig Pen would go for the guitar and I'd say " Uh, listen…that's a Martin." or I'd say "Hey, that's a Fender…maybe you shouldn't…." SPRONG! He later defended his actions by quoting some police publication or *High Times* magazine or whomever which identified guitars as good hiding places for drugs. He had always been—according to him—looking for illegal substances that may have been hidden inside the guitars' hollow bodies. I pointed out to him that at least two or three of the guitars that I had witnessed him "search" had been solid-body electric jobs with NO interior hiding places by design. He stared at the ceiling for a few seconds and then proclaimed "Fuck them. ALL guitar playing leads to using drugs." And that was the world according to Pig Pen.

On a bitterly cold January evening, Pig Pen and I headed over to the Curtis Hotel on Henderson Highway. A little voice had called and told us that a certain hulking high school kid named Wolfie was dealing a lot of dope out of the beverage room every night. We had a pretty good description of him and his vehicle—which was his Mommy's—and one pass through the rear parking lot in Pig Pen's old Monte Carlo was enough for us to see the big Oldsmobile parked close to the back doors.

I went in the back and Pig Pen stomped in through the front about five minutes later. Including the drug dealer and ourselves there was a grand total of six people in the place. We took up separate tables and ordered a beer. With both of us having hair to our shoulders and a three week growth on our faces no one gave us a second look. I always HATED it when I had just ordered a drink and within five seconds of it arriving at my table something went down. Pig Pen never let it bother him as he always just chugged his drink down as he was getting up and often quoted "Waste Not, Want Not" when we discussed the events afterwards. Wolfie nailed down his next customer in three seconds after my beer arrived and I never even got to touch it before he and his new source of income were heading out the back doors to his car. Pig Pen belched once and we met at the back door. We gave Wolfie enough time to get into his car and then we went for them. Pig Pen had the passenger's door open and the buyer out in the snow and was yelling "POLICE!" just as I was passing the front of the Olds to get to the driver's side. I was about three seconds too late. Wolfie already had the big sedan running and just as I was about dead center in front of the car, he dropped it into Low and nailed the gas pedal to the floor. There wasn't a spare second to get left or right to get out of the way and my only option was UP and that's where I went. I landed squarely on the windshield as the car rocketed under me and after orienting myself enough in the next two seconds to roll flat onto my stomach on the hood while gripping both windshield wipers I came to notice that the car was going about fifty miles an hour when it careened over the curb out of the parking lot and Southbound on Brazier Street.

I was yelling "POLICE" about every two seconds and every time I did the car sped up another five miles an hour. I suppose we had covered about a quarter of a mile and were nearing the Speed of Light when I decided I was going to die anyway so I might as well shoot Wolfie before I did. I had a Model 19 Smith and Wesson with a short barrel in a shoulder holster and I managed to get it out with losing it and I jammed the business end onto the windshield about a foot from Wolfie's face. I screamed "STOP THIS FUCKING CAR!" There is no way he could have heard me with the engine noise, but he either read lips well or the gun scared him almost as much as I already was. His eyes were like saucers when he locked on the brakes and took about a full block to slide to a stop. I managed to hang on until the point when the car went back over the curb, but it had slowed considerably. What didn't compute was the fact the car I was riding on was still moving fairly quickly and Wolfie was out and running. Even stranger was the fact that he had only run a very few yards when a Monte Carlo came out of nowhere and mowed him down.

I bailed off the still-sliding Olds and hit the ground running just as Pig Pen was performing The Big Splash on the prone remains of Wolfie. The kid was tough and actually made an attempt to perform a feeble rendition of street fighting, but Pig Pen quelled all further resistance with a round-house right that turned off all the lights. We cuffed him and I said we better start looking for the dope. Pig Pen smiled and matter-of-factly announced that he had seen Wolfie dump it all out the driver's window a few seconds after he took off with me on the hood. He had, of course, paused ever so briefly in his endeavors of rescuing me to recover the evidence and to handcuff the passenger to a handy light standard. The big guy never ceased to amaze me and was truly the best drug cop on the planet.

Much to our combined chagrin, Wolfie turned out to be seventeen years old—by mere days. We threw the book at him, but in the end we wound up in Youth Court on a bunch of charges that covered everything from Trafficking, Possess for the Purpose of Trafficking, Dangerous Driving, Unlawfully in a Licensed Premises and anything else we could dream up. He was convicted across the board but got nothing. I knew the lawyer that represented Wolfie's defence well and he was always a gentleman, but he was very specific in his questioning of our conduct from about the point where Wolfie got run over. He earned the several thousand dollars Wolfie's parents had paid him to keep the kid out of a secure holding facility for naughty little bastards. Wolfie was still cocky and made the mistake of looking less than angelic before the judge. Pig Pen's testimony and explanation of his actions was rock solid as usual and the judge actually complimented us in his summation for our restraint under the circumstances. Pig Pen and I managed to restrain ourselves from laughing and looked properly deadpan and professional. Needless to say, Wolfie endured to get busted as an adult on several occasions thereafter.

In the same era when Pig Pen and I were partners, a number of divisional transfers took place and although Pig Pen and I remained paired up for years, new faces appeared in the Drug Squad from time to time due mostly to promotions and regulated transfers. A short period of mentoring with each new officer occurred, and everyone on that particular shift pitched in to get the new members' feet wet as quickly as possible.

The Ski had come to the Drug Squad after unusually long service in the uniform divisions. He was an officer with enviable enthusiasm. With a slighter build, it had been rumoured that he had never won a fight in his life, although he had likely started several considering his lack of discretion. He was, however, as likable as they came and plunged headlong into his duties as a new narc, despite his lack of experience in undercover police work. Tall John was a highly successful veteran in the Drug Squad and had been partnered with him to teach him the ropes for a few weeks. On a cool autumn night a group of us, including Space and myself, headed out to give The Ski a little "hands-on" instruction.

The Westminster was as good a place as any to maximize a new officer's exposure to street drugs and the criminals who used and dealt in them. There was ALWAYS some kind of action there—either in the bar or the parking lot—even on the quietest of shifts. The group of us utilized every entrance and staggered our arrivals over a period of several minutes until all four of us had settled into various locations in the bar crowd drawing no attention to ourselves whatsoever. The Ski was shaking like a leaf. He had managed to "scruff up" somewhat in his first few days and looked as unshaven and dirty as any of the other patrons. He had managed to get himself seated with an aging biker lady who had tapped him for a double whiskey in less than ten seconds. He had a lot to learn.

The bar was nearly full and within fifteen minutes, Tall John had spied an individual in his end of the bar who had approached a few tables of patrons and had brief conversations with the groups at each table. With the subtlety of slight head motions and eye contact, Space and I picked up on it and were trying to get The Ski's attention away from the biker bimbo's breasts long enough to clue him in. As luck would have it, the dealer headed for the men's washroom with a potential customer in tow right at that time. Tall John gave The Ski a slap on the back of his head to get his attention as he followed the pair into the restroom—with Space and myself moving that way a few steps behind. Just about the time The Ski finally made it into the washroom behind the rest of us, the dealer pulled out The Doobie of Doom.

It was the biggest marijuana cigarette I had ever seen. It looked more like one of those submarine-sized joke cigars that are a foot long. We had told The Ski just to do what we did and not to get too quick to pull out his badge or gun and he remembered. The joint was about an inch thick and contained nothing but about a quarter of a pound of the very highest end Kona buds with nary a trace of stalks or stems. The dealer smiled at all of us as he gave us the sales pitch bullshit about his dope containing only the flowering buds from female plants and how it was worth a thousand dollars a pound. He added that he had lots more—out in his car. Then he fired it up.

This could have been a classic example of "You know you're having a bad day when...four of your five new dope customers are NARCS." It was at this point, however, that the dealer took a huge hit off the burning offering and then passed it to his first potential customer that had accompanied him into the washroom. A semi-circle had formed up in the process, and Tall John was next. He, like Space and myself had already attended the Drugs Investigational Techniques Course which was a two-week educational and instructional course for undercover police officers. One of the earliest topics covered had been how to SIMULATE smoking marijuana when faced with the circumstances that at that moment were occurring. The second goof passed the party joint to Tall John and he perfectly executed the manoeuvre in which he blew smoke and made a great production of appearing to take a hit off the illicit substance. The

Ski was next and it suddenly occurred to the rest of us that we had failed to mention to him that this might occur and what to do. He took a pull off the joint and sucked it in. I gave him a hard look and he smiled back. The joint went around to Space and then myself and back to the dealer where it made another round through the crowd. The Ski got an even bigger face full the second time and Tall John told the dealer he was in for some. About the time the joint burned down, Tall John and the dealer headed out to the parking lot to do the deal, and Space took a fast leak while we counted down a minute or so until we followed the dealer and Tall John out to make the bust.

Space and I started to go after the second dopehead had left to scrape up some cash from somewhere and I said to The Ski: "Let's go." Space and I walked out of the washroom and after about ten steps I realized the take-down team was a man short. I headed back into the washroom and The Ski was standing right where I had left him. I said: "Let's GO!" but he continued to stare at the wall. I yelled at him: "SKI! Time to GO!" He slow-motioned his face towards me and his eyes were crossed. He mumbled: "Huh?" I grabbed him and towed him stumbling along until we got outside and Space took his gun away from him. Tall John was right in the middle of wondering where in the HELL his cover team was and was stalling the dealer, but we made it right after Tall John bought the dope. Space and I shoved the dealer back into his car and Space drove it away while Tall John retrieved The Ski. The dealer never knew The Ski was one of us and we did nothing to change that. The Ski went on to do some pretty good undercover work including popping a local pharmacist who had been supplementing his income for an extended period of time by selling pharmaceuticals without a prescription—at vastly inflated prices—to the area's junkies. He had been a very tough nut to crack and a number of us—including myself—had tried unsuccessfully to make a buy from him before The Ski came along.

There were other times when it was hard to scare up a Drug Squad member even when a very real need for one existed. Towards the end of April was a notably bad period for sustaining manpower in all divisions, as regulations stated that all unused Annual Leave and most other forms of leave must be used up by April 30th of each year so that there would be no carry-over of any leave after May 1st when all the new leave went on the books.

It was a late spring day in that magic time of year in Winnipeg when the snow was melting fast and furiously and there was a lot of standing water everywhere in the streets. The uniform guys downtown made the best sport of it by driving down the flooded curb lanes on Main Street at forty miles per hour causing tidal waves which shot ten feet over the sidewalks and gave a lot of the winos which were shuffling down them the closest thing to a bath they had experienced in months.

It was a Saturday, and for reasons beyond my exact recollection there were only two of us working the dayshift in the entire Vice Division. I was busy hammering out a mountain of paperwork on drug arrest reports and the Acting Sergeant was Bigfoot—who normally was a Detective in the Gambling Unit. There was nothing doing until The Bat Phone rang from the confines of the back Drug Office. We called it that because it meant that there was going to be some business at hand fairly quickly. Informants and potential drug deal sellers were given the number along with some fictitious name all the guys in the Drug Squad gave out to facilitate further contact. I caught it on the third ring and tried to sound sleepy when I croaked a "Yeah?" into the mouth piece.

It was a high school punk who had been supplying most of the West Kildonan school kids with marijuana and LSD for months. I'd done a dial-a-dealer on him about a week before, but he had been sold out for a few days and wanted a number at which to call me back when he got re-supplied so I'd given him the number. He wanted to meet me in an hour outside the shopping center on Leila Avenue just off McPhillips. I said I'd be there and that I'd wait out front by the theatre.

The very first time I had ever seen Bigfoot I was about eighteen years old. It was getting nicely dark, and I was sitting in Browning Park off Westwood Drive with three of my buddies. We were waiting for full darkness to set in before we cracked open the ice-cold twenty-four of Club beer that we had each kicked in a dollar-fifty for. We were laughing and talking and it was just about time to rip open the box of brews when I looked up and I could see my three companions tearing away in a full sprint out of the far end of the park. I was just thinking that they must have lost their minds when something made me look behind me. A giant cop was reaching for my collar. At six foot eight and a quarter and snapping at two hundred and sixty pounds or so he really caught my attention. I could do a 9.9 hundred yard dash in those days and I was forty yards into it in the blink of an eye. A sonic boom echoed in my jet stream: "COME BACK HERE YOU LITTLE BASTARD!" I didn't. When we sneaked back for a look an hour later the giant cop was long gone, with our beer.

Bigfoot had been the product of the very early suburbs' six or eight man police departments which had been assimilated into one of the larger neighbouring ones over time and then finally into the full city amalgamation of police in 1974. He also had some military service, was an accomplished pugilist and was one of the nicest guys I ever worked with. He'd made quite a few of the city's aging bookies suffer the indignity of incontinence just by walking into their places but he just wasn't Drug Squad material. It would have been like trying to make a bull moose in your living room look inconspicuous. As had been the case with myself, once you saw him you never forgot him.

Anyway, I told Bigfoot what was up and he got right on the phone and shopped around to the different divisions within The Public Safety Building looking for a partner for himself so he could cover me while I made the buy. Division 11 volunteered a rookie female officer who looked like she was about sixteen years old and she was back in her jeans and in our office within ten minutes. Bigfoot was pushing fifty, and the female officer came up to his belt buckle when they stood side by side, but we were off and running.

I had a pocketful of script money with recorded serial numbers and Bigfoot and his little partner were watching me from inside the theatre as I stood on the curb out front. Right on time, one of those mid-70's full-sized Chryslers that were about a city block long slid up to me and stopped. The punk behind the wheel had shades on and a smoke sagging out of his lip as he tried to look real "downtown" driving his Daddy's car. He'd brought two other goofs along for muscle. He made sure I was his guy and then told me to get in the back with one of his buddies. The car was a two door model, and he opened the driver's door and I crawled in behind him. He left the door cracked, so I knew it was happening right there. Peach-fuzz beside me was trying to stare me down and hissed "You better not be a cop, man!" I told him to Fuck Off and said to the driver "What have you got? I'm in a hurry."

He pulled out a few bags of marijuana and said "Thirty an ounce." I thought that wasn't bad for a last minute week-end thing—only ten bucks more than it was worth. I said I'd take two and I flipped him the cash. Then I scratched my head and I saw Bigfoot take the cue. He and the mini-cop strolled out of the theatre—holding hands—and moved as if they were going to pass in front of the car. The moron in the front passenger's seat laughed "Look at THIS pair of REJECTS."

All three of them were riveted on the sheer physical magnitude of Bigfoot's close proximity so I fished out my badge. In the next two seconds, I had yelled "POLICE!", Bigfoot was at the driver's door with his salami-sized fingers gripping the top of the open door and the female Constable was giving the front seat passenger a close-up view of the rifling inside the barrel of her service revolver. Stupid—the driver—then decided he would slam his door on Bigfoot's fingers.

Bigfoot reacted instantly and braced a hip against the open driver's door. He then bent the window frame out and down until it was at a right angle to the rest of the door. Then, with his left hand alone, he plucked the kid out of the driver's seat, out of the car and flung him down onto the curb where he planted one of his size fifteen shoes on his neck. The other two became pictures of cooperation and we had it all wrapped up in a few minutes. The dealer gained a bit of his bravado back later on and claimed that he hadn't really pissed his pants when Bigfoot extracted him from the car. He said it was just water from the curb that he had been lying in. He lied.

CHAPTER 9 The Bootlegger

oday's liquor laws have pretty much precluded the possibility of an honest bootlegger being able to make a living—at least in an urban environment. Back in the 1970s and for nearly two decades thereafter this was not the case. One pair of brothers who were well into their seventies by 1978 had taken over the family business that was started by their dear mother before World War Two and made it flourish. They moved from home-brew into beer and whiskey as people became a little more flush in the post-war boom.

From the closing of the bars on Saturday night until the liquor stores and vendors re-opened on Monday they ran non-stop. They had the same telephone number for thirty years. The caller needed only to drop the address and the specifics of the order. The receptionist repeated both back to the caller and that was it. Sometime in the next hour or two at the most, a car would pull up—always a full-sized Ford with a cavernous trunk and always driven by the elder brother. He was a big, tough and street-wise old bastard with built-in radar. He had an uncanny ability to smell a trap and several times had frustrated the Morality Squad members who were set up on an address by making one pass and never coming back. He was particularly shy of any place he hadn't delivered to before. He had the survival skills of a coyote, and as much as he despised any of the dreaded Morality cops, he was quick to pour a few complimentary belts for the criminal investigators from the Detective Division when they dropped by in the wee hours of the night.

It was really just a game. He bootlegged and the Vice Division tried to catch him at it. Since the brothers had known the old regulars in the division for twenty to thirty years, a lot of the enforcement on them was limited to buzzing their house a few times or following the Fords around, which netted nothing for the police.

I was hammering away at reports on a Saturday day shift and the only other guys in the office were the Sergeant of Detectives and my buddy Hector who was transcribing some tapes from a bookmaker's phone tap. Hector had been one of the two original Winnipeg P.D. Drug Squad members back in 1970. He'd made Detective and as he suffered from a bad case of "old face" he moved from the Drug Squad to the Bookmaking Squad but was still up for any kind of mischief at the drop of a hat. We heard the phone ring and the Sergeant of Detectives talking to someone for several minutes. He was a smart guy that everyone liked and respected and he cut us all a lot of slack. When he hung up he walked into the back where we were sitting and laid it out for Hector and me.

The caller had been Clare—a wretch of an old drunk that lived in a dump of an apartment at the south end of Hargrave Street. She had been drying out and was agitated—mostly because she had no money or means of transportation to get herself to the liquor store. While listening to her babble on, the Sergeant of Detectives had ascertained that she was a regular customer of our favourite bootlegger. He unlocked the cabinet that held some seized liquor that was slated for destruction and pulled out two sealed bottles of whiskey. He figured that old Clare would be up for some drinks and after we made friends with her, going back the next day—Sunday—and calling up the bootlegger to deliver some libations to her place would be a natural sequence of events. Hector and I packed up and went for it.

She was half-way through telling us to Fuck Off after she opened her door when she spotted the two jugs of whiskey in Hector's hands. She literally dragged him inside. Securing a sanitary vessel from which to drink was the first big hurdle for us after our noses finally burned out from the stench in the suite. Hector boiled us a couple of glasses and then it was party-time, but we were already four drinks behind by the time we got our first ones poured. You just couldn't beat three year old whiskey with tap water and no ice in such cosmopolitan surroundings. It was like drinking in a garbage dump.

Clare got smoothed out after her sixth drink and settled into a rhythm of a new hit about every five minutes. Hector cajoled her along, and got her to sing a few songs and eventually to give us a Red River jigging demonstration. She started crashing into the furniture after a bit, so we canned the dancing. After we heard her life story, we told her we were having so much fun that we were coming back the next morning with her niece "Lucy". She wasn't sure if she even had a niece named Lucy, but she thought it was a terrific idea nevertheless. The whiskey was running low by then, so we left her with about a third of the last bottle to get her through the evening and we left.

The Sergeant of Detectives had already lined up a savvy female officer for the next day and arranged for me to pick her up at home on my way into the office. I did, but when she opened her front door I almost fell over. She had PINK rollers all over her head with hair sticking out everywhere and no make-up on save the black eye she had designed. With a Band-Aid on one cheek she was perfect— especially with the ratty pink bathrobe she brought along to wear. It was too easy. Hector was off duty that day, so the female officer and I headed over to Clare's while two takedown teams hid themselves inside adjacent apartment blocks. Another team took up surveillance on the bootlegger's house in the North End. A marked patrol unit sat waiting across the river on the South side of the Midtown Bridge in the event we needed them in a hurry.

When we banged on Clare's door she was a little slow in answering it, and had the shakes something terrible. The female officer gave her a big smile and said: "Hi Auntie! It's ME LUCY!" and gave her a hug. Clare was a bit bewildered but remembered me and thought she remembered Lucy. Then she remembered that she was thirsty and asked me what I had brought along to drink. I said that I hadn't been able to find anything on the way over and that we'd have to call for a "delivery." I knew the bootlegger's telephone number from memory, but Clare had it written on the wall by her phone. The female officer dialled it and in a husky voice rasped out Clare's address and ordered two twelves of beer and a mickey of whiskey.

We waited. Twenty minutes later there was a soft knock at the door. The female officer opened the door a bit and peeked out. Tricky Dickie, the old bootlegger's co-pilot and runner recoiled a bit from the sight of her but quietly asked "Did you order something?" Cool as always, the lady cop looked back into the suite and said "Auntie—your delivery guy is here." Clare answered right away with "O.K. Honey" and Tricky Dickie was sold. He went back out to the waiting Ford, popped the trunk and hauled out two cases of Blue and a small bottle of Three Feathers whiskey. The old bootlegger stayed behind the wheel and was rubber-necking in all directions. The runner gum-booted it back up to Clare's suite with the liquor and the female officer paid him with script money that had all the serial numbers pre-recorded. Thirty seconds later the bootlegger and his hired man were handcuffed and the Ford full of booze was on its way to a police impound.

The surveillance team that had been set up on the bootlegger's house had watched him and Tricky Dickie loading up the Ford's trunk. The younger brother had been passing the beer cases and bottles of hard stuff out of a basement window. They got a search warrant and knocked the place over within the hour. About a zillion cases of beer and whiskey were seized and the officers fielded over forty incoming telephone calls in thirty minutes. They recorded all the addresses and the specifics of the liquor orders for court purposes. Clare never did figure out we were cops and that she didn't really have a niece named Lucy.

CHAPTER 10 The Beat

I n my earliest years on the street I probably gained more education than at any other point in my life. I was twenty years old
when I was cast onto the Mean Streets with a book of parking
tags and a whole lot to learn. The department, as a matter of long-
established practice, always started new constables off on night
shift—sort of an Initiation by Fire. Every police officer was required
to attend and pass Recruit Class, but often a year or more of active
service passed before that opportunity to attend actually occurred.
Quite prudently, new officers did not get issued with a firearm nor
were they allowed to operate a police vehicle until they had at least
proven themselves to possess at least a modicum of common sense
and maturity. Contrarily, today it seems that it has become trendy
for police officers to be fully trained and equipped to perform their
duties BEFORE they are tasked with life and death decisions. Who
could have ever guessed.

At the commencement of every tour of duty, the entire shift,
with the exception of the two patrol units which had earlier start
times, would line up for a quasi-formal inspection from the duty
Sergeant. At exactly FIVE minutes before the hour, we stood in a
single line, cars crews closest to the door, followed by the beat
men. All members stood at attention, while presenting unloaded
revolver, handcuffs and billet club for the perusal of the Sergeant

and Patrol Sergeant. Your person and your equipment were given a varying range of scrutiny, usually something between a casual glance and a full strip search. One particularly barrel-chested old Sergeant who could have hired out scaring babies on the side, would squint down revolver barrels as he moved along and often you could hear "There's a FUCKING spider in there with a long, gray beard." Another of his favourites was to look you over and then ask: "When's the funeral?" The blank look on your face would then prompt: "Your FUCKING barber's. If you want to be a FUCKING hippie you're in the wrong lineup!" He would never say much about the always important shine on each officer's boots. If, after a quick look at the footwear, he decided that some weren't quite up to his standards, he would stare intensively at the offender while grinding his right boot sole onto the top of the less than perfect boot. At the end, he would bark "Left FACE! Quick march!" and the boys would turn and quick step it out the door. If any matter of required correction had been recorded, it was in the very best interests of one's personal health and well-being to insure that it had been remedied by the next day's inspection.

New cops walked the beat for about two or three years. Until attrition created a vacancy in a cruiser car regular crew, the beat was your life. In the meantime, if the Gods were smiling, one "relieved" in the district patrol cars on a "as-required" basis, filling in for the regular patrol car members who were on holidays, in court, in the station writing reports or whatever. The stints could be as short as an hour or as long as a week, but it saved on the shoe leather and exposed us to the real world of policing and the adrenal rush and insanity of police pursuits.

Most people don't know that the Winnipeg Police Department made an armed invasion of the United States of America in the late 1970s. It was only two of our guys, but it WAS a surprise attack and was initially deemed to be an Act of War by our neighbours to the south. The high speed pursuit of a stolen car in Winnipeg had somewhat escalated and in those days the term "abort" seemingly wasn't in the police vocabulary. The boys MIGHT have considered the international and jurisdictional issues and thrown in the towel at the border, but—in for a penny...in for a pound...and they blew the gates at Pembina at a hundred and twenty miles an hour right behind the suspect. When the smoke cleared after a spectacular crash several miles into North Dakota and some allegations of shots being fired, the U.S. Border Patrol kept our suspect but were kind enough to later release our officers and returned the police unit which they had seized.

There were no portable radios in the very early 1970s and each of the numerous beats had a number of the now highly collectible police call boxes. Each beat man or crew of two officers was required to make a call each hour from a call box to let the staff in the dispatch center know that they were still alive. If, for any reason there was a call on your beat or an urgent message, the red light went on at the top of all the call boxes on your beat and you attended to the closest one at your leisure to answer, as long as you did it within the next thirty seconds. If you missed an hourly call, or failed to call in within the prescribed time when a red light was illuminated—even if your next call box was three blocks away—someone with stripes was going to hand you your ass in the minutes that followed.

The Patrol Sergeant could be your best friend or your worst enemy depending on how badly you needed support or what he caught you doing. With the exception of one or two, they were universally stone-faced, middle-aged and impeccably turned out. The exceptions were a couple of recently promoted vets who would smile if they saw you fall down a flight of stairs or do something equally entertaining. I swear these guys woke up neat. After a fourteen block foot chase and a two minute all-out brawl with a break-in suspect, they would pull up, fix you with a terse stare and then enquire as to why you were out of uniform, as your hat was not on your head.

Deportment was everything in my earliest days and saluting was a big part of it. EVERYONE got to their feet whenever the Chief or Deputy Chief entered the room and remained at attention until directed to do otherwise. It was incumbent on the senior man present to announce them with a snappy "Ten-hut!" If the encounter occurred on the street, the single officer would snap to attention, salute and hold it until the salute was returned. This included any time the officer might be involved in any other matter—up to and including a gun battle. To really complicate matters, when a gaggle of several newer constables were being "marched" out to their beats from the station by a Patrol Sergeant, only the Patrol Sergeant was to salute and the subordinate ranks were to respond to a sharp "EYES LEFT" (or RIGHT) on his command while on the move. It couldn't be done. Just trying to keep seven or eight young cops with no military experience in step was in itself nearly impossible, but when you threw in the variables of "sometimes you do and sometimes you don't" salute, the whole deal was doomed to failure. Invariably, the Patrol Sergeant who led the circus and had saluted was reflexively aped immediately by about half of the troop while the other half were debating which side left or right was actually on. Usually within moments of the passing Chief or Deputy taking his leave with a shaking head, the Patrol Sergeant would halt the troop and demonstrate which side was the left one and which was the right by waving the appropriate arm and cursing loudly with every breath. To passing motorists, we must have appeared to be in the middle of a Macarena lesson from a lunatic.

One of the young officers who walked the beat adjacent to mine was at his Traffic Point at Portage and Donald at 4:30 P.M. one crisp autumn day when the Deputy Chief's car passed by as it did each afternoon when the Deputy was chauffeured home. Snapping rigidly to attention, my colleague threw up his best precision salute. He was kind of a Lord Baden-Powell type anyway and was really into those Sam Browne belts and other non-functional crap that we had to wear back then. Unfortunately, in his haste he rapped the brim of his forage cap with his saluting hand and it tumbled off his head, rolled off the curb and was promptly flattened by a succession of cars. He had hardly retrieved it and balanced what was left of it back on his head when the red light went on at the nearest call box. The dispatch operator informed him that the Deputy Chief had just radioed in and enquired as to the identity of the IDIOT who was walking Five Beat.

A big part of the Patrol Sergeant's job was to insure that all beat officers had correctly and punctually deployed to their respective beats and that they were patrolling their beats in the prescribed fashion. Matters of crucial importance, such as walking in step if officers were partnered, walking the beat FACING oncoming traffic, and being on the beat's designated Traffic Point during rush hour were the department's original Zero Tolerance policies. The Patrol Sergeant recorded the exact time of each visit that he made to a beat officer and the officer's beat notebook had best reflect the exact notation when the book was turned in at the end of each shift. If you failed to turn in your Beat Book at the end of your shift you received a rather graphic telephone call from the Sergeant on the shift following along with an invitation to return to the station forthwith and do so.

I was walking Eight X (extended) Beat alone on Portage Avenue one balmy January night as the temperature plunged to forty-four below. I hit the street at midnight and was hoofing it west on The Avenue from Balmoral to Maryland. It was so cold the call-boxes wouldn't work and I didn't see another live person with the exception of a handful of cabs. The ONLY thing open was the Mall Bus Station and you could get in to warm up if you could wake up the night security guard who was usually drunk. I couldn't. My lunch wasn't until 4:30 A.M. and I was just settling into the first detectible signs of hypothermia when I spotted the Patrol Sergeant's car cruising slowly up the other side of the street. He raised both hands and pointed to his watch as he went by. I'd been visited.

Main Street Beats One and Two were in the infamous Drag...a combat zone of bars and flea-bag hotels and subsequently there were usually always four beat men—in two pairs—assigned on the late shifts in that six blocks. It was a track meet most nights: running from one bar fight to the next, loading drunks into the Patrol Wagon and quite often scraping assorted drinkers off the road who had staggered off the sidewalks and into oncoming traffic. The day shifts were painfully boring by comparison, but most times at least two beat officers were sent out on a regular basis. In the summer of 1973 I was about as regular as it got and put in about a straight three months on Main Street. The constable I walked with a lot was a good guy noted for his stamina at partying which had earned him the nickname of Lester Liquor. We quickly figured out how to get through a slow day shift on The Drag.

It was a Sunday and one of the two battered movie theatres on our beat had a condemned balcony. It was cool up there on those hot summer afternoons when no one had yet invented short sleeved shirts on Police uniforms. We got to know the guy that managed the place pretty well, and he seemed like an okay fellow despite some loose talk we'd heard about his past involving farm animals. He was good for a large Coke and one of those giant buckets of popcorn whenever the weekend matinees were on, so my partner and I, after about three passes on our beat, headed over, grabbed our goodies and settled in for a quiet afternoon in our private box watching Werewolves on Wheels. It didn't seem like we'd been up there for an hour and a half. Suddenly, our friend, the lifetime banishee from Aunt Sally's Farm came flying up the balcony stairs and breathily announced that he'd seen some old guy in a police car pull up across the street and park about an hour before. He hadn't thought much about it except that he was still there and looked like he was sort of watching the front of the theatre, and that he kept looking at his watch. Just now, he had left the car and was headed for the front doors. He finished up by adding the fact that the older cop was wearing stripes. The movie screen in my head began flashing "Oh SHIT!!!" about every tenth of a second.

Retreat was hopeless. In two seconds, we thought it through. If we ran back down the stairs to the entrance we would meet the Patrol Sergeant face to face—either on the sidewalk if we went out the front doors or in the lobby if he came in. In either case, he had us. Neglect of Duty was VERY serious shit in those days. We would have been royally screwed if he had caught us. We knew that he knew EXACTLY how long it had been since he had most likely SEEN us come in and the old bastard had probably been sitting out there—giggling to himself—as we were lollygagging in the balcony hanging our own asses out to dry! We told our manager friend to tell him that we had walked in quite a while earlier in the day and that we had walked through the theater and out the emergency exit into the alley. And then we jumped off the balcony.

The bottom of the theater was packed with mostly children and young adults from the core area and we didn't squash any of them too badly in the twelve foot drop to the seats below. After a couple of startled cries and a "Whaddaya fuckin' doin', eh??" when we spilled some drinks and stepped on a fat kid's hot dog, we were gone. At full speed we crashed through the back door and into the lane and sprinted North to Higgins Ave. A quick look around the corner at Main St. revealed the parked black and white but the Patrol Sergeant was still inside the theater trying to squawk our savior. We dashed across Main Street in about three seconds and ducked into the alley behind the Mount Royal Hotel. Being young and athletic, we weren't even puffing a minute later, and we were casually spot checking a couple of dirt bags when the black and white wheeled into the alley off Higgins a few minutes after that. We already had all their pockets inside out with the contents all over the ground and were diligently recording all information on the prescribed Spot Check Form when he pulled up. We also had already made a couple of other entries into our Beat notebooks. He was so mad he was purple. When he first tried to talk he could only make hissing noises.

Finally, he could speak. "You two FUCKING PUNKS think you're pretty cute, DON'T you??"

I responded with my best theatrical innocence, "Whatever do you mean, Patrol Sergeant?"

"I know you two were in there watching that FUCKING movie all afternoon. I SAW you go in there! Do you think I'm fucking STUPID?"

There was a long pause. I actually thought about it, but I went with, "Um, well, Sir...we WERE in the theatre maybe a couple of hours ago...for just a few minutes...we regularly check on ALL the businesses on our beat. We did roust a couple of miscreants who were creating a minor disturbance and ejected them from the premises via the alley exit as it was the closest...and then we resumed our foot patrol. I have their names and the time in my Beat Book. Here they are!"

As I held out my notebook he grabbed it and threw it at the row of garbage cans behind the hotel. I knew our guy at the theatre had held firm. When we talked to him about it a few days later he said the old Sarge had been so mad to find us gone he was even trying to get some of the movie-goers to answer his questions, but it appeared they were tired of cops interrupting their show so they threw popcorn boxes at him and told him to fuck off.

The Patrol Sergeants were at least predictable and everyone knew the rules going in. It was when some senior Constable who had stars in his eyes got to be an ACTING Patrol Sergeant for a stint that the guys in my era needed to be extra cautious because these types were out to make a name for themselves—usually at someone else's expense. Some of them were pretty hilarious to the rest of us in their Quest for Stripes. It was in the course of a regular Patrol Sergeant's duties to "view" every person arrested by patrol officers for being drunk and prior to them being detained at the local Drunk Tank until they sobered up. Obviously, all constables of the day were deemed to be too stupid to determine if a person was intoxicated on their own. So, you arranged to meet with a Patrol Sergeant—who sat at The Pinnacle of Knowledge—at a place of convenience, often just outside the Drunk Tank. At that point, the detainee could be officially deemed as intoxicated by a third police officer who was at least as medically unqualified to make this determination as the original two that had made the arrest. The old regulars would pull up in their car and give the two constables a wave without ever looking at the drunk and that was it. The arresting constables had a name for the "viewed by" box on the arrest form and the world kept turning.

Occasionally, one of the really-motivated-to-get-promoted "actors" would pull up in the Patrol Sergeant's unit, jump out of the car and start smelling your drunk. We'd already been trying NOT to for fifteen minutes and we could have told him that the guy stunk if he'd asked us. After checking for the smell of liquor the zealous wanna-be would commence with several questions like: "Sir! Have you been drinking?" I'm sure a lot of the regular old drunks were thinking, "Oh no, I always puke all over myself, piss my pants and smell like a dead sasquatch's ass because I'm a lifetime abstainer. Hellloooo…" Usually, guys in the senior car crews wouldn't put up with it and before long there'd be a: "You gonna read him a fucking bed-time story too, you fucking RETARD?" or something equally demeaning to the perceived respect that the mere presence of one "acting" commanded.

There was one particular senior constable who'd been in the country for about twenty years from Jolly Old but had maintained an uncorrupted British accent. Pip-pip and all that shit. I'd worked a cruiser car with him a few times when I was pulled off the beat to relieve for his regular partner. He was actually okay when he was just one of the boys working the cars, except for the fact that he was a consummate bullshitter. If one just mentioned in passing that they knew a guy who had ten million dollars, three estates, six Rolls Royces and a dozen thoroughbred horses, HIS friend had eleven million bucks, four ranchos in Argentina, nine Rolls Royces and two Bentleys, thirteen horses AND a three legged donkey. As my old Texas Grand-daddy would have said … The first liar didn't have a chance. In any case, when this particular individual hit a tour of being the Acting Patrol Sergeant one night shift, spring was well underway and I was relieving in his spot in a North End cruiser car.

My buddy Two-Gun was relieving on another North End unit and like myself, he loved the action and was up for just about anything. Quite normally for a Friday night in that end of town, the cars had been going like a half-wit pinsetter in a forty lane bowling alley right from the get-go. It was still about half dark with dawn just hinting in the eastern sky when Two-Gun broke the brief radio silence. He exclaimed that they were in pursuit of TWO stolen cars that had been playing Demolition Derby on Keewatin Street when they happened along. Both cars were loaded with punks and when they had dumped the cars and ran west into a newly developing industrial area they had a fair head start. The swarm of cruiser cars were well into Organized Chaos Mode when my partner and I arrived at the end of the pavement and found one little shit-rat cuffed to a light standard and a second farther up the street firmly manacled to the abandoned back and white. Off to the west lay at least two miles of sheet water from the snow melt. Small icebergs floated here and there in it and if you squinted, you could just make out a small herd of fleeing two-legged rodents several hundred yards out throwing up a pretty good spray of water in their haste—with Two-Gun in hot pursuit a couple of hundred yards behind. We had no idea what had happened to Two-Gun's partner until we heard it. KA-BLAM! KA-BLAM! KA-BLAM!

Way off to the north at least a half a mile and a lot farther west, a lone figure seemed to be the source. Quite intelligently, the more senior half of the crew had remained dry by legging it along a collapsing dirt road that was JUST above the rising waters and with some pretty good long distance running had pulled abreast of and actually a little past the fleeing band of street-scum. Utilizing a fair bit of forward allowance and a lot of Kentucky windage he had lobbed a trio of .38 Specials into the water well AHEAD of the fleeing flock who were making it to freedom. The desired effect was immediately noticeable, as the herd of hooligans swapped ends and picked up considerable speed as they began slogging back towards Two-Gun. About twenty minutes later, Two-Gun beached the whole lot at the abandoned cruiser car after making them all SWIM the whole way back from the point where he had rounded them up. Much to everyone's amusement, it had been observed that whenever one of them had attempted to stand back up and get out of the somewhat cool water, Two-Gun would kick them in the ass and knock them back down.

It was at this point that the Acting Patrol Sergeant arrived. Puffing himself up with importance, he announced "By Jove, I thawt I heard SHAWTS." He then began to look around accusingly at the gamut of officers—both wet and dry—who were assembled. A senior member spoke up. "You didn't hear FUCK ALL you crumpet-burning ASSHOLE. Get the FUCK outta here!" One or two other more senior guys threw in a supportive "Yeah. FUCK OFF." He sniffed indignantly and then left. I swear even his sniff had an English accent.

CHAPTER 11 The North End

I loved the North End. It rocked and rolled all night long and the three cars that patrolled it before the amalgamation of the municipal police departments were amongst the busiest vehicles anywhere. Coupled with the fact that a lot of the North End crews were made up of some of the toughest and smartest street cops I ever knew, it was a perfect learning environment for a young officer if he kept his mouth shut and his eyes and ears open. They seemed to have a language all of their own. Instead of "Pull over, Sir" after spotting some road warrior peeling off a half a block of rubber, it was "Grab a piece of the curb, Asshole," over the loudspeaker. While their courage was enviable and their intentions always honourable, I somehow suspected that their sensitivity was NOT what had drawn some of them to police work. This suspicion was borne out with absolute clarity by one incident in the spring of 1974.

As the incident had been related to me by the equally junior constable who was working a North End unit with a seasoned regular crew member, I shall attempt to relay it as accurately as I can. It occurred at about 11:00 A.M. on a beautiful day when spring was emerging into summer. On one of the busier thoroughfares, the patrolling officers observed a frail, elderly lady standing at an intersection, feebly waving her perfectly ironed lace handkerchief in an attempt to catch their attention. The poor dear was obviously distraught and within seconds they were at her side enquiring as to how they might assist her. She was nearly ninety and her spotless black Victorian dress was beautifully adorned with a solitary band of white lace at the fully buttoned neck and descended far enough to properly cover her ankles and just touch the tops of her shiny black squash-heeled shoes. Her hat was pinned perfectly into place over her nearly blue hair, and beneath her tiny spectacles both cops could see her bright eyes were tearing. She steeled herself enough to get it out. "Oh, officers! Just over there a POOR kitty seems to be injured and unable to care for itself. Won't you PLEASE see what you can do to help it??"

Looking to the spot under some low bushes about fifteen feet from the lady they spotted it. Even at that distance they could see the source of her concern for what it really was—a hissing black tomcat the size of a small puma with testicles hanging like golf balls. The old stud was as wild as he was filthy and scarred. His ears had been half chewed off from a thousand fights and he literally spat at the contemplation of being touched by a human hand for the first time in his life. The younger cop moved in for a bit of a closer look, confirming that the cat's back was broken—most likely by a passing vehicle—and was amazed to witness that even with an injury that would totally incapacitate most creatures, Snooky was not going to go quietly into the night. The old fighter coiled his front end to spring when the officer got too close and unsheathed a set of front claws that looked like mini-linoleum knives as it prepared to disembowel anything within reach.

The older cop moved the few feet to the car and fished under the front seat for a few seconds. After extracting one of the pair of two foot African hardwood truncheons with the royal purple braided wrist-bands, he moved past the hopeful lady and towards the bush. The cat was already voicing its displeasure when the three precision, full-powered overhead strikes to its head staccatoed a distinct WHAM! WHAM! WHAM! Both officers then bade the grandma a good afternoon and drove away, with her staring open-mouthed after them.

Not long afterwards, in the same era, a young constable named Super Dave had been assigned to uniform patrol duties in the

North End on his first posting after recruit class. His mentor and partner was the one and only Frenchie—which may have had a lot to do with how Super Dave turned out like he did. One of the first things that Frenchie did when he got a new partner—especially a fairly gullible and junior one—was to explain that he was actually a Siamese twin and that he had a brother. He'd elaborate by explaining that when they were born they had been joined at the groin, but that his brother had never physically developed with the exception of one weepy eye.

They were working dayshift on a beautiful summer morning when they caught the call regarding "an injured man." Sure enough, on the west sidewalk of Main Street just north of the subway, when they pulled up they could see a body sprawled onto its side. It was being totally ignored by the several passing pedestrians as his pockets had already been turned inside out by an earlier Good Samaritan. The fellow was Aboriginal, about thirty years old, and the fact that he was reeking of booze was the very least of his problems. He was lying in a about an inch deep pool of his own blood and it appeared that if his heart kept it up much longer it was going to have to switch over to "reserve."

A closer look revealed that he had just very recently undergone a fairly deliberate tomahawking as there was a vertical, five inch gash above his right ear that had cleaved well into his skull. While the officers were waiting for the ambulance, they got the usual abundance of information—none—concerning a possible identity of the male victim or what might have happened.

After the ambulance went wailing off into the distance, the boys started to backtrack on the blood trail that a blind man could have followed. It meandered north along the sidewalk about a hundred yards to the entrance of the old apartment block on the next corner. They went straight in, followed the blood splashes right up the stairs where they came to a stop outside of a suite door on the second floor. The place was all quiet and they knocked. Nothing. Frenchie hammered on the door a bit louder and hollered "Police." This caused some muffled movements from within but no one made any attempt to open the door. Following correct police procedure for just such occurrences, Frenchie began kicking the door and yelled "GODDAMN IT! I SAID POLICE!! OPEN THE FUCKING DOOR!"

The locked turned and the door opened an inch. The smell of soap and freshly baked bread wafted out. The boys were somewhat taken back, as urine and vomit were the usual olfactory indicators most often encountered from the suites in the area. Upon peeking in, there was no blood inside, and they were met by the fearful glances of a portly and immaculately attired older lady wearing a starched apron. They eased in. Once inside, it all started to make sense. She was from right off the Steppes, and her English was halting at best. She and her late husband had immigrated over twenty years earlier, and she had been living alone in her little apartment since his death as the neighbourhood crumbled around her. The place was so clean you could have eaten off the floor and the colours and floral patterns of her three room group screamed "Kern-Hill Furniture Co-op" from just up the street. The couch, chair and lampshades still had the shipping plastic on them to help keep them in pristine condition.

Super Dave picked it up. "Baba, can you tell me what happened here?" and he pointed to the beginning of the blood trail out in the hallway. She began to tremble and sob, and Super Dave put his arm around her and told her that now that they were there no one could hurt her and she would be okay. She calmed somewhat and then spoke. "Poleets, I tell. Bad man cummit." Ever patient, Super Dave nudged her along. "Baba, why did the bad man come here?" She grew instantly more agitated, and forcefully answered "Bad man CUMMIT! Try break-it door! Try steal my HROSHI!"

Frenchie pulled Super Dave aside and whispered "What the FUCK is hroshi? Is that those little buns with the cabbage in them?" Despite his strong leadership qualities, Frenchie sometimes faltered when persons he was dealing with used strange terminology. Years later, while Frenchie was in the Vice Division, he had accompanied a few of the Drug Squad guys—including myself—on a search warrant over on Stradbrook Ave. Some long haired waste of oxygen we were rousting had called him a Neanderthal, and Frenchie smacked him a resounding open-hander and yelled at him "Don't you ever call me a fucking DUTCHMAN, you lump of shit—I'm FRENCH!!"

Super Dave had grown up in the North End and he explained to Frenchie that the lady was talking about money. Making progress, Super Dave kept it rolling. "Baba, what did you do when the bad man tried to break your door?" Tears began streaming down her face and still trembling she got it out. "I HIT!" Super Dave knew he was almost there and giving her another little pat on the shoulder, he went for broke. "Now Baba, can you tell me what you hit the bad man with?" She walked the few steps to the little broom closet beside the suite door and extracted her Army Surplus fire axe with the four foot hickory handle and the still dripping blade and passed it to them. Super Dave wrapped it up with, "Baba, why did the bad man think that you have money here?"

She left the room for a few seconds and returned from the back bedroom with a small zippered vinyl bag. She placed it on her tiny table and opened it up. There was something over thirty thousand dollars in cash. Amazed that she had lived that long in a place where life and death were often decided by possession of a case of beer, they talked to her for a while and got all the facts. She knew about banks, but her late husband had not trusted them and as a matter of course, she didn't either. Super Dave explained to her that banks were good and that he put his money in a bank. That was good enough for her.

Frenchie filled up on that morning's batch of cabbage rolls and home-made buns while Super Dave hoofed it the block and a half to the bank and retrieved the manager. He was a fine man and after hearing of the lady's dilemma, he insisted on coming down with Super Dave himself. He patiently explained to her how the bank worked and assured her that when she would come down to put money in or take money out he would look after her himself. The boys accompanied the manager back to his bank with the cash after a careful accounting, and then returned the bank book to her. She was all smiles when they left to check on the axe wound recipient and ascertained that he would recover. I didn't read the report myself, but I'm sure it contained all the pertinent information surrounding the male's fall down the stairs in the apartment block due his advanced state of intoxication—where he had struck his head on the handrail—and that he couldn't remember anything about it when they questioned him at a later time in the hospital.

My own very brief first exposure to The North End had occurred in the previous spring just a week or two after I hit the street. I was still on my first two week night shift—walking solo—and I was instructed to remain at the call box when I made my first hourly call as a car would be picking me up as a relief. I waited by the box for about forty-five minutes, but one did not question instructions from the Sergeant. Finally one of the North End's units rolled up, bumped the curb and stopped—it being a station wagon that had a small jump seat in the back along with a stretcher and a bunch of First Aid shit that nobody knew how to use.

The old vet driving had one foot out the door of the downtown station and was due to retire within a few weeks. He was drunk as a rat. Naturally, I would be jumping and taking the reports as my very senior partner wheeled us around. It was an unusually quiet night and he blabbered for a while as we cruised the outlying areas of the District but he wound down and his marginally passable driving began to deteriorate somewhat and then somewhat more. I was just asking him if he knew HE was driving as we were passing a large bottling plant at the edge of the prairie when he keeled over. We were westbound at about twenty-five miles per hour when he just flopped over in the seat. The old boy was a BIG guy—probably six foot three and two hundred and twenty pounds. When I was yelling at him to wake up and trying to push him back upright, the cruiser hopped the curb, crossed about fifty feet of lawn and bounced up and into the middle of the industrial landscaping right in front of the soft drink plant.

After three full laps around the cruiser, I could still only get my brain to compute "Oh SHIT!" I had been around long enough to avoid undergoing complete hysteria and I willed myself to THINK about it for a minute. After ascertaining that my partner hadn't had the big one—and was actually merely passed out—I did a twelve second analysis. I was facing a couple of little problems. I couldn't get him out of the driver's seat and into the passenger's side by myself if my life depended on it. Further, even if I could have, I wasn't approved at that point in time to operate a Police vehicle. The immediate problem I was facing was to get the police car out of the rock garden it was jammed into before some John Q. Citizen drove by and saw it and called the Mayor or somebody. My Probationary Constable's ass was in need of some serious help. I grabbed the radio and requested that another North End unit meet with us as we needed a traffic tag as we were out and I gave the location. I had already picked up on that requesting a traffic tag from another unit could mean The Shit Has Hit The Fan—Come NOW! Unit 25 answered and showed up within three or four minutes. After they stopped laughing, they pulled my old partner out and carried him around the other side and loaded him into the rear jump seat. The two of them—both big Interlake Ukrainian boys off the farm—pushed that hulking Plymouth wagon off the rocks like it was nothing while I steered it back out. They told me to go ahead and drive the car—there was nothing else that could be done. I was worried that I might get a call and they told me they'd make sure I didn't. They were right. I followed them to a quiet spot and parked it while my partner slept it off. I missed lunch but the boys in Unit 25 brought us a coffee about 5:30 A.M. and got the old boy awake. We hit the barn an hour later and when we were getting out he said "Nice working with you, kid." I was thinking "Oh yeah. Likewise, DICKHEAD!" I was walking on eggshells for the next three days after he had signed off and submitted the Unit Activity Report for that night, but it slid through.

Not too long afterwards, I once again was awestruck by my law enforcement colleagues' abilities to correctly decipher a coded radio message. I was sitting in the passenger seat of a downtown black and white while relieving with a jovial and popular constable who stayed but a few years on the job. It was a steaming hot July night—about 11:00 P.M.—and it was still well over eighty degrees. We had all the windows down as air conditioning for police cars had not yet been invented. As we passed Polo Park—one of the city's first mall style shopping centres—my partner nodded towards the land-yacht sized New Yorker that was loafing along right beside us. It was apparent that those inside were not of a mind to pass us even though we were cruising well under the speed limit. It was four kids and they were all looking STRAIGHT ahead. Not only did they not want to pass us they didn't even want to look at us. We pulled them over.

My partner was having a little chat with the driver. They looked like good kids and he hadn't bothered with the drivers license and registration as they hadn't been doing anything wrong. He had ascertained that it was the kid's dad's car and everything was pretty much in order when we shined a light onto the floor in the back seat. There, still sweating from the cooler at a downtown vendor that was a bit less particular about proper I.D., lay TWO sealed twenty-fours of beer. We asked the driver how old he was. Sixteen. The other three were fifteen, sixteen and fourteen—also a might short of the magic eighteen that The Liquor Act required. My partner opened the back door, removed the beer and informed the now scared silly quartet that they may be summonsed. He was already half way back to our cruiser car with the beer when the driver called to him, "Don't you want our names?"

About a minute later, my partner grabbed the mike and announced: "Car Number 3—we need a traffic tag if another unit could meet us," and he gave the cross streets adjacent to a secluded parking lot in an industrial area nearby. Within five minutes no less than seven units had met us and forty-eight very cold ones were gone in less than ten. Even the Acting Patrol Sergeant had dropped by—a really good sort who got his stripes within the year.

I was only assigned to The North End for one short stint when I came out of the Drug Squad after three years in Vice. It only lasted fifteen months or so, as the department was in a period of sweeping changes. Rank integration along with other initiatives had people moving throughout the divisions in a whirlwind of transfers and promotions, but despite it, the North End remained pretty much the same including the demeanor of the officers that policed it. I think, in hindsight, it just required a special style of enforcement.

I had just got my first promotion and was touring around one spring day in the North End's supervisor unit. It was a beautiful spring day—more like early May than early March—and I saw a kid about eight years old pounding away with his fists on an over-turned bicycle on the corner of Charles and Selkirk. I pulled over and got out of my patrol car right beside him. He was crying and still whacking at the bike and in my friendliest public relations manner I asked: "Hey Little Buddy. Is something wrong with your bike?" Obviously a little wise beyond his years besides being very dirty, he looked at me like I was three kinds of stupid and answered, "It's SHITTY and FUCKED-UP!" I threw the bike in the trunk while silently wondering why he wasn't in school, but I took him over to the Dari-Whip a couple of blocks down and he demolished a dou-ble cheeseburger with chili and about a bale of French fries. Three Cokes later I got his life story. His sister—who was fifteen AND a hooker—had this boyfriend who was twenty-three and just out of jail who gave him the bike which later came up as stolen when I ran the serial number. The kid had no idea who his father was and his mother left him alone for days at a time. They lived in a shit-hole in the Lord Selkirk Development known universally in police circles as The Virus Village. He was in Grade Two when he managed to get to school. I made the appropriate phone calls to the social agencies and was told they'd add the case to their list of those that were waiting.

Half a Point Harry had been a Patrol Sergeant in Traffic when I start-ed on the job. Over the years, I got to know him better and I always found him to be personable and professional. He was extremely knowledgeable in the Highway Traffic Act and most other statutes, and was a natural leader with his calm and confident manner. He had picked up his strange nickname from when he had reviewed each cruiser car crew's Unit Daily Activity Report. As part of his du-ties, he recorded the totals of all units' traffic tickets, parking tags and the like, but he only awarded one HALF point to each of the two officers for each offence notice that crew gave out. Most other Sergeants, as a matter of course, awarded ONE point to each officer for each tag, but not Harry. One ticket—split two ways—was HALF a point each-period. Subsequently, it was a bit harder for the crews he supervised to get their personal totals out of the danger zone each month which could result in a first class ass-chewing from the Inspector if one's ticket total was a bit low.

I was down to my last few days in the North End before I was shipped out with my new stripes and was patrolling alone on a dayshift in the Supervisor's unit. 'A man with a knife' call was broadcast to the North End units, and not unusually, all of the regular patrol units were tied up. The place was only a few blocks from the Hartford Avenue station, and I radioed that I was close by and would be taking it in. Half a Point Harry was the Divisional Inspector at the time and I had no idea he was even out of the station. He had been downtown and was just returning to the North End station when he too had heard the call go out.

When I pulled up in front, Half a Point Harry was standing off to the side of the front steps and I parked behind his unit and walked over. The snow was fairly deep, and I had failed to see the prone and unconscious male lying in the snow off to the side of the house's front steps until I got right up there. The Inspector was looking a little sheepish and wasn't saying much, but I did notice that there was a huge butcher knife lying on the sidewalk and a metal snow shovel with the blade dented into the shape of a human head lying right beside it. He always called me "John." He said in his usual calm manner: "John, would you be kind enough to see that this gets wrapped up appropriately?" I assured him that I would and he left. The knife-wielder was as drunk as a rat when he finally came to, and I had a crew convey him down to the Drunk Tank after ascertaining that he hadn't carved anybody up in the neighbourhood.

Red was actually working in plainclothes in the North End that winter, and just the day before Christmas, the entirety of the Detective Division had barricaded themselves into their office to toast the season. No one cared, as it was a tradition of long standing, but after five or six hours, it started to get a little too boisterous in that Indian leg-wrestling, singing and general mayhem had taken over. Half a Point Harry decided to head down the hall and suggest that perhaps the boys might wrap it up for the day, but his knocking on the locked door went unanswered. He was just starting to get a little miffed about it, as he WAS the Inspector, standing in the hallway in his starched white uniform shirt and mirror-polished black oxfords with EVERYONE ignoring him. However, Red suddenly realized that he might have just had a bit too much Christmas cheer and decided to break loose of the fortification of the Detective Office and make a hurried trip to the men's room which was right across the hall. He bolted out the door and failed to even see Half a Point Harry who was standing less than two steps away. Red later told me his vision may have been slightly off and his legs weren't working quite up to snuff, but he was a man on a mission stumbling straight towards the washroom door when Half a Point Harry caught his arm. Red said he remembered seeing SOMETHING white in front of him, which was most likely the Inspector's shirt, and was aware that someone was quite tersely addressing him but he couldn't make out what the person was saying. He had lost the momentum to make it into the men's room, so he said he just bent over right there and did a projectile vomit all over Half a Point Harry's shiny shoes.

The North End's uniform patrol was subjected to the same policing duties as the other five patrol districts in the city besides being subjected to a ten-fold greater call load for fights and other calls of a violent nature. One of the truly annoying items on the slate was the service of Traffic Warrants. In a quiet district where there was NEVER anything much doing, it was no big deal. In fact, it may have been the sole form of entertainment in some areas for the whole shift. Somehow, the execution of a $34.00 unpaid Traffic By-law conviction seemed a little out of place in the Land of Murder and Mayhem, but it was your ass if they didn't get done.

I had just been promoted in the late winter of 1980-81 and was riding with a new kid who was a farm boy from out near Warren, Manitoba. The snow was deep and it was excruciatingly cold for jumping in and out of the cruiser car unnecessarily, but we had been given a mitt full of nickel and dime Traffic Warrants in our patrol area so we went right after them. Our first stop was for some guy who lived on Jefferson Avenue just east of Main Street. I pulled the cruiser car right up in front of the house.

The front of the place was snowed under and it was obvious that the front entrance hadn't been used since the first snowflake had fallen three months earlier. The lights were on in the house, but the curtains were all drawn so we couldn't see anything inside as we took the side pathway through the snowdrifts to the rear entrance of the little bungalow. As soon as we got out of the car, Grace Slick was being heard loud and clear all the way downtown. I had the warrant in my hand as we stepped up onto the stoop by the back door. It was for a whopping $14.00 unpaid fine. I knocked on the door twice without any results whatsoever, and then I really wound up and started to pound on it. It popped open on about the third whack, and the next thing I noticed was that the smoke—as in marijuana smoke—was so thick inside the place that you could have taken a bite out of it and chewed it.

We walked in through the tiny kitchen and could see a group of three idiots staring out at our marked police car through the small part they had made in the curtains. We could also see that the generous-sized coffee table was literally heaped with small bundles of Thai sticks and there were four or five burning in ash trays around the room. I put my finger to my lips so that my partner would remain quiet and we just stood there. The idiots were yelling over the music to each other, "Where the FUCK did those cops go?" and other highly intelligent exclamations until one of them finally turned around. We were standing about six feet from them. I punched the stereo button to "Off" and making sure I used correct wording for the benefit of my very junior partner I said: "You Fuck-heads are under arrest."

I asked the three geniuses which one of them was Mr. So-and-so who was named on the warrant. The scruffiest one spoke right up and said he was. After thinking it all over for a few seconds, he exclaimed: "You got a WARRANT?" I said: "Oh Yeah. Right here—with your name on it." I held my thumb over the Traffic Fine part as I showed it very briefly to him and dejectedly he said "Well, O.K." I called for a back-up unit and when they arrived I gave the joint a thorough tossing. There was some more dope in the basement in a bedroom and all told I believe it was at that time the largest Thai stick seizure in the history of the city. I submitted a very carefully worded report and it all sailed through court with three guilty pleas. The kid I was with must have had fun because he went on to serve several years as the Sergeant in the Drug Squad later in his career.

Trouble doesn't always come in threes. Five was actually the magic number that early spring afternoon at the Lincoln Hotel. Charlie Number One was mostly black while Charlie Number Two was mostly red. The other three seated at the table in the beer parlour were first generation European immigrants whose families had likely been deported by the KGB. They were assholes, loosely raised by assholes with asshole mentalities that lived in a small nucleus of District Three that was inhabited mostly by other assholes. It was likely the only thing that any of them had ever come by honestly.

It went from boisterous laughter, to grab-assing the waitresses and then to dumping beer on some of the quieter patrons that they eventually planned on kicking the shit out of for no particular reason. The bartender quietly called the cops. In all such eventualities, multiple units were sent in the interest of officer safety and to lend adequate support in suppressing the riots that were sometimes already underway. Old Stan had worked in Ident for a long time and was getting way up in his fifties. He probably shouldn't have gone in first as Frenchy and Super Dave were only a few blocks behind but he did. As the acting street supervisor, his 'old school' mindset was that just the presence of the police uniform would quell any disturbance and order would be restored. Times had changed.

Old Stan came shuffling towards the table where the source of the problem lay and just as he came up behind Charlie Two, the volatile Indian leaped straight up and back with a perfectly timed strike and drove the top of his head into Old Stan's face—and down he went. The group went wild and were roaring with laughter as Charlie Two stood there theatrically shrugging his shoulders and repeating: "What happened? What happened?" None of them had seen Frenchy and Super Dave slip into the bar about two seconds before Old Stan got suckered. The group was already seated again as Frenchy walked up on the table and Super Dave got to working on getting Old Stan back upright. Both Charlies and their hangers-on were still chortling and laughing and Charlie Two again smirked: "What happened?"

Frenchy wasn't screwing around with any verbal jousting. He never did. He quietly said, "What HAPPENED, Tonto, is that you just assaulted a police officer." There was suddenly a "VOOP" sound not unlike the laser beam blade of Darth Vader's neon electro-magnetic sword springing to life as a mysterious appendage suddenly appeared in Frenchy's hand. It was a custom nightstick—fashioned from hot-laminating six hockey stick handles together. A uniquely Winnipeg thing. A half-second and a two-handed swing later, the wide flat edge nailed Charlie Two flush in the face. All two hundred pounds of him crashed over backwards in the chair and he was all done for the rest of the afternoon.

One of the hangers-on, a well-known rounder with a record three pages long leaped to his feet as there was just too much audience to be wasted and he was still building his reputation as a very bad dude. He screamed, "FUCKING SON-OF-A-BITCH! COME ON! HIT ME IN THE FACE WITH YOUR FUCKING STICK! COME ON YOU CHICKEN-SHIT COP!" He had his dukes up and he really did have a pretty fair reputation as a tough guy. He had just started another verbal tirade when Frenchy underhanded the narrow edge of the bat straight up from the floor at two hundred miles an hour and into the loud one's nuts. The punk screamed like a burning witch and both hands dropped to cup his very injured testicles. THEN Frenchy hit him in the face as requested—another two handed stroke that dropped him like a rock right beside the prone Charlie Two.

Frenchy then leaned in closely to the alpha rat—Charlie One—who was by then sitting very still and looking only at the table. Usually Charlie drank with his brothers, a family so big and tough they formed their own gang. But not today. In a perfect stage whisper Frenchy said: "You have anything you'd like to add to what the President of The White Trash Retards here just said?" Charlie One shook his head. Frenchy gave him and his two other companions ten entire seconds to gather up their fallen comrades and make themselves scarce. They did. Old Stan had a knot on his cheek but lived to get through his last weeks on the job. The call was cleared on a "suspects gone on arrival" code and no report was ever written. Life was good in the seventies.

There was a lot of internal movement in the department in that era. In the short time I worked the North End in 1980-81, I had a surprisingly large number of regular car partners in the fifteen or so months I was there in uniform patrol. The last one was a big raw-boned hockey player that I always called Little John. I had worked with him occasionally when we were both rookies downtown, and I had a lot of laughs with him. He was steady and tough through anything, which included a "neighbour trouble" call we had taken in where a little fat guy with a big rifle had met us on the side-walk. John was a decent street-fighter and wasn't afraid to drop the gauntlets with anyone, no matter how many of them there were.

Fat Albert was an outlaw biker. He was a member in good stand-ing and some rank—apparently a Sergeant at Arms—of the local Los Bravos gang about the time they had reached the summit of their influence. He was around two hundred and eighty pounds and most likely was about a foot too short for his body mass index. He had long stringy blondish hair, a shit load of crappy looking tattoos and a really bad attitude. His crossed eyes only added to his bad-ass persona and whenever the bunch raised their ugly heads en masse, Fat Albert was usually there.

Little John and I were cruising around on a night shift early that June and dawn was well underway around four-thirty in the morn-ing. We'd been running all night call-to-call with nothing in the form of a break. We finally had a few minutes to grab a coffee and just when we were heading for it, we caught another call for a noise complaint on Polson Avenue east of Main Street near the old cem-etery. We came up St. Cross and turned onto Polson Avenue and drove right into the middle of about a hundred and fifty yelling and laughing party-goers with about thirty of them wearing colours.

Little John was driving and before we could even discuss back-ing up or calling for assistance, he was out of the car. I was tight on his right shoulder as we got about twenty feet into the crowd before we were pressed from all sides and ground to a halt. I wasn't liking it much. Bikers, defiantly drinking beer and smoking weed, strolled up close and personal. No one had yet invented issuing body armour to police officers and I knew there were only about fifty knives secreted in that crowd and likely more than a few hide-out guns as well. Fat Albert parted the crowd and got right up into our faces and smirked, "Hi boys. Looks like these odds REALLY suck for you." He was loving it with the big audience. He went on with, "Which one of you PIGS is going to piss his pants first?"

Little John leaned over to his ear. I could barely hear him say: "Listen you tub of shit. If this goes bad my first shot is going into your nuts. Then my partner and I are going to kill a bunch more of you assholes before we go down. Your call." Fat Albert visibly paled in the early morning light and lost the smirk. He stepped back and waved the rest off. We told them to clear the street in five minutes or we'd be back with an army. We were actually quite lucky that a couple of the gang's regular leadership weren't there as it could have been very bad for us.

Naturally, the mob didn't break ranks for almost half an hour which gave us ample time to call in about twenty cruiser car crews from all over the city. We all laid back and let them leave. They sneaked off a bike or two at a time and as soon as they were at least a few blocks away a cruiser car landed on them with both feet. Tickets flew like leaves in the wind and a few got popped on outstanding warrants, but Little John waited only for Fat Albert. He was one of the very last to run for it and went tearing southbound on his Harley before we stopped him in the middle of the Redwood Bridge. Little John got his nose about a half inch from Fat Albert's and impressed upon him how really alone he was. Then he called him every kind of a low-life piece-of-shit scum-bag he could think of—some stuff I'd never even heard of before—to make Fat Albert fight. He wouldn't. It was "Yes Sir. No Sir." He was a lot of things, but Fat Albert was NOT stupid, at least most of the time. A few years later he was whooping it up in the St. Boniface Hotel with the rest of the bunch of The Scum of the Earth. When they all left,

Fat Albert popped a wheelie on his brand new metallic red Electra Glide straight into the waiting arms of a police cruiser. He was given the demand for a breath sample and full of swagger and attitude he said, "Fuck you. Give me the test. I only had ONE drink." He failed. Afterwards, he kept saying "I can't figure it out. I only had ONE drink." The arresting officers suggested it must have been a really big one.

Albert got himself into a few major problems by getting caught with a load of LSD and a handgun sometime in that era but I lost track of him after that. One summer afternoon quite a few years later I was sitting in the Staff Sergeant's office in the downtown station when a delivery guy banged on the front window. He was a little skinny guy with short blond hair and glasses. I didn't really pay him any mind when I went out and took the package from him. He looked at me and smiled and said, "You don't recognize me, do you?" I looked at him for ten or fifteen seconds before the light went on. It was Fat Albert in the flesh—but a lot less of it. He'd lost over a hundred pounds and looked about as healthy as I'd ever seen him. He told me he'd cleaned up his act. He'd been working steady and out of trouble for quite a while. He'd also given up all of his old cohorts and that way of life forever. We laughed about the old days for a few minutes and we shook hands when he left. He said, "I was REALLY such an asshole back then." I agreed.

CHAPTER 12 Meat

'm not sure if Meat's name was just some usual police bastard-ization of his real name or if in fact he was what he ate. At a little over three hundred and fifty pounds spread over a six and a half foot frame he was worth a fortune—even at rendering plant prices. It was however, his humour value above all else that made him so priceless. He was one of the funniest cops that ever lived.

He wasn't always that big. In his youthful days as a patrol of-ficer it was rumoured that he only tipped the scales at two twen-ty-five, but it was about even money that he was already that big in the fourth grade. He was a product of one of the micro-depart-ments that policed out past the last chicken coop on the North side of the city—part of an area that later fell under the jurisdiction of the Royal Canadian Mounted Police. The remainder was swallowed up by the advancement of urbanization and was eventually policed by the Winnipeg Police Department after 1974.

Meat, like Bigfoot, was one of those cops you never forgot even if you only saw him once. Large as a house, amiable and with a booming laugh, I remembered him more for his darker side from the fall of 1968 when he had awarded me with my very first traffic ticket. It had been about two o'clock in the morning when I was running a little late in getting back home from a hot date in East Kildonan on the opposite side of the city from where my parents lived. I was sixteen years old and was flying my mother's V-eight Ford club coupe a little low on the North perimeter highway at Pipeline Road when I spotted the red light almost a mile behind me. The aging six cylinder police car was over-heated and smoking something fierce by the time I pulled over and the big cop who was driving it turned out to be just as hot. He dinged me for seventy-five in a sixty zone and it later cost me ten dollars in Juvenile Court. That equated to about a full eight hour shift jerking sodas and scrubbing floors at my part time job at T-J's Roast Beef Sandwiches at the Westwood Shopping Centre. Even worse, my Dad had to go with me. Between him and the lady who was the judge I decided I wasn't cut out for a life of crime and drove everything like it was a baby carriage thereafter.

A St. James cop had LIED and said I ran a stop sign about two years later. I hadn't. In fact, I had sat at it for almost five full minutes trying to make a right turn onto Portage Avenue before there was enough of a break in the traffic to allow it. I was polite and respectful and attempted to explain that fact to him, but his parents had obviously told him he could be anything he wanted to be when he grew up—so he became an asshole. I never forgot him either, especially when I became his Staff Sergeant quite a few years later. That one cost me twenty dollars. Amalgamation of the thirteen suburban police departments did have some real advantages. The only other ticket I ever got was from a five foot-nothing rookie North Dakota State cop with a giant gun in the fall of 1976 for doing a dare-devil sixty-one miles an hour in a fifty-five zone at four o'clock in the morning in the middle of nowhere. After he recorded my occupation on the ticket I asked him if he knew when the State of North Dakota was likely to start aptitude testing for police recruits. Twenty bucks U.S.

As time went on, Meat mutated into the always jovial but somewhat more rotund eating machine that we all came to know him as. Meat had naturally stone-gray hair by that time and he too, like myself and many others had undergone a rather pronounced hair loss. His condition was likely best described as bald except for the bushy fringe above his ears and the lush sideburns he retained.

Vanity being prevalent in a lot of people, Meat was no different and he went out and got himself a toupee. I suspected that he didn't dump a lot of cash in acquiring it in that it was less than a perfect match in both colour and fit. It was a vivid burnt orange and contrasted somewhat sharply against his remaining silver locks. I suspected the thing was also a "winter warm" model as it was luxuriously plush. Subsequently, Meat would begin to perspire noticeably if the office temperature got much over fifty degrees or if he exerted himself in any way—which was a fairly rare occurrence in any case. The sweat had obviously made the hair-piece somewhat itchy in my observation, as on warmer occasions when Meat was manning the front desk he could be observed to utilize a ball point pen to scratch up and down well up and under the edges of his coiffeur. This of course, went a long way in explaining why he always had a lot of ink lines on the sides of his head.

Meat worked all three shifts like the rest of us that were in General Patrol in the North End's Hartford Avenue station. Besides dealing with the public's enquiries on a walk-in basis, he took motor vehicle accident reports, received found property and performed a number of other duties that fell to the Station Duty officers. One of them was the recording of voluntary payments for parking tickets.

Back in that era, a lot of the normal fines were five dollars, a few were ten and the most serious were fifteen. The front office maintained a cash float for making change with a receipt ledger for the tickets that had been paid and the transactions were universally made in small bills. Late one evening shift, a couple of the area's more well-known rounders had knocked back quite a number of beers apiece. One of them suddenly remembered that he had a fifteen dollar parking tag that was due THAT day. From experience, he also remembered that in default of any payment by the end of the due date, the matter went for a warrant unless a not guilty plea had been entered on the matter and a court date had been set for the case to be heard by the court.

Up for some public mayhem, the well-oiled twosome appeared at the front desk of the police station just a few minutes before the midnight cut-off for that date's voluntary ticket payments. They flung the ticket over the counter and the ticket recipient stood there grinning like the drunken idiot he was. Meat checked the dates on the tag and grunted "Fifteen dollars." Half-wit, across the counter yelled out, "HERE'S YOUR FIFTEEN FUCKING DOLLARS!" and began pitching handfuls of pennies out of his coat pockets over the counter. They rolled off onto the floor, down the hall, under the counter and after seven or right handfuls they were everywhere. Both of them became so hysterical with laughter they were doubled over and were slapping each other on the back. It didn't last.

Meat never moved. With his lack of reaction, the laughter subsided fairly quickly and he said, "We don't accept pennies. It's the law. NOW PICK THEM UP." The escalated noise level from all the previous jocularity that the pair had conjured up along with Meat's bellow at them to retrieve the coins had alerted the Duty Sergeant to the situation and the intercom went on. "Assistance is required in the Station Duty Office IMMEDIATELY" was broadcast throughout the station just moments before the ticket holder screamed, "FUCK YOU COPS! THAT FINE IS PAID! YOU FUCKIN' PICK THEM UP!"

When the first wave of cops crashed into the front office Meat had already grabbed the pair in a one-arm headlock apiece and although their feet were off the floor and they were dangling like rag dolls they were doing their best to break loose. They couldn't. Like a cave bear, Meat had them locked in a death grip until assistance arrived. Frenchie and Super Dave got to them first, which pretty much precluded the requirement for anyone else to become involved and the pair went from a fifteen dollar fine for a parking ticket to a night in jail and a morning court appearance for Causing a Disturbance. They also received a bonus thirty minute penny-hunt on their hands and knees with some additional motivation to make them look harder. The whole incident got Meat somewhat sweated up and it was noted that he wrote on his head for several minutes afterwards.

Meat's usual lunch from home for a single shift consisted of an entire loaf of bread made into thick sandwiches that would utilize an entire ham or roast of beef. A number of his wife's baking specialties were always included. He regularly supplemented this fare with five or six doughnuts from the two or three dozen that made their way into the coffee room every day AND it was reputed that on the way home from a dayshift he always stopped at the Kentucky Fried Chicken outlet over on McPhillips Street. Meat had a forty-five minute drive home to his residence north of the city, and the twenty piece bucket of drumsticks fortified him enough to make it without the onset of undue hunger. He liked the drumsticks as he could pop them into his mouth whole and then slide out the bone and fling it out the window as he drove.

One of the big bonuses for the Station Duty officer in the North End station was that as such, he was the first line of reception to the public. This included being the reception committee for the nightly pizza delivery. Archie was a super-generous Greek who happened to run a string of pizza restaurants all over the city. Every night, just before closing time, Archie had his staff at the outlet closest to the North End station use up all the leftover dough and pizza toppings and they made up two and sometimes three TWELVE topping extra-large pizzas. Archie then had them delivered with his compliments to the officers at the district police station.

Meat LOVED Archie's pizza. He did not, however, like sharing it so he devised a way to get the most pizza down in the shortest possible time before any other officers would have been attracted by the aroma. After the delivery driver left, Meat would quickly open up each respective pizza box lid and then roll the complete pizza up tightly into a large, burrito-shaped offering which he had to clench tightly utilizing BOTH hands to preclude any chance of it opening up and spilling out any of the multiple toppings. Then, in three or four huge bites, he would devour the entire thing without putting it down. This in itself was not a problem for him in that he had a bite radius like a tiger shark. With practice, he could engulf two and sometimes three entire pizzas in just a couple of minutes and would then surreptitiously dispose of the boxes in the outside dumpster with no one having been the wiser.

However, he was sometimes the victim of his own devices as when he tightly clenched the rolled pizzas while devouring them, the grease would be squeezed out of them and it would then run down his arm and soak the sleeve of his light blue uniform police shirt. This, of course, always tipped off even the most casual of observers as to what had taken place even if the numerous splatterings on the front of his shirt did not. When confronted with this overwhelming evidence, he would only boom out a laugh.

As a matter of course, two or three different patrol car crews would each bring a full dozen box of doughnuts into the station every morning—all scrounged from the area's doughnut shops. Meat would grab a few and retreat back to his office, but if they happened to be jam busters, he'd get four or five which left precious few for the rest of the platoon. Cops having always been diabolical in seeking their revenge, so one morning when I was making a doughnut run I headed down to the Robin's on McPhillips Street. The owner happened to be there and was a good guy so I asked him if it was possible if it was possible to pump enough jam into one of his jam busters so that it would explode if a person was to bite it.

I believe that one jam buster weighed more than the other eleven in the box combined and the pastry was stretched to the limits. Handling it like nitroglycerin, we managed to get it back into the station and onto a plate—on top of all the other ones—without having it blow up. Meat lumbered into the coffee room just seconds after the trap was set. About ten other cops were in on it along with the Sergeant and the Inspector and it was poker faces across the board. He snatched up the booby-trapped offering and all eyes were riveted on him. Meat was NOT dumb and I could never tell if we all leered just a little too much or if it was the fact that that jam buster weighed about four pounds that tipped him to the fact that something was up. He hesitated—which was completely out of character for him—and then he crammed the WHOLE jam buster into his mouth. He picked up three more and left.

In March of 1981 I was promoted along with a couple of hundred others cops when rank integration took place. As the result, I spent most of my time patrolling alone in the District Three Supervisor's unit until I was shipped back to plainclothes a month later. On a calm but very damp spring evening shift the Staff Sergeant on duty asked me if I'd take Meat along with me for the shift as he already had a new kid learning the ropes on the desk. Meat eventually found his winter hat and parka and got his gun belt rigged on the outside of his coat—which was the style of the old all-leather coats, one of which he still had. The rest were in museums. I noticed as he trudged out to our car that his gun and holster were all the way around his back—out of reach—but it was just for one shift.

I soon discovered that the only way Meat managed to land his huge carcass into the front passenger's seat of the cruiser was to tightly grip the roof rack which supported the emergency light bar and then sort of heave himself inside with one motion. I heard the metal creak when he did it, but it seemed to hold. I was in and out of the unit a few times over the next few hours. It was starting to get busy and I stopped at a few calls that other cars were on, but Meat stayed in our car as it was just easier. All the cars were tied up and the calls for service were backing up and since we were a two man unit the dispatcher asked if we could take a call that had been waiting—a noisy party in the three hundred block of Manitoba Avenue.

I pulled up in front and noticed that the place was well lit up inside although there were no lights on outside. It was a decaying old two-storey with a screened-in porch on the front. Meat kicked open his door and reached out with his right hand and gripped the roof rack again. There was an audible complaint as it shifted but held as he grunted his way out of the seat and up and out. The cruiser bounced about six times and then we headed for the house. The four front steps up to the porch were old two-by-eights and I opened the screen door and crossed the twelve feet of the veranda's board floor to the front doors. The music was blaring some George Jones and Tammy Wynette as I hammered on the outer door. Meat had made it up the steps by then and was about half way across the veranda floor when it gave way. With a resounding crash and a roar of surprise from Meat, I spun around to see what had happened to him just as the front door opened.

Meat was right up to his armpits. His pounds per square inch had proved to be a little much for the long-rotted wood and he had dropped through it like a trap door on a gallows. He couldn't budge and was cursing a blue streak. I suddenly became aware of the press of upright bodies from behind me and when I looked there were seven or eight Natives—all carrying a beer—peering at Meat through the effects of advanced intoxication. In unison, three or four of them said: "Holy FUCK, eh?"

Ever obliging, they put down their beers and began tugging on Meat's coat sleeves and collar—in different directions—which elicited a loud growl of disapproval from my fallen partner. I made sure he was uninjured and then I pitched in to help extract Meat from the porch. He wouldn't budge. The Indians all sat down with their beers around Meat in a circle and one of their lady friends brought Meat and I a cold one apiece while we waited it out. It took the Fire Department about ten minutes to get there as I had specified there was no emergency. They eventually chopped him loose. That was the last time that Meat worked the street, but I always remembered the bewildered look on his face when he was stuck in the floor and I had said: "God is punishing you for giving me that speeding ticket—you PRICK."

CHAPTER 13 Tradition

Having the odd pull off the old jug was not an unknown concept in police work in those days and the tradition continued for a least for a couple more decades. It was male bonding at its finest. Today, it has gone the way of the Great Auk. No one can dispute we had to change with the times.

The very first Christmas I was on the job, I was working nights at my Cadet duties in Central Registry. The Detective Sergeant who was filling in on nights and the Detective working Station Duty answering the phones were thirty-year vets who hadn't worn a uniform since the Earth was flat. They were men of few words but when they DID speak people listened or they would beat the shit out of them. I had picked up on that fact just the evening shift before. While I was up front on the phone, some swaggering loud-mouth who turned out to be an ex-con bounced up to the front counter where the older Detective was on duty and alluded to the fact that he was "reporting". I didn't know that he was a recent parolee—for armed robbery—and that he showed up once a week to present himself as one of the conditions of his release from prison. The goof was about twenty-five and had been pumping a little iron in the joint. The old Detective ignored him and kept up with his two-fingered assault on his typewriter. About fifteen seconds later, and with his best attempt at intimidation, Stupid hammered the counter with his fist and barked "Are you fucking DEAF? "

The jailbird was leaning way over the counter to add a little emphasis to his complete lack of proper etiquette in a police building as the old boy turned slowly in his swivel chair, picked up the phone—not just the receiver but the WHOLE phone—and then welded it to the side of Retard's head with a spectacular smash. Before I could even get my jaw dropped the aging Detective pulled the asshole the rest of the way over the counter and was on him—following up with a flurry of body shots from Ma Bell's multi-functional apparatus. I yelled at the constable I was on the phone with "Fight in the Detective Office. Bring help!" just before I bailed over the counter on my side of the foyer. The Detective Sergeant and I got there at about the same second. A team of detectives rushed up from the back office just as four guys from Juvenile beat the three guys from Morality—which was a little farther down the hall—into the fracas. It wasn't another ten seconds when the population of a small town, all wearing uniforms, thundered in from both front and back entrances.

I didn't get an EXACT head count, but I do believe that our new visitor was introduced individually to each officer in the next ninety seconds or so, and then they were gone. The team in the back whipped up a quick report for Breach of Parole (consuming liquor) and Disorderly in a Public Place and then it was back to the joint for another three years for the big loser in the fight to finish off his original sentence. I realized then I had SO much to learn as I hadn't even smelled the liquor on him. I heard that the Assaulting a Police officer charge was later dropped. The sum and total of any follow-up conversation about it that included me was from the Detective Sergeant. He looked at me for a moment and said "You did good, Kid. Now get the fuck back to work."

Anyway, the Christmas Eve night shift was about an hour old and I was busy filing a bale and a half of contact cards into the belt-driven card conveyor. The same old Detective who had amazed me with his phone-to-head combat skills the week previously stood up after he received a three second phone call. When I looked over in response to his whistle, with a slight motion of his head he bade me to follow. He walked into the open door of the

Sergeant of Detectives Office and grabbed a chair. I stood outside. I wasn't getting yelled at. The same older Detective Sergeant was seated behind the desk and he motioned me in and pointed to the last empty chair. He rolled open a drawer in his desk and hauled out a full crock of Cutty Sark. The office water cooler had those little pointy paper cups that only held about three ounces of liquid and a handful of them were already on the desk. They poured three straight up and no doubt as the result of some serious practice they knocked theirs back in one smooth gulp as they bid all present a Merry Christmas.

I followed suit—with just a hint of a shudder as the scotch hit bottom—and entered a Rite of Passage without even knowing it. It was about respect. My part in the office brawl had been pretty small as I had been flung aside nearly at the outset by one of the much burlier Detectives from the back office. But because I had jumped in they were letting me know that they thought I was okay. Those two had a lot of bark on them and are now both gone from this Earth, but I still think of them and that earliest of lessons I learned about the measure of men in the eyes of their fellows. We killed the rest of the Cutty along with the jug that the old Detective had stashed in HIS drawer over the next five or six hours. When it became obvious that I could no longer read the typing on the cards I was filing, the Detective Sergeant had me driven home—right after we had "one for the ditch".

The Police Department ran the jail on the fourth floor of the Public Safety Building for quite a few years until it was taken over by the provincial correction authorities in the later 1970s. Back then, when we still had it, it was the last place in the world even the most stalwart of cons would choose to do any time however short the duration. It was concrete floors and steel bunks with the perpetual odour of vomit, urine, stale sweat and industrial strength disinfectant. The lockup was run daily by three crews on eight hour shifts with a pretty senior Patrol Sergeant in charge of three or four very senior constables on each tour. All of them were past any kind of street duty and in their last year or two of service were posted inside until they hit sixty and had to retire. For the most part, they were grumpy old vets who had seen it all and worked at their own pace booking the assorted prisoners in and out of jail. They had it down to a science and even got a little free chow from the old wino that was on retainer putting together what constituted the three meals a day for the prisoners.

I was walking Four Beat one night when I came across a middle-aged celebrant who had crashed and burned in a doorway on the East side of Main Street. He was snoring comfortably even though it was a cool fall evening. The drunk was dressed in a huge overcoat and had on a three piece suit underneath. I left him lying there until the Patrol Wagon arrived and the three of us carried him into the back. I got the guy mostly awake by the time we hit the basement loading dock in the downtown station and on the rubberiest of legs got him out and before the uniform Sergeant who pointed up—which meant up to the fourth floor Drunk Tank. I was having to really struggle to keep the poor guy upright as his knees sagged about every third step. I got him into the elevator and propped in a corner while we rode up. At the fourth floor landing, there was one of the senior constables up front and he activated the electronically controlled rolling barred door at the entrance to let us in. I pulled in my drunk and leaned him on the Booking Desk.

The older officer stood opposite us and started filling out the form as I began to run through the numerous pockets on my teetery companion looking for I.D. and any personal property he might have. I found his wallet and pitched it to the other officer so he could start recording the name and address as I continued my search. Besides some rumpled smokes in a crushed package, it seemed like every pocket the guy had contained a mickey of whiskey. I had them all lined up on the counter and was just adding the last one—number seven—when the old Patrol Sergeant and another senior constable strolled in from their check of the cells. The first officer was diligently recording the list of personal property while reciting it aloud and had just completed "SEVEN small bottles of whiskey" when the old Sarge and his companion shot each other looks of alarm. The Patrol Sergeant cleared his throat. After looking around, the recording officer made a bold "X" on his form and stated aloud "SIX small bottles of whiskey." He looked up again and met the steely gaze of his supervisor. Another "X"—followed by "OK, let's see if I have this right. One wallet with personal papers, twelve dollars in cash, a pack of smokes and FIVE small bottles of whiskey."

Whenever the four man foot patrol of Main Street was underway on evening shift, one of these officers was generally a Patrol Sergeant or at least an Acting Patrol Sergeant. A lot of these "acting" guys were crusty old constables and couldn't have cared less about a promotion. They didn't RUN anywhere and wouldn't have changed expressions during an air raid. They knew The Drag like they knew their own living rooms—having kept the peace down there for usually over twenty years before we came along. One nippy late-fall evening, the Acting Patrol Sergeant and I were on our second pass of the East side when he feigned a shiver and announced "Goddamn! It's cold out here tonight. I think it's about time for a little anti-freeze, Kid."

By lucky coincidence, we were right outside the old National Hotel and he steered us into the front doors. There was a small office to the right in which the owner—Irving—usually parked himself during business hours and for long periods afterwards. The quality of whiskey in his office was rumored to be of a far superior blend than the watery three year old stuff that was utilized in the bar. My partner approached the door and pushed it open. About a second after we got in and closed the door again behind us, I immediately recognized Irving AND his seated guest. It was the Inspector on evening shift whom I had seen earlier in the day as we headed out to the beat. Irving poured us a straight up twelve year old and topped off the Inspector's. I often wondered how this scenario would have turned out if the Inspector had arrived for a hit AFTER we did, but he always struck me as a capable leader and a lot of guys liked and respected him—including myself.

On one of the very first Christmas Eves that I worked after I hit the street, the shift was lined up for inspection and just as we turned to march out, the old Sergeant said "Don't get drunk." I noted that he didn't say "Don't drink." Some months later, I chased a break-in suspect on foot for about a mile in deep snow and finally ran him down with the very last ounce of energy I had. My uniform was soaked from sweat and my lungs felt like I had been under water for a week. I got the suspect back into the station with the help of a car crew and was just barely able to breathe again when the same old Sarge motioned me towards the locker room. He said "Good job" and poured us a pair of whiskies. I was on the verge of puking BEFORE I had the whiskey, but I knocked it back and gritted my teeth to keep it down for about the next hour.

It was just another almost subliminal lesson from those early years. Rank didn't mean much to men I recognized as being respected. Many years later, a newly promoted Duty Inspector who had actually spent a few years in Robbery/Homicide—being one of the boys—made a couple of quick jumps in rank and suddenly found himself to be an officer. Being the officer-in-charge after hours, he was moving around the six floors of the old Public Safety Building when he passed by his old Robbery/Homicide office and from behind the locked doors heard some guffawing and noise from several members inside. Using his pass-key to gain entrance, he strolled into a group of three teams of investigators with their Sergeant who were celebrating another successful conclusion in a recent rash of armed robberies.

The jug of whiskey was in plain view on the desk with a couple of empty ones and the mix and ice. Despite the fact that he had actually worked—and drank—with most of the detectives present, he grabbed up the open bottle of rye and began a tersely presented lecture regarding drinking in a police office and what consequences that would be forthcoming when he finished making his report. Super Dave was one of the old crowd and had actually worked on the same shift with him just a couple of years before, and he didn't get the nickname from doing retarded stunts on television. With his usual off-handedness and easy dialogue, he informed the new Inspector that he should "shut the fuck up and sit down and have a drink with the boys" or he would be thrown THROUGH the door on the way out—without the whiskey. He wasn't kidding. And, having said that, he removed the bottle of whiskey from the offending hand that clutched it and began pouring another round. The Inspector stayed for two.

CHAPTER 14 Making it Right

A lot of guys who achieved a little rank wore it with dignity, but never changed in their ways of thinking and how they treated other officers. They never stopped being cops. Unfortunately, others did. One particular incident back in the mid 1980s pretty much summed up what working cops thought of high-ranking officers who did little else but run around causing unnecessary grief. The particular newly promoted Duty Inspector had been, in all fairness, a pretty good investigator in his day and had an admirable level of expertise in some fields. Then, it became all about politics and mostly through some first rate apple-polishing he rode the power wave all the way to officer rank. Part of the duties of a Duty Inspector in those days was to attend serious incidents all over the city to insure that adequate supervision and manpower requirements were utilized in addressing the incident, and to visit the outlying district stations just to make sure everything was basically going to plan. It was easy duty, and the vast majority of these new officers really provided a welcome sense of support to the men and women out on the street. Not this one. Somehow, it became his personal obsession to have as many police officers charged under The Rules and Regulations for chicken-shit breaches as humanly possible. REALLY glaring offences, such as: more than one cruiser car at a coffee shop at one time OR taking more than fifteen minutes for a coffee break were his Hit List specials. Not wearing your uniform hat when out of the cruiser car was also huge.

While some of these minor breaches might have carried a reprimand after a little session in "Kangaroo Court," a lot of officers were losing a day's pay or a day of weekly leave as the result, and it stuck on your service record until Hell would freeze over twice in the same afternoon. Emotions were starting to run a little high after about thirty were charged, but much to his personal glee he kept at it and to add insult to injury, made such exclamations as: "These young guys are like shooting fish in a barrel". Something had to give—and it did. On a bitterly cold winter night, the Duty Inspector in question pulled into the underground parking area of the downtown police station, and parked. Some observant type with a long memory saw the Inspector head upstairs and noted he was not wearing HIS hat. Officers have traditionally been issued a fur hat which is an expensive satin-lined otter skin job. About fifteen minutes later, the Inspector returned to his parked unit, jumped in and wheeled out of the garage and into the frosty night. It is unclear from all reports whether or not he actually got the fur hat jammed onto his head or not before he discovered the steaming human turd that had been lovingly placed inside.

Along the same lines, I did a tour in The Holy City as a new Sergeant in the mid 1980s. The old St. Boniface Police Station on Provencher Boulevard had become the District Five Headquarters on amalgamation and although cramped and terribly out of date, it housed some pretty funny cops. My Number Two was "O"—a crusty old Patrol Sergeant who'd been on the department for several years before I joined. He had been in the district for some time, and had already grown to despise one of the other Sergeants from another platoon. I soon picked up on why. At Supervisors meetings the idea was to identify any problems in the district and to formulate plans to remedy them. That one particular Sergeant would stand up and say intelligent things like "The problem is that the men don't fear the Sergeants any more." The rest of us would look around and at each other and ask, "Did he REALLY say that?" He was serious, too.

The guy was continually denying guys time off for no reason, formally reporting officers for even the most minor of regulation breaches and generally being adversarial and contrary to all of his subordinates and most of his peers. Something had to give—and it did. "O" had his wife buy a pair of petit-sized black lace panties and he marinated them in Oscar de la Renta for about a week in a plastic bag. A quick call was made to some friendlies over in the Stolen Auto Squad downtown who attended the Provencher Station and they quickly and quietly unlocked the passenger's door on the miserable Sergeant's personal car with a Slim Jim where it was parked on the street near the station. The panties were placed just right under the edge of the passenger's seat, so that they would be out of sight from anyone in the driver's seat, but would certainly catch the eye of anyone getting in or out as a passenger. The car was locked back up and a multitude of cops watched Grumpy wheel away after work. It only took an hour. When he called the station he was hyperventilating as he attempted to make a report of his car being broken into and damaged while it was parked at work and was the obvious work of perverts. His wife was STILL screaming at him in the background when he called it in.

Cops have always been quick to let those in the ranks that were making life miserable for others know that it didn't go undetected. The message could have been devious or deliberate but it ALWAYS came. Back then—as now—each of the six patrol districts in the city was manned by uniform officers and Sergeants spread over six platoons. Each platoon also had a Patrol Sergeant—a second in-charge that was also a supervisory rank. In the early 1980s the department went with a computer aided dispatch system and it nearly killed a lot of the older cops with stress as most had never even seen a computer before. However, old dogs can learn new tricks and over time everyone settled into the regimen of posting rosters for upcoming shifts on a computer and a number of other information storing functions. It was just a lot easier for some than others.

Through normal attrition, vacancies on the platoons occurred from time to time before a transfer or promotion could fill it and the vacancy was historically filled by the person next in rank. It did occur on another platoon in The Holy City when "O" my Patrol Sergeant and I were in charge of a District Five shift in the late 1980s. The Patrol Sergeant on the shift following ours was first and foremost an alright sort of a guy, but he got stuck "acting" as the Sergeant on his shift for an extended period of time and stepped up to the plate to fulfill the duties to the best of his ability. He lived out near Anola, Manitoba where a lot of other Winnipeg cops lived. Unfortunately, he became such a nit-picker about EVERYTHING and was so afraid that he'd make a mistake while acting in a higher rank that he became almost unbearable to be around. He bounced his guys reports for miniscule errors and got to be a regular pain in the ass about haircuts and coffee breaks his guys had taken two extra minutes on. "O" started calling him the Ayatollah of Anola to his face.

With the advancement of technology, it was inevitable that the department had to upgrade its use of computers when the time came, and it came when The Ayatollah was acting Sergeant. No one really knew what a complete boob he was at mastering functions on a computer that a rhesus monkey could get right on the first try. The complete roster entry protocol changed drastically, and "O" and I stumbled through the training and eventually got it right, but The Ayatollah just couldn't grasp it. And, as the Acting Sergeant it was up to him to perform exactly that function—every day. Most of us were down to eight or ten minutes getting a new roster for the next shift entered and printed for posting. We only had a few entries to put in—Sergeant, Patrol Sergeant, three to maybe five cruiser car crews and each car's two officers' names and badge numbers. That was it. It took him and hour and a half and if someone even spoke to him while he was hunched over and sweating onto the keyboard he went berserk. He would scream at the interloper and talk to himself for several minutes afterwards as he pecked away. When he finally finished, he waved the printed roster in a flourish of triumph and relaxed visibly. "O" said he'd had enough.

After a particularly nasty and lengthy session one evening, The Ayatollah, on the brink of a breakdown, printed his next day's roster and stuck it on the duty board in the Sergeant's office. Then he went for coffee. When he came back up he saw some of his guys that had come in from the street laughing while they were looking at the roster. "O" and I had already left for the night. When the Acting Sergeant got up for a look, his roster had been re-entered in the computer and re-printed as:

Acting Sgt. The Ayatollah of Anola
Acting P/Sgt Donald Duck
N501 Pluto
Goofy
N502 Chopper
Yakky Doodle
N503 Mickey Mouse
Snow White

I don't believe he REALLY broke down and cried like one of his guys said he did, but I did believe it took him another two hours to straighten it all out. Naturally, "O" and I denied any knowledge of the occurrence.

Even a lot of the old Sergeants didn't take much bullshit from anyone. That came across loud and clear in the turmoil of the amalgamation of the city's thirteen suburban police departments in October of 1974. Someone in the planning stages decided that it would be a smashing idea to have a Disciplinary Sergeant appointed to keep all the troops in line in the first months after the big move. In the History of Bad Ideas, that may have been a contender for first place.

The guy that was picked for the job came out of Hooterville in the extreme east end of the city from the old Transcona P.D. I didn't know him at all but I later worked under him back in that same patrol area eight or nine years later and I never met a finer guy. He went into the new job with a mind to do what he had been assigned to do and it just didn't work. I doubt if anyone could have been told to Fuck Off more in six months than he was. One of his focuses was of course on deportment of all officers—which included both appearance and conduct. His example was exemplary. The first time I saw him was at a morning inspection of the day shift when I was still working downtown as a beat officer.

His tunic and forage cap were spotless—not a speck of lint on him anywhere. His shoes could have been used for mirrors and his gold buttons and sergeant's chevrons gleamed. I think he shaved and got a haircut every fifteen minutes. He stood unsmiling just behind my shift's Sergeant—who was a crusty old veteran—and was having his usual look at the troops that were heading out onto the street. Just a fraction of a second after my Sergeant called for a "left face" from the lined up officers, the Disciplinary Sergeant barked "HOLD IT." He walked down the line tapping shoulders as he went. "THIS officer needs a haircut. THIS officer's shoes are a not appropriately shined." That was as far as he got. My old Sarge looked him right in the eye and said, "THESE are MY men. They have passed MY inspection. I don't need you to help me—so FUCK OFF."

I think it was the same day I heard the Disciplinary Sergeant had wandered into the back of Detective Division up on the second floor. Pete and Jack were nationally famous as tough Winnipeg Detectives and they had an audience of about twenty other guys as Pete was telling some hilarious story for several minutes as the Disciplinary Sergeant stood by. Pete maybe only used some explicit form of profanity six or seven times, but up stepped the shiny new Sergeant and said: "Detective, you will REFRAIN from using profanity in this office at all times in the future." It was said you could have hear the proverbial pin drop in the pregnant pause that followed. Pete walked over to him and yelled at him: "FUCK YOU, SONNY! GET THE FUCK OUT OF HERE!" He did.

Even doing some sneaky surveillance on the guys coming and going out of the downtown station's underground garage didn't go well for him. The Disciplinary Sergeant had slipped down and into the garage just before shift change and secreted himself in the back of the parked Patrol Wagon. From there he could peep out at the officers while undetected. Flagrant breaches of discipline, such as smoking in a police car or being thirty seconds late going on the air for patrol by junior officers were easier to handle than big detectives that would knock the slobber out any potential source of annoyance. However, somebody saw him, and with a little planning, a distraction was set-up while a still unidentified member sneaked up and slammed the wagon's back doors shut—and locked them. He was in there for quite some time before one of the old chauffeurs heard him yelling and pounding on the walls.

CHAPTER 15 Fun and Games

C ertainly the old adage of "too much of a good thing" was never more true than on a cold winter night a few years later when Pig Pen and I were working 7:00 P.M.–3:00 A.M. in Drugs. We had burned it at both ends for weeks as we'd been running with two very productive informants and the overtime coupled with court some days had us all so exhausted that The Shadow and Space had taken a rare night off. Pig Pen had stopped at the liquor store on his way to work and picked a full case of assorted wine for an upcoming family function and had it in the trunk of his car.

After the usual couple of coffees and catching up on what had taken place in the department in the previous sixteen hours, our old Drug Sergeant told us to rack out in the back for a while if we had to. Mort was like a second Dad to everyone in the Drug Squad. One minute he was reaming you out royally and the next he was staying all night making the guys on overtime coffee and helping out with the reports until the sun came up. And, like a second Dad, we didn't tell him EVERYTHING. Pig Pen indicated that we had to retrieve the case of wine out of his car and run it back to his place before it froze and then we'd head over to The Midtown Café and pig out on the all-you-can-eat menu. The plan was good in theory, anyway.

We made it back to Pig Pen's in the suburbs and carried in the wine. His wife had gone over to her mother's with the kids and Pig Pen began to put the whites in the fridge and the reds on the counter before we left. About halfway through this little chore he commented that the whites already had a nice chill on them from the stint in his trunk and that we should probably try a glass to insure that the wine hadn't been bruised from the sudden changes in temperature. The first bottle was a crystal clear, off-dry South African Cape Riesling. We killed it. Deciding that we couldn't fly on one wing, Pig Pen snatched a second bottle from the fridge, a younger but perky Napa Valley Chardonnay with smooth subtleties of oak and refreshing burst of citrus on the palate.

To the untrained eye, we may have appeared to be merely a couple of bingo-chugging, long haired, filthy-looking, bearded boors clad in ripped jeans and T-shirts with nasty slogans on them. Pig Pen's said "Nuke the Gay Whales" and mine decreed support for "The Jewish Vegetarian Lesbians for Jesus." Jointly, we had always strived for success in offending EVERYONE. In actuality, we bantered lightly back and forth, discussing the sundry origins of the numerous essences within the wine. We switched to red. I had previously attended number of wine tastings, and had picked up on the fact that each connoisseur's methods of evaluating a vintage was a law unto itself. Pig Pen's unique modus operandi became evident sometime after the second bottle of red. He could stick his tongue out far enough to touch the bottom of the filled wine glass and would then gargle continuously for a full forty-five seconds with a full glass of Cabernet Sauvignon. When I tried it, I inadvertently laughed, and it shot out my nose. Somewhere around the eighth bottle we began mixing the reds and whites and created a passable looking rose, but it tasted like shit.

In the end, we drank all twelve bottles. I was doing pretty good until we got up to leave and I noticed that my face was going numb and I couldn't get my boots back on. Pig Pen was hovering around two hundred and sixty pounds and always had a fair bit more capacity for liquor than I did. I was junkie-thin and well under my usual hundred and eighty-five or so, and hadn't had a thing to eat all day. I made it out to the car, carrying my boots, and we were off. Somewhere in the whirlwind of the next few hours, I had made it into the back seat and was awakened only briefly here and there as Pig Pen careened around a corner at some location unknown to me. He had stopped a couple of times to hammer down a rum or two at other cops' places while I grabbed some much needed rest.

When I woke up, it was two thirty in the morning. Pig Pen had just slammed on the brakes and I sat up as my head and body shrieked at me to lie back down. I was still in La-La Land when my partner, in his advanced state of inebriation barked: "Let's go!" I got out and put my boots on while standing in the snow in my socks and realized we were outside the Lincoln Hotel. We made it inside the lobby and it was quickly evident that the bar and the lounge were closed due to the late hour. I was just starting in on Pig Pen to the effect that we should get the FUCK out of there when he heard it. It was music from the downstairs banquet room.

I don't know why I followed him, but I did. At the bottom of the stairs was a cloakroom of sorts and then a wide doorway opened into the banquet area. I stood in the doorway as Pig Pen stomped on into the facility where it became evident that about three hundred people—all dressed in formal attire—were waltzing around the dance floor in celebration of what appeared to have been a wedding. Pig Pen, spying the well-supplied bar near the door, sauntered over up and requested a rum and Coke from the bartender who had already shot us a few dubious looks. Probably because he was more than just a bit fearful of us, the bartender put together the drink and pushed it across the bar. Looking up at the wall behind the bar area, Pig Pen pulled out his tin and flashed it announcing in a LOUD voice: "Where is your liquor permit?" The bartender shrugged. Now that he had EVERYONE'S attention in the entire place, my partner then stuck two fingers into the drink and pronounced: "I'm SEIZING this drink" and then inverted it as he held it aloft—the result being that the drink ran into his jacket sleeve. The music stopped.

Not to be deterred from whatever insanity at that moment was inspiring him, Pig Pen then turned to the crowd, held his badge AND the spilled drink aloft and shouted: "You're ALL under arrest!" It was at precisely that moment that the rigours of the evening caught up with me and I vomited.

We had beaten a rather hasty retreat without my partner's three hundred prisoners and at the onset of sobriety later in the morning, we realized we most likely hadn't heard the end of our little perfor-mance at the hotel. By mutual agreement, we decided it was not a time to lie back and wait for it, so we took the offensive. Professing that we had a totally unmanageable workload of reports, we report-ed at the office HOURS ahead of our regular starting time the next day. No one yelled at us when we came in so we knew we were still okay—if not out of the woods yet. Every time either of the two in-coming office phone lines lit up, one of us immediately snatched it up before the dayshift Detective Sergeant could get to it. We didn't have to wait very long.

Not even a full hour after we had arrived, I grabbed the phone before the first ring had died away. After properly identifying my-self, I breathed a sigh of relief as the caller identified himself as the manager of the Lincoln Hotel. He went on to relate that he had a complaint to make against whom he believed might be two mem-bers of the Winnipeg Police Vice Division as the result of an inci-dent the night before which had been brought to his attention by his staff. I informed the manager that he should direct his com-plaint to the on-duty Sergeant of Detectives and that I would be pleased to transfer the call to him.

Pig Pen took it on the phone in the farthest recesses of the rear Drug Office and identified himself as the officer in charge. He lis-tened politely for several minutes, injecting the odd "I see" or "Yes, Sir." After the manager had finished relating his knowledge of the alleged incident, Pig Pen then informed him that his was in fact the THIRD such complaint that had been received that morning, and that the entire Police Department was investigating a pair of culprits who had been passing themselves off as police officers at various downtown locations in the past couple of days. Pig Pen ob-tained the names of any hotel employees who actually saw the sus-pects in case it became necessary, in the course of the investigation, to interview them or perhaps show some mug shots at a later time. The manager, satisfied with Pig Pen's professionalism and with re-newed faith in the local constabulary added that he really hadn't believed the pair were real cops and wished the force every success with their investigation. I haven't been back to the Lincoln since.

CHAPTER 16 People Are Strange

illy had been a permanent fixture in the North End commencing sometime around 1977. In my entire thirty-three year career, he was the MOST completely dysfunctional human being I have ever seen. He was about thirty years old, and even at that relatively young age he had foiled the very best efforts of every social care-giving agency in the city. He was never NOT filthy in those days and emitted a permeating fetidness of human waste, gas, paint thinner and glue. The modern heroes on the "survivor" shows on television who eat a few live worms and have to pull a couple of leeches off themselves are nothing but weak sisters by comparison. Survival is about conquering your fears. Billy had none because his brain was fried, so he made quite a few less than appropriate decisions regarding the size and tenacity of the opponents he selected for sparring partners—moving cars and buses being a couple of examples that immediately come to mind. I believe he hailed from Shamattawa or some other northern Manitoba resort town and it was rumoured that he had come from a close family—maybe extraordinarily close considering Billy looked like an extra from *Deliverance*.

Billy was a substance abuser without peer. He had probably sucked back more toxic fumes than the Texas City explosion and the Bhopal disaster had spewed out together. Subsequently, he spent all his time snickering. His eyes were perpetually crossed which I personally thought did little to enhance his depth perception as he seemed to gear up for a fight when the nearest person was still several blocks away. He'd get his trademark fiendish smirk on his face and begin engaging multiple foes in mortal hand-to-hand combat. It's my guess that just before the main breaker in his head blew up, he must have been watching Teenage Mutant Ninja Turtles or something else with an equally riveting martial arts theme.

Many a time, he could be observed to move into what appeared to be The Stance of The Crane and hold it for several seconds—albeit a mite unsteadily being on one leg—and then attempt a high kick but with the same leg that was holding him up. It didn't work. However, it did lend some level of understanding for the myriad of scars he had on his face which had been incurred upon his crashing head first onto the roadway or into assorted fixed objects. He had long since lost his ability to speak and the totality of his vocabulary consisted of a few high-pitched yells similar to those heard from combatants in Japanese movies with English sub-titles. Reason had slipped away and Billy was left homeless and on the continual prowl satisfying his most basic needs. Eat. Sleep. Shit. And sniff.

Billy calls were quite common. Billy had just gone to the Seven Eleven and eaten sixteen candy bars. Billy had just mugged a hooker; he left her cash but took her lipstick. Billy had stopped traffic at King and Dufferin and was defecating in the street. Each time he was removed from public contact and deposited at the Drunk Tank, or the hospital Emergency Ward if he was scraped up, or City Welfare in repeated attempts to get him off the street. If nothing else, in warmer weather, cops would hose him down in the wash rack to clean him up a little as putting him in a shopping cart and running him through a car wash may not have been construed by some as good public relations. He had undergone more psychiatric examinations than Charles Manson. Social workers found him unresponsive. He had been given flop-house apartments, lodging at the Salvation Army and other shelter initiatives but they just hadn't worked out for him. When he left them for a day's outing he could never remember that he might go back and never did. In the brief periods he had been institutionalized in his best interests, it never lasted and he had a bag of sniff clamped onto his face in the same hour he was released. He actually existed in this fashion for years.

It was about three o'clock in the morning on a rainy and cool April night when another Billy call was dispatched to a North End unit. I was the Acting Patrol Sergeant and attended way out west on Jarvis Avenue where Billy had taken a fancy to pouncing on all the cars that had been stopping to chat up the hookers and was ripping the windshield wipers off them. Most of the working girls in the area were huddled under the bridge to keep dry and had created a natural bottle-neck of vehicles going both ways. It had made it easy pickings for Billy. None of the victims were getting out of their cars to try and stop him either as between grabbing the wipers he was a blur of spin-kicks and jabs while shrieking like a banshee. I was just pulling in from the east side and the responding two officer unit from the west when Billy saw us. Still clutching his new windshield wiper collection, he began running, spaghetti-legging it past the approaching cruiser on the other side and about two blocks farther while slipping and sliding in the mud and water on the north side of the street.

He made it to the fenced compound of one of the city's bigger lawn and garden retailers. They had endured so many break-ins over the years that they had gotten real serious about protecting their property. The compound was one of those seven foot chain link jobs and it had three strands of barbed-wire stretched as tight as banjo strings all around the top. For an even better deterrent to unauthorized entry were the five guard dogs that were inside—a low budget pack consisting of mostly Shepherd-looking mutts with a couple of huge mongrels in the mix. From previous experience with them, I knew that three of them were just for noise—slinking fear biters at best that would usually just whirl around snapping at their own tails while barking their brains out. The other two were something else altogether. The best dog in the bunch was a no-nonsense hundred pound Shepherd with good lines that came STRAIGHT at the fence whenever you got close and always made a pretty good shot at coming on through. He lived to bite and would even ignore food if you threw a corner off a doughnut in there. There was also a seventy pound bitch. Although a little small, she shadowed the big alpha male and you could tell she had NO back up in her whatsoever.

Billy hit the fence at top speed, and ignoring the pain of the barbed wire chewing into him as only those in a chemically-induced stupor can, he hurtled on over with the three of us just a few steps behind. Just as he hit the ground inside the compound the dogs were out from behind the tractors and other equipment and were moving on him. I was just thinking that we'd likely have to shoot the dogs if they got him down. The big male that was ALL business was picking up speed in his usual straight-on rush and Billy was holding his ground and coiling into one of his versions of some kind of gung-fu stance. The big dog actually made contact with him and then recoiled like he'd just hit an electric fence. He trotted off a few feet and sat down as the little female started—and then stopped just as fast. The other three were whirling around in the background—growling and snapping—and pretty much ignoring Billy. The ONLY explanation I could think of was that Billy stunk so bad that the lead dog and his sidekick had abandoned all aggression when they got a snootful. I mean, even ATTACK dogs have to draw the line somewhere. The big male started a long moaning howl and Billy—smiling insanely—answered him in what he probably felt was Japanese. The senior cop from the pair who were fielding the call looked at me and said, "Whatever he's on...I want some!"

In the same era, I was working the evening shift on a smoking July afternoon with my regular car partner in the core area patrol district. It was 3:00 P.M. when we rolled out of the downtown station and had almost a full minute of free patrol time in when we got the call. We were given the address of a rooming house south of Portage Avenue which was not our area and the happy "Suspicious Circumstances" code which meant "somebody's dead and getting stinky" with the caveat that no one had actually SEEN the dead body yet. In all cases where the death was confirmed, the call code was simply "Investigate."

We rolled up to the two story converted house and the owner met us on the curb. He explained that he had a tenant on the second floor whom he had not seen for at least a week and when he went to collect the rent in the hour previously, he had found the door bolted from the inside and an overpowering smell was coming from the suite. It is at this point that you'd love to say "Well, if the smell doesn't clear up on its own in a few days, maybe give us a call back." And then leave. With a little more questioning, we learned that the tenant was a Chinese fellow about twenty-eight years old who kept to himself and never caused any problems. He had always paid his rent on time and had been living in the room for several months.

We arrived on the second floor and were immediately assailed by the one of the worst stomach-turning stenches that either of us had experienced thus far. Fortunately, both of us had guts of iron and had been to some pretty bad ones. You knew from previous experience that when you pulled up and the Fire Rescue crews were sprawled on the lawn out front puking into their gas masks that it was not going to be pretty. The owner couldn't handle it and bailed. To make it worse, it was over eighty degrees outside and the upstairs in the old place was well over a hundred.

We banged on the door with no response. Red shouted "Police" three or four times with still no sign of life coming from inside the suite. We had already informed the owner we would probably have to force entry and with the perfection that comes only with practice, my partner took it straight down with one boot. We may have thought at some point in those first few minutes that the door wasn't actually holding back the smell for the most part. We were SO wrong. We'd be burning our uniforms again. The room was very dim as the lights were all off and the big shade on the one window was down. I could see the poor son of a bitch slumped in a half sitting position on the edge of the bed-grimacing and rigid in death. What distracted me when I was moving to the bed itself was the presence of a forty-five gallon oil drum with an open top just a couple of feet away from the body. My flashlight revealed that it was just about half full-of human urine and feces which were fermenting nicely in the nuclear heat of the room. My partner had already been whacking at the window frame with ever-increasing intensity in his attempts to get it open but was still being cautious not to contaminate the scene in case it somehow turned out to be a homicide or something else other than a natural death. He gave up but did carefully raise the shade. It brightened up the room enough that with the one bare light bulb on the ceiling we could see well enough to have a good look around.

The place was a shit-hole of the First Order. There wasn't a crumb of food in there which was no big deal, as it looked to me like the guy was a bit past entertaining company, anyway. I had my notebook out and thought I'd check out the body to see if it had progressed to the maggot stage. My partner was already downstairs calling for an Identification Unit crew and the Medical Examiner. It had appeared strange that such a young man might die of natural causes, and the door and the window had been securely locked from the inside. At those kinds of calls you were always thinking there might be more to it. The usual possibilities of accidental overdose or possible suicide were going though my mind when I bent over the body for a closer look. For some reason, and despite the incapacitating heat, the cadaver, which appeared to be an Asian male, was wearing several layers of clothing including heavy overcoats AND one of those ear-flap fur hats that you'd wear if you were a yak herder in Tibet.

My sidekick had just walked back into the room and informed me that the M.E. said he'd be about thirty minutes and I waved him over to the body. I asked him what he made of the goofy get-up the dead guy had on. He considered it for a few seconds and then proclaimed: "The dumb Fuck probably heat-stroked." It was at exactly that point that the dead Chinaman opened his eyes. He then cracked a big smile and looked at us with the look that only someone comfortable in the deepest depths of madness could manage.

The sweat was pouring off the little guy's face and I remembered thinking that I MIGHT have taken note of that fact a little earlier as not a lot of dead people sweat. I figured we had better get some of the coats and crap off him before he DID heat stroke. I went to pull the heavy fur hat off his head, but it was securely tied under his chin and he clamped both hands down on his head and tried to fight us off. I finally reefed it off his head, and found it to be extremely heavy for some reason. Upon looking inside, I could see that our not-so-dead friend had saved up about thirty or so of the metal ends off oval-shaped ham cans and had taped them together and crammed them into the top of his hat. I just had to ask "Sir, what the FUCK is this in your hat?" Rising to the question, the little guy stopped fighting and enthusiastically—in pretty good English—explained that he had in fact invented that particular apparatus and was utilizing it to keep himself cool through heat displacement from his head. The conversation went downhill from there. After ascertaining that he was at least not injured physically we got around to asking him who he was. With utmost sincerity, he proclaimed himself to be: "The Inventor General of The Universe."

We began to peel off the layers of clothing off him and he struggled and squirmed a bit in the beginning but my beefy partner clamped a hand on the back of his neck and held him still while I gave him a good look. A winter parka and fur hat, a blazer over a wool sweater, five shirts, three undershirts, four pairs of pants and seven carpenter's aprons later we had him down to his very nasty skivvies. I'd collected about a wheel barrow full of junk from all his pockets and the carpenters aprons. Along with the over three dozen toothbrushes for which it was quite apparent he had yet to master their intended use, and about six pounds of bottle caps were a couple of hundred pencils and pens and about fifty notebooks—the kind with lined pages inside and not unlike a police notebook. Further examination revealed that on each line of every notebook there were FOUR hand-written lines all compressed into that one line of the book. The entries were a chronological history of everything our somewhat confused little friend had done for the past four or five months and the entries were sometimes only a few minutes apart. I was still trying to read some of them to gain a few insights for the psychiatric staff at the hospital and he was busily explaining several of his latest inventions that we had stumbled upon in his pockets.

One of the purest forms of sheer drudgery in a police officer's life is to have to take a person to the hospital for a psychiatric examination. All hospitals had a strict protocol wherein the patient must first be seen by a general practitioner from their Emergency Admitting area to insure that their physical well-being has first been addressed. This in itself could take hours as the cases are all addressed by priority and the most serious injuries are always treated first. Unless the place is very quiet, the healthy-but-hallucinating guy being babysat by two cops is never too high on the priority list. Bribing one of the old Triage nurses with chocolate sometimes helped, but long waits were still quite common. Once the patient was deemed to be physically out of danger, the hospital's psychiatric staff was notified and again the officers were subjected to waits of seldom less than one hour and as long as twenty-four before the psych exam actually started. Even when the psychiatrists had attended and undergone a fairly lengthy examination of a patient, one could not count on a quick decision pertaining to their diagnosis and the ultimate disposition of the patient.

We had allowed the little Chinese fellow ONE shirt and ONE pair of pants and whistled him off to the hospital with a few of his notebooks to show the shrink. The physical with the Emergency doctor went off in near record time and other than a little dehydration he was good to go. We were informed that a resident psychiatrist was on his way down and we geared ourselves up for another LONG wait. The hitch was that as police officers, we were required by law to remain with the patient until the hospital admitted him or he was released.

The bearded psychiatrist attended and carrying a briefcase he announced he would be commencing his examination of the patient in an adjacent secure room. We would remain just outside for the usual one to two hours until he was finished, and then remain still longer for next hour or so until a determination had been made by the psychiatrist—considering all factors—as to whether the patient should be admitted or not.

In just under two minutes the shrink was back out. I stood and approached him to see what the problem was, suspecting that our little friend had become resistive again. The doctor, without any alluding to a specific neurosis or psychosis as they usually did at length, quite simply stated with a tired look, "He's staying." I was just opening my mouth to enquire as to a possible diagnosis for my report and he added, "He's fucking nuts."

It occurred to me somewhere in those early years that a LOT of people were nuts, and still running around loose. I was working a downtown unit with an English guy who didn't stay on the job for a great length of time. He had that dry, British sense of humour and was an extremely nice fellow who would never purposely offend anyone. I had worked the front desk with him a couple of nights previously and was amazed at the calm and professional manner he could keep up even when tested by some of the rudest callers possible. On one occasion, the female complainant SCREAMED into the phone at him for over ten minutes voicing her displeasure over the fact that her neighbor's Great Dane kept defecating in her yard and that the police had done nothing about it despite her numerous calls to register a formal complaint. Whenever she had paused to catch her breath—for even just a second—he would politely say "Yes, Madam." She went on forever, but consistent with his manner, he got in about ten or twelve "Yes, Madams'" before she finally finished venting and hung up. He replaced the handset and calmly stated to the hung-up telephone "Fuck off, Madam."

One night, we were cruising around right downtown around 9:00 P.M. when we received a not uncommon call of "A woman refusing to leave." We got a fair bit of that in the area, as a lot of one night stands that got past the original point of their visit decided they were going to set up camp on a more permanent basis and were sometimes a little hard to get headed back out the door by the fellow who was paying the rent. It was a suite on Vaughn Street and when we knocked, we were met by a very pleasant lady in her late fifties. She had a very nicely decorated suite which was, in every way, orderly and clean. My partner, with his best charm, asked her how we may help her. She informed us, in low tones, to avoid being overheard by anyone else who was inside the suite, that a young Negro girl who was about eighteen years of age sometimes visited her. She was, in fact there at that time in her living room, but for some reason was refusing to go home. The lady went on to explain that she was tired and usually went to sleep at about nine in the evening, but the girl just wouldn't leave—even when asked to.

We assured her that we would remedy the situation quickly and without any undue embarrassment for her and both of us walked around the corner into her perfectly appointed living room. There was no one there. Thinking that the girl may have slipped into another room or the bathroom, we checked out the whole place while the lady remained at the suite door. There wasn't a trace of anyone. My partner motioned the lady over to the living room entrance and asked her where exactly the girl had been in the suite as we were unable to locate her. With grace and poise, she walked over to a three foot tall china urn which was in a corner, looked into the top and then back at us. She pointed at the urn and with a smile, stated, "She's in there." I HAD to look. It was empty. I knew I would feel stupid afterwards. My partner never missed a beat. He smiled back, and leaning over the urn, in a school-master voice barked "All RIGHT. You come out of there at ONCE and leave this lady's home!" He paused about ten seconds, and then informed the still smiling lady that the girl was now gone. With gratitude, she walked us out and graciously bid us a good evening.

Graciousness and good manners were not, however, always in the equation when the core area's strangest were encountered on the streets. One particular young fellow whose name was Gerry was as weird as they came. He was about eighteen and a tall, gangly sort. He was gaunt as a corpse and had bleached blond hair to his shoulders. To enhance his appearance, he had taken to wearing a heavy application of pasty-white makeup on his face and he was usually about half gooned out on a mind altering substance of some description whenever patrolling officers came upon him. The kid kept worse hours than Dracula. He was only on the street between midnight and four or five in the morning but made excellent use of his time away from home satisfying his predatory urges as a professional mugger, thief and pervert.

Gerry had been imprinted much earlier in his life on the streets to generate programmed responses to all circumstances. If he caught someone elderly, weaker or smaller than himself he robbed or sodomized them. If he saw the police, he ran. If the police caught him, he got his ass kicked. And so on. My earliest experience with Gerry came one hot summer night in the mid 1970s when I was riding with a more senior North End patrol officer who was driving our unit north on Main Street from The Drag. We were cruising along and taking it easy as the bars were just closing when my partner suddenly jammed the accelerator to the floor. I looked ahead to try and spot what he had seen, and a lanky figure with long blond hair flowing behind him was running for all he was worth, trying to get across the street before we got to him. When it became apparent that he wasn't going to make it and he'd be mowed down by our car, he did a complete 180 and started to run back the way he had come. My partner fired open the driver's door just as we passed within two feet of him at forty miles an hour, and knocked him somersaulting over the centre boulevard and into the southbound lanes of traffic.

My partner then shut his door, slowed down and resumed our previous cruising speed without saying a word. I HAD to ask. I got the low-down on Gerry and I had many more encounters with him before the passage of time swallowed him up like all of his kind and he was gone.

CHAPTER 17 Tough Guys

Throughout my years on the street, I tangled with a number of men in the course of my duties. Bikers, lounge lizards, drug dealers and a variety of others of every colour and creed. I can state with absolute sincerity that the two toughest human beings I have ever encountered were Indians.

The second toughest man was a pretty brief encounter, and not unlike literally dozens of others I have had in similar circumstances, it occurred when I was walking alone on Main Street on a slow dayshift. I was standing on the west side of Main Street right at Higgins Avenue when I saw the guy stumble out of the old Patricia Hotel. He was Cree, about thirty-five years old and weighed about two-forty with a pretty good Molson Muscle in the front. He started to cross the street without even a sideways glance and as he careened out into traffic cars began slamming on brakes and running up the curb to avoid running him down. He retreated back to the sidewalk and I double-timed it over there to get him in tow before he tried it again.

He gave me his name and I told him he was going to have to take a ride with me over to the Drunk Tank for a little nap. I radioed for the wagon to pick us up and stood back to wait. My new friend decided he wasn't waiting around and started to lumber off south on the east side of Main Street. I caught up to him and grabbed his arm and he promptly tore the cross strap off my Sam Browne belt and made a grab for my shirt. Over the next two or three minutes, he threw about two dozen bombs at my head and I hit him with everything but the barn door. Fortunately, he telegraphed everything he did, and I was in my early twenties and in good shape, but I was by then missing my hat, my tie, both shirt sleeves and my epaulets. For the third time in ten seconds I drove him one right on the button with every ounce of strength I had and each time he just grunted, took a half-step back and came on for some more. I was starting to look behind him to see what was holding him up. He had taken the second line drive in the nuts and was still on his feet and the short jabs I was raining on him might as well have been flower petals.

A bus driver stopped and despite being pretty portly wanted to jump in and help me. I waved him off and asked him to call me some assistance on his bus radio. I did manage to make the Cree's nose bleed but it seemed to only make him madder and the shots to his ears seemed to hurt him the most so I worked on them for another minute. Out of nowhere, a Native girl about thirty walked up and pushed my fellow combatant up against the brick wall along the sidewalk and slapped him a dandy right on the side of his head. She said something to him in Cree and then he sat down. She told me she was his wife and that she'd take him from there. I was thinking "Thank CHRIST!" but I said: "Well, okay, I'll let him off with a warning THIS time." She towed him away by one of his fattened ears. My hands hurt for a week but it was an excellent lesson in humility.

The Number One tough man and I never laid a glove on each other, nor did we even try. In fact, there was virtually no hostility between us whatsoever. I was assigned to walk the beat on a dayshift, and I was informed by the Duty Sergeant at morning roll call that I was to escort a prisoner from the fourth floor lockup to the hospital. I reported straight to the old Patrol Sergeant who was running the jail on dayshift, and he had one of his crew bring out a very large Indian prisoner from the back.

The fellow was in his late twenties and a solid six four and two-fifty on the hoof. It was cool in the jail, but his face was beaded with perspiration, and it was evident that he was in a lot of discomfort. I asked the jailers what the nature of his ailment was and I received a fairly lengthy explanation involving a myriad of medical terms, and I quote: "He can't piss."

So, I cuffed myself to the big fellow and travelled down the elevator to the basement area and into the back of the waiting patrol wagon. En route to the Health Sciences Centre I asked him, "What's wrong?" He softly stated "Clap." I resisted the urge to leap away from him but I did only then notice the large dried spot of encrusted bodily fluids on the front of his trousers. I got him through Triage and was waiting in the Police Room but for a few minutes when one of the nurses came in and told me to take my prisoner into the back treatment area. I stayed cuffed to him, as he was in custody for some fairly serious offences involving violence. The doctor came in and under the circumstances requested that I remain and he had the big fellow drop his pants and shorts and stand up.

The doctor wheeled in close for a look and announced that the infection appeared to be quite pronounced. When he asked how long it had been since he was able to pass urine the answer shocked us both. Over two days. I then understood why the guy was sweating. They had a little verbal exchange about when he thought he had become infected, and if he had the name of the lady who imparted the gift that kept on giving and the like, and then it was down to business. The poor guy's privates were a horror show with some serious discoloration and swelling and it took the doctor quite a few minutes to clean him up enough to start the procedure. When he did, I started to sweat.

Out of the tray of medical instruments, the doctor selected a stainless steel tube about an eighth of an inch in diameter which was about ten inches long. It looked pretty innocuous until he tested out the mechanism that was retracted inside the business end. When he cycled the spring on the rear end of it, a stainless steel umbrella with razor sharp rear edges snapped open on the business end. Despite a lack of medical training, it took me about a half a second to figure out that the tube was going into my prisoner's urethra and when it was fully inserted, the little umbrella was going to snap open for the trip back out. And, those little razor edges were going to clean out the runway. I was just going to tell the doctor that I'd have to call in to get the other nine cops that were going to be required to hold this poor bastard down when he just did it. The rod went in and I almost fainted, but the big guy never flinched. Only a telltale marked increase in his sweating let me know he felt it. The doctor popped open the umbrella and in a long, smooth stroke withdrew it.

The only sound, faint as it was, that the big Native boy made was "uh." He shuddered for a second or two and the sweat was pouring off him in buckets but that was the only sound he made. I would have STILL been screaming. Just as the instrument was nearly fully withdrawn, the blood, urine and pus shot out nearly three feet and did wonders for the doctor's white lab coat and most of the area around him. I think I was up on the arm of the chair by then. About two million units of penicillin later, most of it shot right into the poor guy's left gluteus maximus, we got down to some serious clean-up. The doctor had him shuck out of everything and gave him some new green surgical duds to wear as the disposable blue paper clothes were way too small. His clothes, the doctor's lab coat and all the gauze and toweling got bundled up for burning. My prisoner got a prescription filled for cookie-sized antibiotics and a follow-up appointment. Never threw a punch but he was the toughest man in the world. Period.

CHAPTER 18 Emergency Response Unit

I n the mid 1970s, a lot of the larger municipal police departments in Canada started to get on board with what had been developing stateside in the wake of the Vietnam War. Returning Special Forces vets began to join the L.A.P.D. and other notable pioneers in the specialization of police functions, following their discharges from the armed forces. The S.W.A.T. (Special Weapons and Tactics) movement began and the F.B.I., with an earlier version of today's Hostage Rescue Team tactics provided a lot of the expertise in the early training.

The Winnipeg P.D. jumped in about 1975 with an unprecedented enthusiasm by sending five Detectives from the Robbery and Homicide side to receive their basic training in the doctrine from the F.B.I. at their facility in Quantico, Virginia. The idea was to enable them to bring it back to Winnipeg and to be able to expand their newly acquired knowledge with further training at home. The long range plan was to eventually expand the unit as funding and advanced training became available.

It was early in 1976 when a number of officers from all divisions—uniform and plainclothes—were recruited to bring the Emergency Response Unit (E.R.U.) up to numbers. A co-ordinator, and three team leaders—each in charge of a five man team—began training one day a month separately by teams, and then a second day that month as the complete three team unit.

Red and I got selected for it, and were always on the same team in our many years on the unit. He quickly proved himself to be the best shot—ever. Funding was a little slow equipment-wise, and even though we started off with an old Dive Unit truck as our official E.R.U. wheels, we later acquired what looked like a giant blue bread truck that was purchased by the city. After it was customized to hold all the gear, it served the unit well for almost twenty years.

The early weaponry came from a variety of sources. We evolved fairly quickly from the Smith and Wesson .38 Special revolvers which were standard issue in those times—and may still be in Uruguay—to some new Colt .45 automatics. Despite the somewhat limited magazine capacities they had in comparison to today's Glocks, it didn't take a lot of shots to win an argument with one. Our sniping rifles were something else. I believe ALL of them had been pressed into service after they had been seized by a number of the municipal departments that made up the Winnipeg P.D. after the fall of 1974. They came in an assortment of calibers, .270's, .308's and others and were really just standard hunting rifles with low dollar scopes and even cheaper scope mounts. Red got assigned to put together a few from what we had to make them as serviceable as possible for the unit until we got us some bona fide sniping rifles and scopes.

A course came up and the unit coordinator selected Red and another member to attend the very prestigious, week-long Ontario Provincial Police (O.P.P.) Sniper Training Course at Camp Borden, Ontario. This was THE course for snipers and was taught by and demonstrated by some of the best funded and allegedly best sniping teams in the country. If you didn't believe that, you could have just asked them. Red torqued down the action screws on his off-the-rack budget Model 70 Winchester with a straight six power scope, a stock trigger and still intact iron sights on the sporter weight barrel. He grabbed about ten boxes of the seized factory .270 ammunition and away he went to be enlightened.

On the first morning, our boys were virtually laughed out of the briefing room and were informed by the instructors that they were just wasting their time with the junk that they had toted along for rifles. The O.P.P. boys were fielding fine-tuned Remington target guns—all .308's—with telescopic sights on them not much smaller than the MacDonald Observatory. Their after market triggers were down to ounces—not pounds—and their ammunition was all match stuff built for serious accuracy. They were still laughing when everyone headed out into the stiff morning breeze to do a little plinking out to six hundred yards. They weren't laughing when they came back in.

Much to their repeated dismay, Red started a week-long tradition wherein every day, he totally and completely humiliated the best shooters that any of the other police forces could field. Being one of those very rare, natural born riflemen, he could calculate wind drift and bullet drop in his head in about a quarter of a second. When the O.P.P. boys were cranking away on the elevation and windage adjustments of their eighteen power scopes trying to find something close to adequate correction, Red was squinting through his forty dollar six power Bushnell and drilling the black ten ring with boring regularity. Red's partner told me later on he could hear the O.P.P. Coordinator who was hosting the course SCREAMING at his troops in their barracks and pointing out that some "Fucking STUBBLE-JUMPER from Winnipeg was kicking their asses with a rifle that should have been used for a JACK HANDLE."

Even quite a bit later on, a lot of huff and puff went into a certain caliber of cartridge supposedly being inherently more accurate that some other. To some extent, that may have been the case, and the .308 with a couple of others pretty much standardized what "police" rifles evolved into. Despite what may or may not have been the best, it had always been foremost in my own thoughts that the rifle was only as good as the man on the trigger.

In those early years of training within the unit, I realized that I had a bit of a natural aversion to a number of things, including getting shot, blown up or dropped from great heights to my death. Furthermore, I found I wasn't a real hardcore tear gas fan, either. My first trip to the rappelling tower could only be described as sheer terror. I think I developed a nosebleed on about the second rung of the ladder going up. The whole unit was sent to Canadian Forces

Base (C.F.B.) Shilo to get whipped into shape by a really gung-ho Warrant Officer from The Princess Patricia's Canadian Light Infantry (P.P.C.L.I.). He was a sawed-off little rooster and about as ruthless as they came. To add even further to his persona, he had an exqui- site command of profanity and could—several times in the same sentence—use the "F" word as a noun, pronoun, verb, adverb and a past pluperfect. We were in awe. The guy was ALL blood and guts and I'm positive he would have charged a machine-gun nest single- handedly with nothing more than a sharpened toothbrush.

We were lined up on the tower-standing as far from the edge as possible-while he was stomping around in his combat boots with one foot in outer space as he explained the basics of plummeting backwards—and then forwards—off the tower. To demonstrate, he snapped a young Private's caribeener onto the rappelling rope and told him to go. The kid took about a half of a second too long, so the impatient instructor threw him off. The safety line caught and jerked him to a halt about four inches from the ground. One of our team leaders was next in line, and snapped onto the line and began inching to the edge of the tower to give it a go. Numbnuts the Warrant Officer bounced over and took hold of him—most likely with a mind to repeat his demonstration of the technique of advanced freefalling—when he was suddenly surrounded by about ten much larger cops who weren't picking up on the humour value in being tossed off the roof. After a short conference he agreed that it was probably a much better idea to let our guys do it slowly for the first couple of times until they got used to it.

It was going pretty good, and everyone did about a dozen back- wards descents down the forty foot wall to the ground. I was just thinking that it hadn't been TOO bad when G.I. Joe announced that now that we were experts, we would be doing the "Austrian Rappel" which entailed RUNNING off the tower FORWARDS. As he explained the technique in detail over the next six seconds, I believe, in hind- sight, I was thinking that running off a perfectly solid and safe plat- form into thin air several stories above the ground was about the highest attainable degree of Human Stupidity. To pretty much sub- stantiate that theory, the instructor didn't even hook up, but merely looped the rappelling rope over a shoulder and under the off arm and bailed. It was not considered good form if one "thundered in" at the end of a rappel, meaning you had lost control of your descent AND the safety rope failed. This was exactly what he did. Fortunately, he landed for the most part directly on his head and was uninjured.

My Team Leader was standing first in line to try it out and for some reason still unclear to me all these years later, I was next. I told him that I didn't think he should do it, and when he asked me why with a perplexed look, I explained that if he did that meant that then I'd have to—especially with everyone else watching. He and I tended to disagree about most things, and as the years progressed we unfortunately digressed into some real personal flare-ups, but I can offer no dispute into the fact that he always had admirable intestinal fortitude. The crazy son of a bitch snapped onto the rope, and yelling louder than the Rebs charging up Little Round Top, he went over.

It was my turn. With shaking hands I hooked on, and braced the brake rope across my chest with my right arm. I discovered some bastard had nailed my boots to the deck when I started to go, and only with super-human effort did I manage to break them loose. However, for some reason, my feet felt like they weighed about two hundred pounds apiece, and I only managed to hit about three miles per hour when I stumbled over the edge with "GO, TINMAN!" from all the voices behind me ringing in my ears. I think I hit the wall the first time about half way down and the brake rope got wound around my left foot but it slowed me right down. I did manage to invert myself into to some semblance of an orderly, controlled descent and made a few running steps—actually touching the wall with my feet—in the last fifteen feet to the ground. I did a few more and we learned that the Austrians, who invented that particular form of madness, would fire their sub-machine guns as they ran down the wall. I suspected that it was for the purpose of being able to shoot themselves to achieve a quick, painless death rather than lingering for weeks awaiting death in a hospital with multiple fractures and internal injuries.

Explosives were probably the one thing I was never really comfortable being around. Like most of the guys in the unit, I had a
very limited experience of them save a one day job with a trapper
friend when I helped him blow up some beaver dams with some
really scary stuff called PowerFrac. We air-mailed beavers into other
postal code zones where they had previously not existed. All the
training after our first couple of years started to get more and more
sophisticated, and the use of explosives to facilitate an "explosive
entry" came into play. Basically, what that meant was that if an
assault team needed to get inside a secure premises in a lightning-
quick, surprise assault the "explosive entry" technique would allow them a door for entry where seconds before none existed. It
sounded good in theory.

The unit co-ordinator and his three team leaders—one of which
by then was myself—headed out into the country about eighty
miles from the city where our Bomb Unit guys and the R.C.M.P.
Bomb Unit and E.R.T. leaders had secured a log farmhouse for our
mutual benefit in doing a little informal blasting. A video crew
came along to capture it all for the purposes of future training. The
Bomb guys had some stuff called DetaSheet which looked a lot like
thick tape. They'd bend the edges in after taping it onto the edges
of a sheet of Styrofoam the size of a door, lean it on the log side of
the old farmhouse, and blast out a perfectly rectangular point of
entry in the foot thick walls. After a couple of dry runs, it was time
for the E.R.U. and E.R.T. guys to get right up close, behind a tiny, but
allegedly indestructible transparent umbrella called a Bomb Shield.
It was one-two-three KA-BOOM and then the assault team would
enter in the micro-seconds following the blast and catch all the dis-
oriented villains inside unawares. It also sounded good in theory.

The first time we tried it, we found we were too far from the
house when we had placed the bomb shield at twenty feet away.
We were too slow getting inside. The object of the whole exercise
was to develop a REALLY fast entry, so we cut the distance down to
about fifteen feet and the film crew set up for Take Two. We were
crouched and ready to spring the second the blast ripped an opening and we waited it out. One, two…somebody MISSED three…

and then we sprang—I supposed right where three should have been a half a second before. I was just into my second running step towards the house, when "Oh-Oh!" popped into my brain—and then it went. When I viewed the videotape several minutes later and my hearing was beginning to return, there I was. The blast took two of us almost STRAIGHT up into the air for over twelve feet and then deposited all of us in various positions of repose quite some distance from where we had started off. My moustache and eyebrows were singed almost completely off, and I had several deep burns from the molten Styrofoam that had been blown onto my exposed face, arms and hands. I was dizzy for an hour and didn't re-gain all my hearing for a full week. That video was used for several years following, for the purpose of instructing what NOT do to when conducting an "explosive entry". It got some great laughs. Cops I had never met would come up to me and say "Hey! I know you! You're the RETARD in that training video who got blown up!"

CHAPTER 19 Professionalism 101

The place was out in upper middle class suburbia on a secluded bay in The Bible Belt. North Kildonan was a quiet, desirable community in which to live and was far removed from the violence and crime of the inner city. The house was a comfortable bungalow on a nicely treed lot and it showed a lot of care from the honest and hardworking couple who had lived there for over a decade. Their oldest child—a daughter—had left the nest and lived close by and their sole remaining child—a twenty-year-old son—had just begun working full time after two years of community college.

Life was pretty good on the home front until that very eventful late spring morning in 1984 when Mom and Dad headed out for their ritual grocery shopping trip early on a Saturday and left Junior at home presumably catching up on his sleep in his professionally finished basement bedroom.

When the folks arrived back at home around 10:30 A.M. the kid's car was still parked in the driveway and after unlocking the house and making a start at hauling in the week's worth of groceries, the head of the household yelled down the basement stairs for the kid to get up and give them a hand. Five minutes later, he yelled again with the same absence of any response, and he headed down to roust the kid out of the sack.

The parents knew that their son had been in a seemingly unshakable relationship of very long standing with his high school sweetheart and assumed that in time the pair would marry. Apparently the son had made the same assumption, but when the young lady announced the termination of the relationship late on the evening before, his devastation was total and even his crying and pleading was for naught. She dumped him. From within the recesses of his despair, and with little consideration of the fact that he was going to live for another sixty or seventy years, in a classic move rife with "I'LL SHOW YOU" he ended his suffering in the two hour period his parents were out of the house. After penning a scrawled note proclaiming his eternal, undying love for his now departed lady friend, he laid back on his thousand dollar free-flow waterbed, and put the business end of his father's shotgun into his mouth. Then he touched it off.

No one has ever effectively described in words what actually occurs in that micro-second of time when a human head explodes from a point blank shotgun blast. Too many things go wrong all at once and those that have actually witnessed it are so horrified by it that most cannot speak at all for extended periods of time. In this case, the ounce and a quarter of extra hard birdshot that exited the twelve gauge's muzzle at around 1330 feet per second hadn't even begun to spread and the effect was not unlike that of a small cannon. Everything from the kid's bottom jaw on up was just gone and blown into trout food all over the headboard and the wall behind the bed. The kid's body was swimming in blood and parental despair could never be more pronounced. Much to their credit, they sucked it up within seconds and got to a phone and called 911.

Within moments, a parade of ambulances, EMS supervisors, Fire Rescue units and cops began to converge on the innocuous spot in quiet suburbia. The rescue units had one very quick look and pronounced there was no further need of their services at that location. One young lady who was enjoying her very first day in the field as half of an ambulance crew was puking on the front steps when the police supervisors pulled up. They were a jovial pair of veterans with an average of twenty-five years or so service apiece and both had been moved into the amalgamated police department from two of the smaller thirteen police agencies that had merged in 1974. Both were Sergeants—a Level I and a Level II and both had a myriad of police experience.

Upon moving into the residence, they could see the very distraught parents were being comforted by a neighbour in the living room on the main floor. Both officers moved into the mode of somber-faced and caring professionals taking charge of a crisis with due consideration of the level of devastation the family was enduring at the moment. After insuring the parents were as good as they possibly could be under the circumstances, the boys headed down into the basement where a pasty-white junior constable was guarding the open bedroom and an Identification Unit photographer was just wrapping up the end of his grisly photo session. The blood splattered note was located and retained as evidence for the Medical Examiner who was reported to be en route and did in fact arrive within the next couple of minutes. After some rapid preliminary exchanges of information, the M.E. prepared to get up close and personal with the deceased son and as he was snapping on his latex gloves he requested that the officers present remove the weapon in the interests of safety. It was at this point that it all went very wrong.

For reasons he took to the grave with him, Junior had decided that ONE twelve gauge shotgun shell might not be enough to totally decapitate himself. Or, he conceivably may have even considered that he might even miss with the first shot. No one will ever know, but the fact was is that he had stuffed THREE shells into the shotgun—one in the chamber and two into the pantry—again a mystery in itself as the weapon in question was a pump action and required a live person to actually pump out the empty and chamber a second live round after it was fired. One's head turning into red mist after the first pop normally would preclude any form of reloading but the kid WAS distraught and probably wasn't considering all of this in his plan for self-destruction nor would he have given a shit about what happened after he was gone.

There was another underlying complication. What really was the cause of what was about to take place lurked within the makeup of the weapon itself. It was a Winchester Model 12—named for the year 1912 in which it was introduced. Discontinued in 1963 as rising costs of production in hand-finished firearms made the cost too prohibitive, the company began mass producing weapons made up of machine stampings with much lower production costs the year following. The Model 12 was a symphony of steel and Dad's was a particularly nice one with a highly collectible solid raised rib on the barrel and in like-new condition. But, like its predecessor the Model 1897, it had no disconnector in the trigger mechanism. What this meant, was that as long as the trigger was just held back and the weapon was pumped to shuck out the fired empty and chamber a new live round, when the action was slammed shut on the new round it would fire instantly. This was a real joy to the many G.I.'s who toted one through the close fighting in the jungles of the Pacific in World War II. With the magazine plug removed, the Model 12's would hold a gaggle of shells—seven to be exact—and many a group of Japanese marines were swathed off their feet with rapid fire involving Uncle Sam's buckshot belched out of a Model 12.

Today, police firearms instructors preach a very simple rule to all qualifying officers with all forms of weaponry: "Gun OFF target-finger OFF trigger" It is repeated so many times in all training sessions so that even the dimmest communication dwarf in the ranks will get it. But, this was in 1984.

Stepping up to the task, the junior ranking Sergeant snatched up the Model 12 and possibly assuming that there was a fired round in the chamber he pulled the trigger and held it there which did nothing as the action was not cocked since the firing pin had already struck and fired the shell resting in there. Pointing the weapon down—as in down into the waterbed beside the prone body—he proceeded with his version of how to unload the fired casing and making sure the firearm was rendered safe. When he shucked back the walnut forearm the empty popped out the loading port on the right side. Everyone there must have thought "So far so good." However, in the next moment when he slammed it shut with a forward sliding motion, true to form, the old Winchester flawlessly chambered the next shell and fired it quicker than anyone could believe.

The resounding BOOM under the low basement ceiling was only slightly overshadowed in total shock effect by the geyser of water, blood, brains and bed parts that were blown up to the ceiling and several hundred gallons of water were unleashed on the crime scene. But, unfazed by this minor set-back in his professional image, the old Sarge—squeezing the trigger tighter than ever at this point—reflexively stroked it again and shell number THREE went BOOM right beside where number TWO had just a second before reduced all present into a quailing, open-mouthed state of sheer horror. All except for the more senior ranking Sergeant who calmly stated: "Pump it again, you FUCKING IDIOT!!"

For some reason, the parents didn't sue the city for stress and duress, or for any of the extensive counselling sessions they likely attended for the rest of their lives.

Firearms fiascos haven't been limited to only one or two little mishaps in the last few decades. Fortunately, no one was ever injured with the exception of a range officer plugging himself in the hip with one of the old Smith and Wesson .38's while attempting to free up a locked cylinder on the indoor firing line. It took the spring out of his step for a bit, but he lived to laugh about it.

Throughout my years on the job, I only bore witness to a single incident of an accidental discharge. Every year, each and every member of the organization that carries a firearm in the course of their duties was required through an accreditation process to re-qualify with that weapon. And it meant everyone—regardless of rank. As it worked out in somebody's planning, the entirety of the Senior Officer ranks, which included everyone with the rank of Inspector on up to the Chief of Police, was included in a single day's refresher which precluded any participation from members of the rank and file—most likely so that the diminished marksmanship of the majority of the leadership could remain a guarded secret.

The old but very serviceable Smith and Wesson revolvers were replaced in the mid-1990s with the state-of-the-art Glock Model 22 semi-automatic pistols in .40 S&W calibre. Each officer was issued three of the fifteen-shot magazines with the thinking that no one was going to lose a gun fight for lack of shooting back. Or at least one could keep the enemy pinned down until help arrived. However, the transition from carrying a revolver for up to thirty years and then switching to a semi-automatic pistol was less than smooth for a few members and qualifying was tougher for some than others.

Preceding any time spent on the firing line was a full morning of classroom instruction, hands-on maintenance and a little test to make sure everyone was paying attention. All issue pistols were brought in and safely unloaded at a "loading station" which was present in all police buildings and would trap any fired rounds in case of a discharge while loading or unloading. The guns were then inspected by range officers who confirmed which members had which pistols and then it was class time.

One very warm June day, about twenty Senior Officers were sitting in the range facility classroom about mid-morning in the session. As the instructor droned on about how far the actual projectiles of various rounds could travel the impact of his words was slightly overwhelmed by a resounding KA-BLAM about two rows from the back of the room. No one keeled over but the silence that followed the many coffee cups spilling over and people resuming their seats was pronounced and accusing looks were shot all over the room. Finally, the instructor recovered enough to speak and asked "Is everyone O.K.?"

A small voice from another Inspector sitting near me offered, "Well…if blood is BROWN, I'm hit!!" Another member of the class who had been fooling around with his new Glock under the table where he sat later explained that he thought if the magazine was removed the gun was safe, so he pulled the trigger. It wasn't Good Idea of The Day. This was a guy with a degree. Despite the fact that the magazine was removed from the pistol there was a live round still in the chamber which hadn't gotten jacked out and Glocks WILL fire a round in the chamber even when the magazine is missing so that officers don't get killed in the middle of a magazine change. He shot the floor about halfway to the guys sitting at the desks in front of him and was immediately dropped from about a dozen Christmas card lists.

CHAPTER 20 Making It Work

S ituations occasionally arose that fell outside of any possibility of being addressed by normal operating procedures. Some even required a fair bit of special planning and the assignment of a temporary task force to overcome the problem. Most often, it was the result of public outcry or unfavourable media coverage that prompted police to act on such issues, but act we did. The term "proactive" was just getting warmed up back then.

One of the more memorable problems we crushed was the perpetual activity of male sex trade workers and their vast following in the area around the Manitoba Legislative Building. From early evening—especially in the warmer months in the early 1990s— every street corner for a six block radius around Government House was posted by hustlers of every description. The all night traffic was murderous up and down the usually quiet streets and alleys off Assiniboine Avenue and it had even spilled over to the riverbank area behind the old curling club on the west side of Osborne Street. Literally hundreds of potential customers and thrill seekers cruised the zone in their vehicles and area residents had decided enough was too much. They were unable to leave their apartments after dark, their children were being continually solicited and many had witnessed wide-open sexual activity in the alleys and area shrubbery.

I was working downtown as a uniform Staff Sergeant at the time and my boss approached me and told me to make it go away. I always knew when he was taking some major heat from the fifth floor as he was a lot less particular about the "How" part when we had those little talks. I also knew he still had an eye on the Deputy Chief's chair and some seriously positive results were expected forthwith. I proceeded to recruit about twenty of the biggest and nastiest uniform cops I could find. I submitted a "plan" which was ninety-eight percent bullshit and two percent smoke and mirrors, but it did allude to the fact that the project would involve my draftees and myself being out on the street for five successive nights from dusk until the early morning hours. That part WAS true.

The only real experience I had in dealing with the usually secretive illegal activities of male prostitutes had come in one brief encounter when I assisted some of the Morals guys in a sweep on a North Main Street steam bath which was operating back in the late '70s. Just about everyone who was working in Vice that night got dragged along so a few of us from the Drug Squad were there just to bolster the police numbers. It was forty below outside and eighty-five degrees inside. The place was dark and steamy and smelled like mold, baby lotion and body odour with just a hint of shit. There were a lot of naked men wandering around in varying states of obvious sexual excitement—some with towels but most with nothing on whatsoever. A catacomb of little rooms with drawn curtains and dim lights that were rented out by the hour were everywhere and you couldn't really tell who was where or how many we were dealing with. Frenchie, with his usual diplomacy, took charge by yelling: "O.K. POLICE. ALL YOU FUCKING TAMP-A-TURD ARTISTS STOP JACK-HAMMERING EACH OTHER'S ASSES AND GET THE FUCK OUT HERE WHERE WE CAN SEE YOU!" Weird had been one of the first cops through the door and had snagged a twenty-something wisp of a man with long hair, a lot of runny mascara and black lace panties who had been playing Musical Mattresses in the joint all evening. He was performing oral sex on a senior citizen in the first cubicle when we hit the door. Aside from remembering being very uncomfortable in the steam wearing my goose down parka, probably more so from all the very creepy people in there, I can recall little else from the experience, except Weird addressing his new arrest as "You disgusting, perverted, sicko, low-life piece of human SHIT!" Not offended in the least and standing there wearing only his panties and Weird's handcuffs, he lisped back in a hoarse whisper, "It dothent mean you're a bad perthon."

Anyway, back at the Legislature, I commandeered the police patrol wagon, about six boxes of Spot Check Forms and a Polaroid camera with a hockey sock full of film. The four dozen or so books of blank traffic tickets came in very handy as well. Then we went for it. On Night One, I had assigned pairs of officers to be placed throughout the problem area just to reinforce the perception that there was suddenly a high police presence in the neighbourhood. Every corner seemed to have suddenly sprouted two scowling cops. I reserved a half dozen or so of the boys that I considered to be the cream of the crop to accompany me in the patrol wagon as we would be interfacing with the numerous persons that would be stopped throughout the project. Naturally, it was extremely important for us to portray a positive professional image, good public relations and an understanding of persons with alternate lifestyles, so I chose them after considering each of their past performances in such areas.

The Jewish guy in the new Mercedes had made his third pass in the area checking over the male prostitute prospects that were available. He was a little leery because of all the uniforms and police units in the area, but not to be deterred, and with practiced diligence he kept looking. He obviously wasn't just passing through the neighbourhood, so I directed Mack to pull him over. As I wheeled the patrol wagon up beside the coupe at a stop sign, Mack leaned out the passenger window and bellowed, "HEY TINKERBELL, PULL THE FUCK OVER!"

The thirty-something curbcruiser in his Gucci jeans leaped out of his import and began howling with indignant outrage. Even when he was still exiting his vehicle he was yelling, "Do you know who I am?" Mack calmly answered him with, "Yes Sir, I do. You're "I'm A Little Light On My Loafers Number Fifty-Six" out of all those that we've observed down here this evening." Quivering with rage, our new acquaintance retorted with the usual, "I'll have your job!" With a big smile, Mack came back at him with, "Cool. You get the Patrol wagon, I'll take the Mercedes."

He was howling even louder when he was pulled into the back of the patrol wagon, issued with a traffic ticket for failing to come to a complete stop at the previous stop sign and had all his personal information and vehicle description recorded on the Spot Check Form that was attached to the color Polaroid picture that was taken of him. Mack explained that since he didn't live or work anywhere near there, EVERY time he was seen in the area in the future he would again be spot checked with the identical thoroughness including a new traffic ticket if possible. The concept in which we considered him to be a part of the very big problem we were in the process of eliminating from the city's streets was made abundantly clear to him. Mack asked him if his wife knew about his evening activities and when the guy didn't answer he went on to the part where we were going to give the names of everyone that got themselves arrested in our little project to the newspapers. Gucci Man gulped about forty times and became very polite. There were no wants on him, so we punted him loose and never saw him again. He was Entry One into The Book.

After thirty or forty similar encounters with other motorists and pedestrians we started to get their attention. After a hundred or so it was clear we were making real progress. The vehicular traffic was way down and area residents began to approach the police officers in the area to thank them and shake their hands. Applause could be heard from balconies in the high-rises whenever we were conducting a spot check in front of them. One nice elderly lady brought cookies and Mack ate them all without sharing. I didn't care because I knew the all extra sugar would keep him on top of his game.

It was a very rare occurrence to spot check the same person twice. Once was usually enough for anyone but I suppose somewhere in the Law of Averages there are exceptions to everything. Ours came in the form of a five foot two, one hundred and ten pound little fellow who looked a lot like Peter Pan. We'd seen him tip-toeing around the area being hit on by numerous passing vehicles and somewhere on Day Two we snagged him. He managed to tee-hee out his name between nervous giggles and we recorded all his pertinent personal information and got around to taking his picture. He gave us his best Pepsodent smile and the subtle shadows of his make-up and teeny ear-hoops were captured perfectly in the flash. He'd dyed his page-boy hairdo a muted crimson and his tights were a perfect match. Mack even complimented him on his elf boots with the curled up toes with the little cat-bells on them. He had no wants and we suggested he disappear. He was back in an hour. So we pulled him in again, went through the drill like we'd never seen him before and noticed that he posed just a bit more provocatively for the photo session than he had the first time. He must have passed himself getting back the third time as it couldn't have been ten minutes. It was becoming a little obvious that Pixie LIKED getting into the back of the patrol wagon with all the big policemen. I left it to Mack to dispose of him and I saw him leaning down to whisper something to the little guy as he clenched the back of his little pencil neck with his giant right hand. I knew Mack was only shining the wee fellow on when he mentioned stuffing him down a storm drain if we saw him again and I felt bad that it made him cry. I got over it.

The Book was looking pretty good with about sixty pages of upstanding citizens that had been enlightened about our new stand on curb crawling. Even the security boys at the Legislature were on board and we added more than a few of their recent captures to our files. About fifteen had hit the lockup on old warrants and a handful that were underage got to gain "Child in Need of Protection" status and hauled off the streets. We towed a few cars, dinged a few suspended drivers and in general openly harassed them all with tickets and terse words until they were almost gone. One particularly hard-core hustler was a filthy twenty-year-old that had been living on the street for months. He wore a fringed leather jacket and we started calling him Buffalo Bill—not so much for his attire but for the fact that he smelled a lot like a buffalo wallow in July. He was about the stinkiest LIVE human being I had ever encountered. The kid wasn't homosexual or bi-sexual but willingly participated in any form of sexual activity for money. We tossed him three times daily but he just wouldn't go away. Unfortunately, the old vagrancy laws that had served the city so well earlier in the century for just such eventualities had been trashed when someone decided that even the disease-ridden dregs of society should have rights too. Then, he was gone and I heard he had turned up mysteriously fifty miles down the road in Portage la Prairie the next morning on his way farther west.

After Day Three we were getting a little hard up for business as nearly everyone was gone and the few stalwart hangers-on started to run when they saw a police unit. It was important to keep up the high police profile in the area, but we switched to a new tactic to ferret out the last few who had burrowed more or less into the woodwork to ply their trade. The area behind the old curling club just west of the Legislature grounds was just a gravel parking lot that bumped right up against the wooded riverbank, but whenever the officers on the project pulled in there all of the people we were targeting were on foot and took off into the undergrowth.

I selected a particularly baby-faced young officer who looked about seventeen. He'd only been on the job for a year or so, and was a good looking shorter kid with dark curly hair. We got him back into his jeans and he drove a Monte Carlo coupe that was a few years old and was as perfect for the job as he was. I told him to pull down into the parking lot, sit in his car with his radio and revolver hidden, and wait for one of the hustlers to approach his vehicle. It would look good on the arrest sheets if our project nailed down a few "Communicate for the Purpose of Prostitution" arrests in addition to all the other initiatives we had undertaken to clean up the area for good.

The little cop wheeled it down into the lot and parked about forty feet from the bushes with his window down. He said he hadn't been there for five seconds when a tall guy with his pants pulled down to his ankles sprang out of the trees pogo-sticking it straight to his car. He said the guy would have won the World Potato Sack Race hands down as he could cover about fifteen feet in one bound. In two seconds he was at the window of the kid's car attempting to pogo on into the open window with his fully formed erection jousting at the kid's head with every bound. The kid panicked and took off—forgetting to make the arrest or to radio his cover team—and was unable to talk properly for about an hour afterwards.

When I rolled into the office the next afternoon I sought out my boss as I usually gave him a daily verbal report on how things were progressing. When I walked into his office I knew something was up as he was generally about as poker-faced as someone engaged in an epileptic fit. He asked about The Book which I had kept under lock and key until the task force headed out each evening and that he should have had no knowledge of whatsoever. Lie, Deny and Act Surprised was my first impulse, but you can only go to that so many times in a month so I went with: "What about it?"

He said that he had to take it and that our project was finished. He wasn't a bad guy and really didn't have the will to deal with the seemingly endless unpleasant duties that leaders are faced with. He went on to elaborate that he had been called upstairs earlier in the day regarding some of our actions on the street. The Executive, while silently applauding our results, had been contacted by a City Councillor—not the one from the area we were policing in the project—but who was a respected member of the city's gay community. It had been brought to their attention that some people's civil rights may have been infringed upon by our practice of photographing each person we had spot checked. I argued that it was NOT a project targeting GAY men but male PROSTITUTES, and those that would indulge in them. I added that the area public was supportive beyond belief and that the activity that had been taking place constituted CRIMINAL offences in many cases—and as such was our DUTY to address. It was for naught and reinforced my belief that there was not—and never would be—any place for politics in police work. I forked over the book and still laugh about how fast the city's Legal Department must have burned it.

CHAPTER 21 Professional Association

Getting along with most other police officers was easy. There was, however, the occasional controversial type that required some extra understanding and effort to keep all relations on a positive basis. One classic example of this was an English guy that had about twenty years on the job when I was working the Drug squad. He had been a patrol officer in various divisions and in all honesty I found him to be a bit of a test on a good day but I never had much to do with him. However, when his kid was busted for the THIRD time for dealing in drugs, his state of total denial must have pushed him over the edge for he took it upon himself to attend to the Vice Division in person and straighten out the whole place for picking on his son.

The Vice Sergeant on duty at the front desk was a gentleman first and foremost. I don't recall ever hearing the man swear or speak harshly to any other human being in the time that I knew him. He was taken completely off guard when the irate father/police member stomped into the front of the office and broadsided him with a loud and rapid-fire series of allegations ranging from planting evidence to a personal vendetta against him by Drug cops. Frenchie just happened to be near the front of the office—performing some of his Detective duties—as he had been monitoring some wiretap tapes from a local bookmaker and he heard the opening barrage from around the corner. The Sergeant had only managed to stammer a few interrupted "Now see here…" and "Now calm down and…" as the little Englishman rose another octave in his tirade.

I was sitting in the back Drug office and when I saw Frenchie punch off the tape recorder, tear off his headphones and fling them onto the desk. I knew something was up so I followed him up to the front along with Trapper and Tinker who had been checking over a mountain of skin books they had seized. I hadn't been involved in any of the three arrests involving Junior, but when the officer saw me he screamed "I want to talk to YOU!" Frenchie stepped into his path and pushed him back through the short swinging gate that separated the public area at the front from the rest of our office. Using his best diplomacy, he stared at the much shorter officer for about five whole seconds and moved his nose right up to his face. I noticed the veins were sticking out on the side of Frenchie's temples as they always did when he was at least minorly annoyed. In a low voice that I could hardly hear from behind him Frenchie laid it out for him with "You get the FUCK out of here now or you'll be eating fish and chips through a FUCKING STRAW." We experienced no further signs of displeasure from that particular officer in the future.

There was always a lot of good-natured bantering between the plain-clothes officers from the various divisions of Detectives on the second floor. When we'd see guys from the old Juvenile Branch we'd refer to them as the Sandbox Squad and ask them if they had been issued a red pail or a blue one when they got transferred there. They'd leer at our long hair and filthy jeans and enquire if someone had taken us to a shit fight and used us for a shield. No one took any offence to any of it.

Some of the Break and Enter Squad guys from across the back hallway were a little tricky sometimes. They'd be really curious about exactly what, in the form of stolen property, might be inside of a certain address on occasion, but were obviously lacking in the area of evidence or reasonable and probable grounds to obtain a search warrant. So, they'd off-handedly mention to a Drug Squad member that they'd "heard" there was likely some DRUGS in the place hoping to tag along and seize anything stolen when the unsuspecting Drug

Squad guy obtained a search warrant—and usually found NOTHING that looked like dope. It didn't work—at least with anyone who had been in the Drug squad for more than a week.

The Homicide guys were something else. They were always dolled up in their expensive suits—even when they got called out at 3:00 in the morning. We told them they looked like pimps and that they best be watching out when the Pussy Posse members were out and about. After they told us to fuck off and asked what we really did with our Clothing Allowance cheques, we'd tell them that Vice guys faced imminent danger every day on the street and that Homicide was the safest place in the whole department to work. We pointed out the fact that by the time the Homicide guys arrived anywhere, everyone was already dead and asked how dangerous THAT could be. You could hear them laughing even after the elevator was gone.

In the course of our normal patrol duties in my early days in the department, we often attended many of the same calls as the then private ambulance firms that provided the paramedic services in the city along with Fire Rescue. I was working a smouldering hot day shift one summer day with Two Gun before either of us achieved permanent cruiser car assignments. We were patrolling in the West End when we were dispatched to one of the numerous "man collapsed" calls near Langside Street and Portage Avenue. We weren't far away and Two Gun got us there at just about the same second the ambulance crew arrived. A man had been walking down Portage Avenue on the south side of the street and had just dropped to the sidewalk with a massive coronary attack. The ambulance two-man crew were on him in seconds and Two Gun and I popped their stretcher loose while they worked together on the victim. Their vehicle was a 1972 Cadillac ambulance which was a sort of giant station wagon with about five hundred horsepower under the hood in the form of a four hundred and seventy-two cubic inch power plant with all the bells and whistles on it.

Much to their credit and life-saving skills, the ambulance crew brought the victim back from the brink of death and managed to maintain a feeble pulse in him while providing some assisted breathing with an air bag. The senior crew member asked me if either Two Gun or myself could drive their ambulance as it was going to take both of them to keep the victim alive on the ride to the Health Sciences Center. He tensely added that we didn't have any time to waste as the victim was extremely critical and was just hanging by a thread. Always obliging, Two Gun jumped behind the wheel of the ambulance as I wheeled the police unit out in front of him to run interference at the traffic lights ahead of him all the way to the hospital. I had figured I'd get ahead of the Cadillac somewhat to make sure the intersections were clear for him and save him from slowing down but it didn't work out that way. We both lit up our respective vehicles emergency lights and sirens and were off. At eighty miles an hour north on Sherbrook Street, Two Gun was right on my back bumper. I realized I was just slowing him down for most of the normally eight minute ride which we covered in about ninety seconds flat. When we all bailed out at the hospital, I had the medical staff waiting in the parking lot and they whisked the patient away in about five seconds into the Emergency Department. It was at that point that things turned ugly.

The senior ambulance crew member was up into our faces and screaming at us which sort of put a damper on our laughing and high-fiving with each other. We had NO idea what he was upset about until he calmed down—although just a little—a few minutes later. Neither of us had ever heard of a flight recorder, but he told us that ambulance was equipped with one which recorded the speed of the unit at all times. In unison we both said "So what?" Still visibly agitated, he went on to explain to us that the ambulance crews were prohibited from exceeding SIXTY miles per hour at any time and that in the city it was even less than that. I think Two Gun said "Oops"—which seem to agitate the poor ambulance guy even more. He countered with a loud "So now WHAT am I supposed to tell my BOSS?" Two Gun looked at him in a brotherly sort of way and said "It's very simple, Ace. Tell him that I was driving as circumstances required that AND that if he doesn't like it, he can KISS MY ASS." The victim survived and apparently likely would not have if the ambulance had rolled in a minute later than it did, so we told him to tell THAT to his boss, too. Two Gun said later that he had heard the two ambulance guys yelling from the back end of the Cadillac all the way to the hospital, but he couldn't make out anything over the wail of the siren and had just figured they were urging him to go faster—so he did. We never heard another thing about it.

Besides the ambulance people, we had a constant and nearly always positive working relationship with the Fire Department. Only once in my entire career did I experience anything that could be construed as a negative encounter. It was a beautiful warm summer day and I was working a two man patrol unit in the downtown. We'd caught a call of a house on fire in the West End. Police attended fires as a matter of course to perform traffic control if necessary and to submit a basic report on the fire cause, estimated damage, any injuries and other pertinent information that may have been required by arson or fire investigators.

The place was a bungalow and the fire had started in the kitchen area in the rear of the building. The place was filled with thick smoke and the Fire Department crews were just winding down after extinguishing the fire and were pulling their hoses and equipment out of the home. I was standing on the front lawn near a sweated-up burly fireman in his early forties who was just pulling off his mask. Just at that moment, I saw a large white cat inside the front picture window that was in obvious distress from the smoke and was trying to get out of the house through the solid window. I didn't even like cats, but it was somebody's pet and I hated to see any animal caught like that. I moved over to the fireman and said "Hey. Any chance you can get that cat out of there?" The guy went berserk.

He shoved me away—quite forcefully—with an open hand and screamed at me, "FUCK THAT CAT!" and flung his mask on the ground. He was tearing at his protective coat to get it off himself and there was little doubt that when he did he was going to take a run at me. I snatched up one of the discarded fire axes and smashed the front window. The cat bailed out. I dropped the axe and yelled at the fireman who was about ten feet away "Just what the FUCK is your problem, ASSHOLE?" He flung off his coat and started towards me so I sailed my uniform hat onto the grass and we squared off. I was just deciding on which side of his face I was going to nail that ignorant bastard first when I caught a white Fire Department helmet in my peripheral vision and I heard a "HOLD IT RIGHT THERE!"

It was Uncle Ray. He was the father of two of my best buddies from the lake when I was a kid. He had about a zillion years of service in the Fire Department and was temporarily assigned as the Acting District Chief or something at the old Number Five Fire Hall. He looked a little miffed and told his fireman to pick up his equipment. He then simply stated "I'll see both of you in my office in fifteen minutes." I believe he saw it more my way, but the direction he went with was more along the lines of the total lack of professional conduct he had observed in both of us. It went no further.

Quite conversely, on another occasion, I was working the dayshift in the Drug Squad a few years later. The Zoo had been a perpetual hot bed of drug activity in that summer of 1977 and I was down there hanging around the bar trying to make a buy. I saw a couple of filthy-looking rats talking for a few minutes in the lobby and then again a few minutes later near the back doors in the bar. It looked like something was about to happen. My partner had a bad case of well-known face and was across the street in our car. Our arrangement was that if I made a buy I'd go out front and give him a wave. The pair headed out the back door and into the alley before I could do anything, so I gave them a fifteen second lead and followed them out. I walked right into them right in the middle of the deal.

It was take them down alone or lose them so I went for it. I had no gun as I rarely carried it when I was making buys as some bright type was always patting you down before they sold to you. I had my tin in my boot and I flashed it fast and grabbed both of them and spun them onto the brick wall at the back of the hotel. I got the dope out of the buyer's hand and the cash from the dealer, but I was sure the dealer had more on him and I didn't have a clue about any weapons. I pocketed the evidence and grabbed one in each hand and started marching them north in the alley to get away from the hotel before they got some help. The dealer was starting to act up and I cracked him a fast one as I pushed them along. Then they both started and I was going to lose at least one of them if I didn't catch a break pretty quick.

Then I saw them. A group of firemen sitting in lawn chairs in the shade just outside the open doors of the fire hall about fifty yards ahead of me. I yelled, "Police Officer! I need some HELP!" The two assholes were going for it and I was just hanging on to them as the firemen all stared for a few seconds at the three dirty long-hairs fighting in the alley. I yelled again, "I'm a COP! Give me a hand!" In the next five seconds, I had about six or seven young firemen off the Fire Department Beefcake Calendar gleefully choking the shit out of my two arrests. I got my badge back out and they obligingly dragged my prisoners back to the fire hall where I skinned them right down and got a bunch more dope off the dealer. The Captain came out and asked how he could help so I gave him my unit number and he called it in. My partner was there in two minutes. We dropped off a couple dozen doughnuts at the fire hall the next day.

CHAPTER 22 Darker Moments

I used to shoot a lot of skeet with a psychologist one summer back in the late 1970s. While he couldn't hit the low-house bird on the last station to save his ass, he did know something about human nature. I learned a lot from him. He talked a fair bit about sex, love, nurturing, relationships and the limits of the human mind's endurance. Most evenings, the Perazzi over/under that he shot and that had cost as much as a good used Cadillac had let him down on that twenty-fourth bird again—the one we always bet the two rounds of clays apiece and a couple of drinks afterwards on—and the lesson would commence thereafter. I was taking it all in and was really developing an understanding about how each individual undergoes a metamorphosis into a "survival reflex" when dealing with stressors beyond the normal scope of their ability to cope. It was fascinating stuff—until my coach went home one night after a few too many vodkas and ate the business end of his Perazzi. I knew there was more to it than just losing at skeet.

Over time, I began to recognize that the vast majority of my co-workers dealt with their own personal stressors fairly effectively. Usually, it came in the form of cop humour—an ingrained mind-set that a little levity could get you through anything. Some of the guys were masters at it. As a fairly junior constable with an even more junior partner one morning, I stood in the single bedroom of a welfare dump of an apartment on Young Street. The Thai-born transvestite prostitute that was dangling from an extension cord tied off on an exposed pipe in the ceiling had already been with his ancestors for at least two days before we got there. He was clad in fish-net stockings and black high heels which matched his camisole. There was some evidence of sexual activity and I was just pondering whether or not the little guy had offed himself on purpose or if it was one of those accidental autoerotic things when the Acting Patrol Sergeant arrived. He leaned in for a close perusal of the corpse and seeking his more experienced opinion, I said "What do you think?" He looked at me like I was a bit slow and without missing a beat matter-of-factly answered, "Slope on a rope."

Cop humour existed everywhere. In every district, on every platoon. In the fifteen months that I was assigned to uniform patrol in the North End the sole caretaker that looked after the janitorial duties for the Hartford Street station was a dour old Slav named Henry. He never talked to anybody and his only verbalizations came in the form of rants and growls if you asked him to look after something when a prisoner threw up in a holding cell or something like that. He had a rather pronounced hunchback and looked a lot like Igor. It was in the days when people could still smoke in police stations, and early one morning I spotted Henry shuffling into the men's staff washroom carrying a large cardboard sign and a roll of tape. The sign letters were in bold capitals a full three inches tall: PLEASE DO NOT THROW YOUR CIGARETTE BUTTS INTO THE URINALS. It was a custom job with the words perfectly balanced in two lines in the center of the signboard. Soon after, I had to drain off some of the four or five cups of coffee I had knocked back earlier in the shift and I hit the men's room door. There it was—taped perfectly center above the full wall of urinals: PLEASE DO NOT THROW YOUR CIGARETTE BUTTS INTO THE URINALS…with a small felt-pen addition underneath…HENRY FINDS THEM TOO SOGGY AND HARD TO LIGHT.

Nicknames abounded at all ranks—rarely hurtful and most-ly hilarious—which were really the foundation stone of the end-less humour and the comradeship that ultimately made the place run in those decades past. Practical jokes, teasing, and regular after work get-togethers involving liquor and laughter worked for most of us who were fortunate enough to rarely encounter circumstances that numbed your mind and turned your guts to ice. Only twice in my life have I felt at least partially overwhelmed by what had just landed on me with both feet.

The first occurred in the form of an unsuspected tragedy in which I had no part. I was seventeen years old with a year of high school still ahead of me. Three of us—two of my closest buddies and me—were out shooting gophers north of Stonewall about forty-five minutes from the city. It was a beautiful July Saturday afternoon, calm and sunny, and I had no idea that my life would change before the day was over. Up until that afternoon, my existence had been a carefree and never-ending party and I had the world by the tail. Swapping gob at the Odeon Drive-Inn and burning the tires off my parents' Ford filled in the days around a summer job at the moving company and the biggest hurtle I had faced that far had been passing Math 200. We were cruising the dirt roads and running seriously low on .22 ammunition when it started. Coming pretty fast out of a small two-tire track from a series of low hills we spotted a Ford pickup with NO ONE driving. As it got close to our road, we stopped and it ground to a halt just a few feet from my buddy's Fairlane sedan. Three little boys in bathing suits, with the eldest—the invisible driver who was about nine years old—bailed out and ran to our car. They were all hysterical and one finally blurted out, "You have to come QUICK. He's DROWNED!"

Collectively, we had enough smarts not to wait for a lengthy elaboration and we yelled at the boys to find a telephone and call the RCMP as we tore off towards the hills. The three of us were out of the car and up to the top of the sand hills in about twenty seconds and when I looked down onto the quarry pond of about an acre in size. An older fellow in a bathing suit was floating on an inner tube out near the middle of the water and I could see a couple of women in bathing suits on the far side shore. The younger one appeared to be sobbing.

I yelled down at the guy on the tube. "Is someone else in the water?" He looked up at me and sort of waved towards a spot about thirty feet over from where he was and calmly answered "Yes…he went down right over there." The eldest of us, who had been out of school and working in the trades for a couple of years piped up with, "Well, why the HELL aren't you OVER THERE looking for him?" The man just as calmly answered, "I can't swim. None of us can." I asked the guy how long it had been since the victim went down and he said "Five…maybe ten minutes." That was it. My other high school buddy and I kicked off our track shoes and socks and hit the water on the run. The forty-five degree slope ran about thirty feet down to the edge of the pond and the last ten of it was the consistency of wet cement. I yelled at our third guy to stay out of that quagmire on the high side as we'd never get anyone out of there if we were all at the bottom end. We started diving.

The first couple of underwater attempts to find the missing man at least developed a bit of valuable information about the pit for us. The dissolved limestone in the water was at the saturation point and the cobalt-coloured water was right at zero visibility. We also found the pond to be just seven or eight feet deep. We also found we were tiring pretty fast, swimming at top speed trying to find the guy before it was too late and from holding our breath for extended periods. Maybe another six or seven painful minutes after we hit the water we got lucky. I noticed on my previous plunge that the water seemed a bit deeper in one spot and I began some straight up and down dips from the surface to the bottom. I was getting more air that way and could cover the bottom in a widening circle. On about the eighth or ninth dip down I stepped right into the middle of the man's back.

I broke the surface like a Polaris missile out of sheer panic recoil and my friend had just popped up nearby. I tried to sound calm as I communicated to him that I had found the man but I knew I was screaming. I caught a breath and hit the bottom and grabbed the guy under the arms. That was the magic moment that I realized the man weighed about two-twenty, was slippery as oil and that I had nothing to grab onto but his bathing suit. Trying to push off the bottom was impossible as it was just ooze and I'm still not sure how I pulled it off, but I fought his limp form to the surface and tried to get his head out of the water. The two of us powered him to shore and tried to maneuver him onto his back and get his head back to commence C.P.R. but the slope gave away and dropped us all back into the water each time. I knew we were running out of time.

We were exhausted and running on pure adrenaline, but we hit the shore one last time and running straight up we made to a point just past the quicksand. Our third buddy was dry, fresh and strong and he pretty much took it from there and got the fellow over the top as we crawled out of the pit. My high school friend and I both had completed Senior Life Saving through swimming classes we had undertaken years earlier and we started C.P.R. The water never stopped coming out of the guy. We flipped him about four times between breaths in and it literally ran out of him each time. There was no pulse. He was blue. We tried for over twenty minutes. The next half-hour after that was a blur—people coming, an ambulance, a country doctor and finally a lone Mountie—a constable from out of Stonewall Detachment who was about the classiest cop I ever met.

I wanted to puke but I didn't. My high school friend did. Even our older buddy was ashen gray and his ever-present jocularity was gone. That young police officer knew we were pretty shook, but none of us were losing it because we didn't want to look like a wimp in front of our friends. He asked us about time and in the end it appeared to be more like fifteen minutes or more before the kids left for help. Then it was at least another ten minutes—after we talked to the boys—before we got the victim out of the water and maybe five more before we were able to start C.P.R. effectively. It was just too long. He shook our hands and called us "young men"—not "kids" and told us no one could have done more than we did. He took our names and asked if we could attend to Winnipeg Detachment to give written statements when they called us as he just had too many other duties and the deceased man's family to attend to at that time. Wet, muddy and beaten down, we headed home and no one spoke a single word on the drive in. I got my .22 rifle out of the trunk and went inside my parents' house and told my mother what happened. I don't think a guy is ever too old to cry in front of his mother and I'd held that in about as long as I could. I tried to sleep that night, but I stepped into the middle of that man's back every time I dozed off.

My Dad took us all down to the RCMP headquarters sometime the next week. The Sergeant there and my Dad were acquainted and the officer took fairly lengthy statements from each of us. We learned the man was a newly-wedded area resident and that the younger lady who had been present had been his wife. When he was finished he shook our hands and thanked us all on behalf of the RCMP and commended us for our actions. He summed it up by telling us that law enforcement always needed good men and when we got a little older to keep that in mind. It obviously made an impression on me, and although I was leaning in that direction by then anyway, it was likely the final nudge towards police work as a career.

That was my first encounter with death and the sense of help-lessness I felt at the time in being unable to prevent it. I knew that I had done all I could and I had no sense of culpability about it, but the despair I felt was very real and I had no idea how to deal with it at the time. I have since grown somewhat hardened to death in its many forms and like most cops I've seen an abundance of it: beating, stabbing and shooting victims, overdoses, jumpers, and drowned ones. I've scraped them off the road, cut them down from trees and taken them out of freezers. There is only one that I recall with any frequency and most likely because I was stunned by the brutality of it and once again was so helpless to change even a sin-gle thing about it.

My first tour in plain clothes came in the fall of 1976 and I was assigned to the Juvenile Division for six months with a crusty old Detective who was a dead-ringer for Archie Bunker. He had a houseful of beautiful little girls that were his whole life and he did about everything to protect them from the evils of the world. He was also about the biggest practical joker in the whole department and did it all: dumping pails of water off the roof onto unsuspect-ing officers, burning your hand with the hot coffee spoon—the works. He was a lot of fun to work with in the short time I was partnered with him and we encouraged quite a few under-aged little bastards into coming clean about their suspected criminal activities. Around Christmas time we were working the dayshift and were assigned to investigate a suspicious infant death.

I'd already been to a number of autopsies in the course of my duties in uniform patrol. I'd always viewed them as extremely interesting and a couple of the old pathologists in that era really enjoyed having a few laughs with the boys during the procedure. One of them loved to pull a rookie cop at his first autopsy right up into the procedure as soon as he got the rib-spreader in place. Then he'd eat a cinnamon bun with one hand as he was poking around with the other and the crumbs would be falling into the chest cavity of the cadaver. It usually only took one to two minutes before his new observer was puking into the adjacent sink. It was great fun and everyone usually had a hit off the bottle of Haig he kept in his desk when it was over.

This case was different. You could pick up on that the second we hit the doorway in the morgue. The old doc wasn't smiling. There was no jerking around or making jokes. He geared up and we moved into the stainless steel world of the dead. I didn't know what to expect when he pulled back the sheet as he had been openly evasive in my opening round of questions for background information about the fatality. He only said, "You best see for yourselves." It was a tiny, blue baby boy about a year old. He had extensive and pronounced dark bruising around both ankles and an assortment of older and paler bruises on his buttocks, upper legs and back. The back of his head was smashed to a pulp and it was evident that there had been extensive bleeding and skull trauma despite the fact that the body had already been washed. My partner went pure white and I could see he was grinding his teeth. He kept staring at the little body and the pathologist gave us a moment before he spoke.

He told us the death was clearly a homicide. He added that, unless he found any trace of evidence to the contrary after opening the cadaver and completing his examination, he was positive that the cause of death was the result of the massive head injury which had been caused by someone of clearly adult strength grabbing the infant by both ankles and very forcefully smashing his head into a fixed object with a straight edge—likely a door frame. He further alluded to the fact that death had been nearly instantaneous, but he suspected that the fatal blow had followed a pattern of regular physical abuse in that in his observation the oldest to the newest bruises spanned weeks in duration of occurrence. He let that sink in as I fumbled for my notebook. The Identification Unit photographer showed up and started getting his preliminary pictures before the autopsy began. My partner still hadn't moved or spoken so I hooked his arm and pulled him towards the door to the hallway and told the pathologist we'd be right back.

I saw the anger rising in him as his colour started to come back. Instead of grinding his teeth he began to breathe heavily and his hands were shaking. I was still stunned. I couldn't believe what I had just looked at. I wanted to be anywhere but where I was at that moment. Between us we had probably seen a couple of hundred dead bodies and yet both of us were numbed and then incensed by the death of that baby. It turned out to be the result of children having children. An eighteen-year-old army private had been thrust into fatherhood when his sixteen-year-old girlfriend had delivered him a son and neither of them had a clue about caring for a baby. The frustrations had led to abuse and then that final act of insanity which ended the infant's short life.

Reflecting back on it, it was clearly several steps past where our personal lines had been drawn regarding what we could shrug off or make a joke about. There was no defence from it. Nothing you could have done and nothing anyone could have said would have made it better. You just shook it off, never spoke of it and how helpless it made you feel. It made you tougher if you could force it into the Pandora's Box you kept in a tiny corner of your mind where you kept all the bad stuff and you nailed the lid down on it. Then you moved on. Or, it made you crazy in varying degrees if you couldn't. It was the reason some cops drank, or became non-communicative and withdrawn. Or why some just quit within spitting distance of a pension. It was all about self-preservation.

While the vast majority of us turned to camaraderie and tombstone humour to offset the cumulative stressors of shift work, fatigue, and the years of dealing with death and the dregs of society on a regular basis, others were permanently affected to the point where they had to leave the environment permanently.

I had a good officer about thirty years old working on a platoon in the downtown area when I was a Staff Sergeant. He had six or seven years on the job and was an easy-going and steady type that was destined for a successful career until he was the first unit on the scene of a multiple homicide in the south side of the city. The parents were both drug addicts but they had two small children—an infant boy and a little girl. Their drug debt had become markedly in arrears and a couple of local thugs with a nine millimeter handgun came calling. Daddy bailed out of an upstairs bathroom window and escaped, but his junkie wife's history of running her mouth at inappropriate times got her dead in short order. The intruders then shot both children before they fled.

The little girl was killed instantly, but upon police arrival, the baby was still trying to crawl even though there was a gaping bullet wound in his abdomen. He died despite the officer's best efforts to save him. Through no choice of his own, that officer's life was changed forever. The incident affected him so adversely that he broke down in court when the two suspects were brought to trial months later. He was never the same and though he stuck it out for a few years, he couldn't get past it and he resigned. There was no police psychologist on staff then as there is today—nor any procedure in place that assured the well-being of officers that had been involved in traumatic incidents. Facing daily tragedies, all we could do was laugh. And move on.

CHAPTER 23 The Russian Bear

The Russian Bear—who was a well-known rounder about town—was running a booze can on Bell Avenue just off Donald Street. The silent partner in it was another hood that had been a private bailiff in previous days and had come up on just about every wire-tap that was ever run. That in itself was not a huge issue, in that the city sported numerous other after-hours joints of varying quality and longevity of operation. The problem was that it was located directly across the street from the old American Consulate. The diplomatic types had delivered a rather harshly worded and official formal complaint which was channelled all the way down from the Mayor's office. It appeared that the dozens of empty liquor bottles, passed-out drunks and the occasional naked woman that were all lying on the consulate property's lawn every morning had been received with rather a dim view.

When Taras (my last Drug Squad partner) and I got called in by our Divisional Commander, his instructions were simple. The fifth floor wanted it to go away—as in immediately—and they weren't really too particular about how it happened. We were already well aware of the place as there was some intelligence dribbling in about the drug dealing going on there. It was also quite a bit more upscale than the usual hovels that were normally utilized by the speak-easy crowd. The eighty year old house had been completely renovated like most of the rest of the block's old residences which had been transformed into trendy studios and offices. We staked it out for a couple of nights in a row. It was long enough. At around 1:00 A.M. both nights the traffic just flowed into the place with numerous private vehicles and cabs dumping off dozens of patrons. The Bear himself was posted right on the front porch each night and he personally scrutinized every person that was admitted inside. At 4:00 A.M. the place hadn't even started to slow down.

Normally, standard operating procedure for after-hours joints was just to lay back and wait. When a vehicle full of the party-goers left, we'd normally just follow them to a point well away from the targeted premises and pull them over. Usually, with a few judicious threats of arrest, the vehicle occupants would all give a nice signed statement indicating that they had been sold liquor illegally while inside the premises and by whom. Then it was just a matter of getting a Search Warrant under the Liquor Control Act and knocking the place over. We then seized all the liquor and cash and then charged the principles with Unlawfully Selling Liquor and Unlawfully Keeping Liquor for Sale. However, we knew that in this case, that wasn't going to work as everyone who frequented the place knew it was worth their life to rat out The Bear. We also needed reliable police testimony for court instead of a vanishing witness regarding the illegal sale of the liquor. That meant we'd have to buy it ourselves so Taras and I went date shopping. There was NO way we were going to get in there without some company that would be well received at the door.

We came onto a pair of live ones who were regulars in The Zoo. It cost the city a few drinks, but we ascertained that they went to The Bear's joint almost every night. The ladies were a bit shop-worn but they knew all the players and we were pretty sure we could ease into the booze can with them in tow. We arranged to meet them back at The Zoo the next night and then when the bar closed the plan was that the four of us would all head for Bell Avenue and have some laughs. By 6:00 P.M. the following day, we had forty uniform and plain clothes officers lined up for the knock-over and we had secured the search warrant from an accommodating magistrate. Taras and I headed down to The Zoo about midnight and met up with our new dream dates who were already bombed. The bar closed and the four of us piled into the front seat of my old Chevy half-ton.

The place was going wide open when I drove up onto the curb right in front. There had been four of us jammed in the cab of my pickup which was quite a squeeze as neither of the girls were anything close to a size eight, but all the cops in the area were already staked out on the place in a loose four or five block perimeter with all the marked units out of sight. The Bear was perched at the top of the front porch chatting up two hookers that had unloaded from a cab just as I was doing my version of parking. We were all laughing and dancing across the lawn to the porch when he turned and focused on us. There was no doubt that he immediately recognized our escorts as he broke into a big smile and bellowed to the boldest of our new friends: "Hiya, Doll! Show me your TITS!" She did. And they both had a good laugh. He then turned to Taras and I and was instantly sombre again. He alluded to the fact that he didn't know either of us "from shit." The girls cajoled him and introduced us as their new beaus and The Bear thought about it for a few seconds. Then he got right up into our faces and said, "If the cops come here the booze is FREE. Got it?" We roger-wilcoed, high-fived and nodded affirmatively and we were in.

The booze wasn't free. It was FIVE dollars for a beer which could have kept Taras and I drinking on The Drag for most of an afternoon in those days. There must have been over two hundred people in the place. Every room was jammed shoulder-to-shoulder with revellers and you couldn't move on any of the staircases. The bar was a formal affair with a tiny little brunette taking the money and serving the drinks. The beer and liquor cases were stacked behind. They weren't short on supply—the hitch was just getting to it as you needed a locomotive with a snowplow on the front to push your way towards it. I went for it and pin-balled my way through the surging mass and marijuana smoke until I sprawled onto the bar. I got four beers and paid the little barkeep with a script fifty dollar bill. I saw her stash it in a box under the bar. She gave me my change—all in five's. I made it back out near the stairs to the second floor just in time to see Taras having a leak in the gas fireplace—which was burning. He hadn't been able to fight his way up the stairs towards the sole bathroom a floor above so he opted to pee in the nearest and handiest spot. Only about forty-five people saw him do it, so it was about ten seconds before we were on our way to being kicked out which was okay as we didn't have to come up with any lame excuse about why we were leaving so quickly. I saw the Ejection Squad heading our way so I grabbed one of the girls' purses and jammed the four beers into it as upright as possible. I told her that at five bucks a pop we weren't leaving them. In reality, that was our evidence on which it all hinged and we had to get it out—intact.

We all got back outside without getting a tune-up although I got the impression Taras wasn't welcome there any more. We loaded into the truck and careened away into the night. Hino and his army were waiting on the nearby shopping center's parking lot and I bailed out and gave them the details of the bar set up and where the script money had gone. After I passed over the four bottles of open beer and the thirty dollars change to the exhibit officer, we dumped off our drunken dates and headed for the office. In traditional form, the knock-over crew crashed in after The Bear had seen them all coming and had run inside and locked the front door. The Vice guys present had found the little brunette that had been slinging drinks and also located my script fifty dollar bill in a box of cash under the bar which could have eliminated The National Debt. The liquor seizure had been enormous and in itself represented quite a hit to the profit margin of the booze can. Also true to form, The Bear said NOTHING and the little brunette bartender was scared enough to pass out, but she had been well-coached and didn't even admit to being in the place. In the end, we popped The Bear for Unlawfully Sell Liquor and Unlawfully Keep Liquor For Sale based on the surveillance that we had done which put him at the door of the booze can for several nights and for his comments to Taras and I when he admitted us. The little bartender took the same hit and we waited for court.

The Bear did show up for court with a high-dollar defence counsel and a smug attitude. In total, about fifteen police officers testified regarding the evidentiary chain of continuity concerning the seized liquor and cash, the observations of the police surveillance from several nights previous to the raid, the number of noise complaints that had been received in the area also previous to the raid, and the fact that the liquor had been tested in a manner prescribed by law, and had turned out to be—liquor. Taras and I were lead by a very qualified Crown Attorney through our testimony in which we were both specific about The Bear's comments to us and the obvious fact that he was in charge of the premises through actions and words. The judge threw it out.

It was the court's decision that while the police had an air-tight case on both charges against the little bartender who had mysteriously vanished, the Crown had not in fact sufficiently proven that The Bear was a partner in the operation of the premises. With the total lack of a confession or further evidence to implicate him, he was found Not Guilty on both charges. Hino and I met to discuss the judge's decision in the hallway of The Law Courts Building just moments after The Bear swaggered out of court and gave us the finger. Hino was fairly easy-going and remained unruffled by the adversity we normally encountered in our line of work. However, the first thing out of Hino's mouth was: "GODDAMNSONOFABITCH." I asked him if I was to construe that response as being indicative of him being somewhat displeased with the judge's ruling. He then growled: "MOTHERFUCKER!" I took that as a "yes".

CHAPTER 24 More Antics With Taras

Not long after that, Taras and I were busy for several weeks watching a group of criminals out of Quebec that had a flop house just off the back lane between the rear doors of the Patricia Hotel and the Mount Royal Hotel around the corner. They were bringing in Talwin and Ritalin by the car-load and the demand was way past what they could supply. They were also running a series of drug stores break-ins locally to boost their product availability and in general were very bad people with a history of violence. It was mid-summer by then and smoking hot outside every day— especially four floors up in the hotel without air conditioning. We had watched the slumdominium from above for about all the time we could endure and we needed a light moment. Lady Luck smiled, and two very rough-looking ladies with really high mileage that we recognized as addicts and the lowest end of the prostitution trade walked around the corner off Higgins Avenue and were standing around—obviously awaiting some kind of drug delivery.

We couldn't hear everything they said but a few remnants of street drug terminology were recognizable and one of them kept counting the few bills she had in one hand. It was about ninety degrees in the shade and there was not a cloud in the sky. Taras was leaning a bit out of the window—I suspected for a better angle from which to overhear their conversation—when I realized he was urinating onto the metal fire escape grating directly above the two hookers. A diffused spray of urine had been settling over them for about ten seconds when one of them held out her hand and said "It's fuckin' rainin". The other nodded in affirmation and they left and Taras said "And THIS is your brain on DRUGS!"

Despite all the funny stuff that Taras did, his most hilarious moment came along quite by accident. Taras, like myself, was a member of Emergency Response Unit Team Three and another younger officer that was also on the same team with us was a full-time Canine Unit member. At that time, the K-9 unit was run out of the District Four station as the area had a large fenced compound for dog training and a heated kennel building for the animals when they were not actually in the mobile units with their respective handlers.

On an Emergency Response Unit training day, Taras and the K-9 member had attended to the District Four facility to retrieve some piece of equipment that was required for the day and upon their arrival they found a lone service dog that did not belong to the K-9 officer with Taras loose in the compound area. This was not an unusual occurrence, as the handler could have been in court or at some other duty which required him to be away from the facility without his dog. All of the service dogs were familiar with all of the other service dogs and their handlers through constant training and were not normally a safety concern to other K-9 officers. The dog came bounding up to the fence with a flurry of challenging barks and growls and a sole command from the K-9 officer backed him off. Both officers then entered the compound and the dog strolled over for a quick scratch on the head from the K-9 member and then he was off again out onto the lawn area.

Taras was standing around—out of uniform and in his jeans—waiting for the K-9 officer to come back out of the enclosed kennel area when the service dog approached him. Taras had the good sense to stand still, avoid any eye contact and appear as non-threatening as possible to the four legged biting machine that was eying him up. The dog slowly made his way over to Taras who was standing rock still and stuck its nose right on the crotch of his jeans.

Taras stood his ground—much to his credit—with the hundred and twenty-five pound German Shepherd with a reputation as a serious biter nosing his nuts. He said afterwards that he could hear the wheels turning in the dog's head as it interpreted the new fear scent as too good to pass up. In a blink he snapped his jaws down hard on Taras's most private of parts and stood staring up at him.

Strangely, the dog did not commence the standard side-to-side mauling motion that big canines adopt as soon as they clamp down on something they want to maim or kill. It just stood there staring up with those empty eyes at Taras who was by that time becoming at least slightly anxious as he could feel the blood soaking through his jeans and the pain was really starting to kick in. After an eternity, the K-9 officer FINALLY came out of the kennel area and began howling with laughter as soon as he spotted the big dog clamped down on Taras's testicles. After he managed to control his hysteria, he shouted a command for the dog to back off—which was promptly ignored. The handler then ran through the A to Z of dog commands in an attempt to make it spit Taras out. There was no way—the dog stayed locked on without moving a muscle.

Concern was starting creep into the situation on both officers' parts, and the K-9 member finally grabbed the dog and attempted to pry its jaws open. This, however, caused some extra bite pressure to be exerted onto Taras's somewhat already compressed testicles and was met with some extra squeals of discomfort from Taras who was afraid to move or speak whatsoever. In desperation, and after several more thwarted attempts to pry the dog's jaws off, the K-9 member finally shut off the dogs air supply by pinching its nose shut and sealing off its lips with his hands. About a minute later, when the dog finally ran out of oxygen it let go and walked away—wagging its tail. Taras tip-toed ever-so-carefully into the security of the kennel area and sucking up his courage he dropped his blood-soaked pants for a look. He said afterwards that his penis looked like one of those sprinkler hoses with a hole in it every half-inch or so. The doctor said he'd live after he splashed on a little après-bite antiseptic and Taras went around afterwards saying, "Don't try this trick at home, folks."

CHAPTER 25 Miscarriages of Justice

I was somewhat disappointed in the Justice System myself after the court's decision on the booze can raid, but in the end The Bear paid about two grand for his lawyer, and lost thousands more as his cash stayed seized along with his liquor which equated to a lot more than The Liquor Control Act fines would have been. Even more irritating was the fact that it represented the second of two cases I had in my career which got pitched out of court when the accused was guilty as sin.

The first had come a few years before on a balmy autumn evening when I was out walking Five Beat alone on Portage Avenue. I was standing on the north-west corner of Edmonton and Portage watching the traffic when the sounds of a set of back tires burning on a high-powered car really caught my attention. About three blocks east of my location, but coming right at me I could see a set of headlights surge well ahead of all other traffic at a very high speed and then brake sharply to stop for the next light. I watched a repeat performance as the light changed and the muscle car burned it off the line again after some serious revving of the engine and the driver was really pouring the coal to it. It quickly got up to about double the speed limit and had to squeal to a stop again at the next red light. It was then just a block from me and as the light changed the driver stood on it once more. It was a Camaro—all jacked up—with foot-wide tires on the back and two assholes sitting in the front. I jumped off the curb and began waving it over with my flashlight as it neared. It slowed down and then rolled past me about six feet from where I was standing. It continued to slow and finally pulled over to the north curb almost down to the next traffic light.

When it was approaching and as it passed, I saw two very distinct things. The first was that there were two younger men in the front bucket seats—the driver had DARK hair and the passenger, whose face passed the closest to me had very BLOND hair. The second was that in the two seconds after the car stopped, I could see some major leaping around going on inside the car as the occupants had traded seats. As suspected, when I walked up to the driver's side window, Mr. BLOND was sitting behind the wheel. He'd had a couple of drinks but was NOT impaired by any means and he produced his driver's license and registration before I could even ask for it. Mr. DARK was lounging in the passenger's seat—so drunk he could hardly stay upright—and by sheer coincidence was a lifetime suspended driver.

Both of them gave me the same line. There was no way Mr. DARK had been driving. I arrested him and took him in where he promptly refused to provide a breath sample for analysis as required by law so he got locked up as he was too drunk to release from custody. He had a lawyer spring him the next morning. Court rolled around about six months later and I met with the Crown briefly before the case was heard. He indicated that the accused had maintained his innocence and that he was adamant that he had been arrested and detained without cause. The case unfolded very quickly. I gave my evidence and was very specific that visibility had not been an issue—even though it was night—as the streets were well lit and the vehicle had passed within a few feet of me. I had also illuminated the passenger fully with my flashlight as the vehicle passed by. I was positive Mr. DARK had been the driver.

Mr. Blond jumped on the stand, and testified that the vehicle had been registered to him and that he and he alone had driven the vehicle on the night in question. The Crown was so positive that my evidence would stand he didn't really press Mr. Blond's perjuries for discrepancies. The defence rested without even putting the accused on the stand and the judge announced that he had already made a decision—not guilty. I couldn't believe it. The judge addressed us and proclaimed that he had found "the police witness" to be "credible and believable" and that he felt I had acted with an "absence of prejudice". He went on to say that he felt the "police witness" did not have a sufficient period of time in which to observe both males in the vehicle and therefore it was incumbent on him to return a Not Guilty verdict on all charges. He had failed to consider the fact that in the SAME period of time I had managed to also ascertain the vehicle's make, model, licence number and color in addition to looking at the persons within. Personally, I thought it might have been constructive to the Crown's case if somewhere it had been brought forward in evidence that the accused was suspended from driving a motor vehicle for life because of his EIGHT previous Driving While Impaired convictions. I did make a concerted effort to consider the court's decision based on how the evidence must have been interpreted from the judge's perspective—but I was unable to get my head that far up my ass.

CHAPTER 26 Courage

At the end of my career, I took some time one day and reflected on all the thousands of people I had been in contact with in thirty-three years of law enforcement and in the brief periods of my life before and after police work. It stood to reason that three of the four bravest human beings I ever encountered were cops. I believe everyone would expect that as with police officers there has always existed—at least to some extent—the macho, hairy-assed cop image that has gone with the turf. However, having said that, it most certainly has been without question individuals who have risen miles above anything that any form of training could have provided to pitch into a life-threatening crisis head-first with little regard for their own safety.

It was early afternoon in that period of time between very late winter and very early spring when the calendar means nothing and it could have been forty above or forty below. The daytime temperatures had in fact hovered near the freezing mark for days but the rivers and creeks in the city were taking early run-off. Pockets of open water were showing in the ice on the waterways and the streets showed a lot more concrete than snow. I was sitting in the Duty Office with my coat still on when the 911 call came in. An eight-year-old had fallen through the ice on the Assiniboine River at the foot of the Maryland Bridge—and had disappeared.

As with all emergency response, a plan which addresses the particular type of emergency reported is instituted within seconds. Uniform patrol units, a Supervisor and the Underwater Search and Rescue Unit from the police side were dispatched along with EMS and Fire Rescue Units. I arrived within five or six minutes and was briefed by the patrol officers on scene. Three eight-year-old boys—all from the same class at a nearby school—had ventured down to the riverbank on the North side of the river during their lunch hour. The ice remained intact to a point approximately forty feet from the shore where it was abruptly and completely eroded for five or six feet by the swift flowing river beneath it. All three had shuffled out onto the ice to within inches of the open water and were throwing chunks of snow into the current and watching them disappear back under the solid surface ice. The one in the middle slipped, fell in and was gone in one second.

Some time—and no one really knew how much—had gone by before the other two boys managed to retreat, decide how much trouble they were in and finally seek some help. Much to their credit they did so quickly and precious little time was lost. Two members of the Dive Unit with nothing more than the personal diving equipment that one of them had in his vehicle arrived within the next minutes and while the rest of us stood helplessly pondering our next move he began to suit up. He was a quiet young constable with ten or twelve years in and I didn't know him that well. I asked him what he was doing and he looked at me like I was anything but the Officer-In-Charge. He told me he was going to dive under the ice to try and find the child. I said, "HOLD IT!" in a voice too loud and began pointing out to him things he already knew. There was a protocol in place with the Dive Unit that dictated the requirement of a back-up diver before any member went in the water. The water was ICE COLD and UNDER the ice, the current was mega-strong, visibility was ZERO under there AND there was only one other member of his Unit on the ice instead of a full Dive team at that second. He said, "I know." And then he and the second Dive Unit member began to tie him into about a quarter of a mile of braided rope. I said, "Listen boys...that kid is already dead.

I just can't let you go under there. I can't risk losing an officer for someone we can't save. That's IT!"

The other Dive Unit member I knew very well and had a lot of respect for. He went on to have a brilliant career riding herd on the country's outlaw motorcycle gangs. He took me by the arm and made his pitch. In a very abbreviated version, he told me about a similar incident that occurred just a couple of years previously in Grand Forks, North Dakota where a six year old had gone under the ice in the Red River. He was located five or six HOURS after he went under the ice and was revived by some miracle. It was called The Golden Hour in police dive team circles. It was a strange phenomenon in which children that have been submerged—especially in colder water—can be resuscitated after extended periods. Then he said, "He's going. We have to."

The other officer who had suited up and was triple-knotted into his single life-line started backing up to the black water surging through the hole in the ice. The line was secured to four uniform members and his dive partner and then he too was gone. For twenty agonizing minutes he pulled himself along under the ice and by the Grace of God did not become entangled in any of the cast-off debris that always lies at the base of bridges. Only a shred of communication through tugs on the line let us know he was still in control as the rope was fed in and out of the hole. When he was finally pulled out he was blue from the cold, exhausted and in the first stages of hypothermia. He was also ultimately confident that he had done everything humanly possible to save that lost boy's life. The body was recovered months later from a location quite some distance downstream. There are no words that could adequately describe the level of sheer courage that young officer displayed, but I was destined to witness such bravery again and to be awed by it once more.

It wasn't too long afterwards, in the heat of summer, when catastrophe struck again on the banks of one of the city's rivers. A young father had parked his vehicle on the docks at the extreme east end of Pritchard Avenue in the North End. He left his two young children in the Chevrolet S-10 pickup as he made some inquiries regarding some marine repairs in the adjacent buildings. In his very brief absence, the truck began to roll on the uneven dock surface, and slid down a boat-launching incline built into the dock. Had it been a couple of feet in either direction, it most likely would have bumped up against the two larger vessels that were moored on the docks and would have been held fast against a boat hull. However, it virtually threaded the needle and went on into the river between the bow of one boat and the stern of the other. The truck half-floated to a point some fifty feet out from the dock and the current took it some one hundred and fifty feet downstream before it sank. Through another twist of grim fate, a civilian mechanic who was nearby had seen the truck with the two screaming children inside and had sprinted a couple of hundred feet to the water's edge and made it to the truck before it sank. The windows were up and the doors were locked and the hysterical children—a boy and a girl—couldn't get them open before the vehicle disappeared beneath the surface. The mechanic sprinted back up the hill and summoned help.

Only one Dive Unit member managed to respond within the first critical minutes. The Dive Unit was still at that point not a full-time operation and members were utilized strictly on a call-out basis from their full time duties within the police divisions or while off duty. Without hesitation, the lone member contacted a second team member whom he knew was working and had the Dive Unit truck with the teams' equipment en route to the scene within minutes. Another civilian who worked in the area volunteered to attempt a rescue dive using his own equipment, but the Dive Unit officer found the air tanks to be severely stale-dated and could not allow it as the civilian would have likely died in the water as the result of utilizing bad air. They waited the few tense minutes out until the Dive Team truck arrived.

Still well within The Golden Hour the lone police diver suited up as the second member was suffering from severe head congestion which precluded any form of diving whatsoever. The protocol dictated yet again that a second back-up diver must be present before any Dive Unit member hits the water. Again, there just wasn't time to wait for that to happen. The approximate sinking location was known and on the second pass with the diver being ripped along the bottom through the current by a River Patrol boat—in thirty-three feet of murky water and with unheard of luck—he hit the truck broadside instead of being impaled on a piece of cast-off rebar. He made one quick trip to the surface to let his backup team know he had found the vehicle and to tell them to get both ambulance resuscitation teams on the spot and he was gone into the murk again. The vehicle was shifting and turning in the swift current and it was a calculated risk to break a window on one side of the truck as compared to the other because of it. He had secured his life line to the truck so that he could get back down to it as quickly as possible. Then he snatched up a rock off the river's bottom and smashed out a side window.

He told me afterwards that he found both the kids within seconds of getting into the truck. His biggest fear was getting them out without losing one of them in the current or having the truck flip over from the constant buffeting it was taking. He bear-hugged the closest one, blew out all his internal air and went up dangerously fast. Ambulance personnel that were in two boats were all over the little boy in the first second he broke the surface and the officer was back down the rope trying to get his air regulated on the way. By Divine intervention he truck hadn't moved and he had the little girl out and up to the surface within a few more seconds. One child resisted death for a short time, but in the end both succumbed. Only their deaths over-shadowed the level of bravery that this police officer contributed in an attempt to save them.

One late spring in the mid-1980s, a young woman had been stabbed to death in her suite at an upscale high rise apartment block way up on Henderson Highway. She had lived on the seventh floor and when her concerned family members finally were admitted to the premises by a caretaker after days of being unable to contact her, the suite door had been locked AND the safety chain was latched. To a thinking person, it lead one to believe that the suspect(s) had left by another means as it was impossible to latch the chain from the outside of the door. The Homicide Unit worked on the case for an extended period of time, and in the end had come up with a pretty sound theory about what had taken place and who was responsible. They did that sort of thing all the time, and that in itself was not outside the normal parameters of homicide investigation. However, in this case, there was one small twist. They had to prove the theory before the Crown would support a murder charge.

The victim had been estranged from her husband for several months prior to her death and he was not handling the rejection well. He had constantly stalked and harassed her. The Homicide boys had taken at least three separate runs at him for it as they were fairly positive he had been wielding the knife that killed her. Hubby was lying—albeit poorly—and denied climbing up the outside of the apartment block, balcony to balcony, from the ground to the seventh floor balcony. He had then popped the flimsy pot-metal lock on the sliding patio door and was inside where he promptly delivered a flurry of fatal wounds to her. He had then left the way he had come. The BIG hitch came in that it was a crucial part of the Homicide Unit's theory that he had pulled it all off in the forty-five minutes he couldn't account for his whereabouts on the night his wife was killed. The Medical Examiner had provided an estimated time of death and it all fit.

One of the investigators from the Homicide Unit was also a team-mate of mine from the Emergency Response Unit. He was a slightly built and athletic Brit that could run like a greyhound and was a gutsy, stand-up cop in any kind of bad scenario. He had a pronounced Cockney twang so I had told him years before he was a Manitoba Mexican and I always called him Miguel. He announced he was climbing the apartment block. I promptly re-named him Miguel The Retard. On a warm May morning, E.R.U. Team Three reported for a day's training and we secured about six miles of rappelling rope out of the unit's truck. The suite was still under police control although the Identification Unit's people were long finished with processing the crime scene. We opened the sliding patio doors and stepped out and onto the balcony and I looked down. I almost threw up. It was a very long way to the ground. But, since we had all done the Austrian Rappel at least once apiece, we were experts and we got to the business at hand.

Miguel opted to go with one safety line as he felt two would encumber his ability to climb too much. We hog-tied him into a modified rappelling harness so that the rope was secured to his back area between his shoulder blades. If he free-fell his arms and legs would not become entangled in the rope which the rest of the team would just keep the slack out of as he ascended and then descended. We strung out the one-piece rope after giving it a careful inspection and snaked it down the outside of the building to the ground where Miguel got hitched to it with about thirty knots. The top end was wrapped three times around the middle of the chesterfield in the suite and the other four of us took up a procession of belay positions on the rope to take up the slack. Miguel could only have dropped two feet if he fell. In the briefing that was held earlier in the morning, he explained that he needed to get up and back down in under forty five minutes—less if possible.

We grabbed on the rope, Miguel gave us a thumb's up and the radio man on the ground who was also the timer crackled a "Go!" He started off slow and careful and even stopped on the fourth floor for a brief look around. Then he got his rhythm and seemed to climb about as fast as the rest of us could the slack out of the rope. In seven minutes he was standing next to me on the balcony. After a five-minute breather in the suite he was back on the ground with a total of nineteen minutes expired. Hubby went to jail and I changed his name back to Miguel again. He and many others never ceased to amaze me about the level of commitment and guts that the Winnipeg Police Department cranked out when the need arose. All buffoonery and joking aside, there were always heroes in the ranks.

The bravest human being I encountered in over three decades of police work was not a cop. He was a father and a husband. I was working alone as the uniform street Supervisor in District Four on a late winter night shift in 1985. A call was broadcast to a residence on a quiet street in North Kildonan just off McLeod Avenue. The details were sketchy and it appeared to be some kind of domestic situation but the female 911 caller had been hysterical and the call handler couldn't get much out of her. I was about four blocks away and there were no other units available from my district. A District Three Supervisor was attending to back me up but he was fifteen minutes away. I radioed that I was out of my unit at that address.

It was a cold night and I noticed that the outer door at the front of the residence was closed but that the mostly glass surface was completely frosted up. The inside door was obviously open as bright light was showing for the full length of the outside door glass. I eased up onto the front step and listened for several seconds. There wasn't any sound whatsoever coming from inside. Normally, police officers will knock at almost all calls before entering, but something told me to check a little closer before I did. I noiselessly eased the outside door—which was unlocked—open slightly and looked in. The carpet from the door to the point several feet down the hallway—where the hall turned ninety degrees to the right—was SOAKED in blood.

I slid my four-inch Smith and Wesson out of the holster and held it down at my right side and eased into the hallway. After stopping and listening for at least another fifteen seconds I still couldn't hear a thing and then I could just make out a stifled female sob coming from somewhere around that next corner in the hallway. As I moved in complete silence up to the corner, the blood in the high-end carpet was oozing over the soles of my uniform boots. I took a quick look and I couldn't believe what I saw.

Kneeling in the center of the hallway about six feet around the corner was very thin man past middle age with silver-white hair. He was literally drenched in blood and was tightly clutching the fourteen-inch blade of a kitchen knife with both of his hands. His own blood was running off his elbows and I could see he was cut deeply on his hands, shoulder and upper arms. The knife handle was caught in a death grip by a second younger male. He looked Asian and very spaced out on something. Neither of them was moving. I eased up to within a couple of feet of the older man and quietly said to him as he looked up at me, "Does he speak English?" He answered with a very slow affirmative nod of his head. In slow motion, I raised the Smith and Wesson and touched the skin directly under the knife guy's closest eye—his left—and then I cocked the piece. He slowly moved his eyes to look at me and I quietly said, "Drop that fucking knife or I'll kill you."

He did. And then I launched him onto his face into the blood-soaked carpet and cuffed him. When I looked back at the older man he was praying out loud. With a foot in the suspect's back to keep him there I barked at the older man, "Is anyone else in the house?" He nodded again and then said "My wife and my daughter, he was killing them." I hauled out the radio and turned it back on and told the dispatcher to send EVERYONE. The older man got up and I finally got him to go and see where his family was after he told me there were no more suspects involved. About thirty seconds later two females—obviously mother and daughter—stumbled into the hallway from the kitchen area and I could see both were in serious need of medical attention. Both had been slashed deeply on their shoulders and backs and both had taken some defensive cuts on their hands but neither had been stabbed. The combined blood loss was staggering—the house was swimming in blood. Two ambulance crews worked feverishly for fifteen minutes and got the three victims stabilized for transport to two different hospitals. Their combined sutures numbered in the hundreds and all three underwent emergency surgery. I got my first police backup unit to guard my prisoner for a few minutes while I spoke to the old man and he filled me on what had taken place.

The suspect—a Cambodian refugee—had begun to date the daughter for a brief period of time several weeks back. She had found the male to be volatile and she had some fear of him so she broke off the relationship. He had followed her almost continually, had been calling her at work and at home and had attended the family's residence on a few occasions to try and convince her to reconcile. She refused. On this particular evening, he had knocked on the front door and the daughter had answered. Without saying a word, he pushed her inside the entrance and began to slash at her with the knife he had brought with him. The daughter had sustained four or five very deep lacerations to her arms and back and her screaming brought her mother out of the kitchen area where she was almost immediately attacked by the suspect. The lady had also sustained a half dozen deep slash cuts to her shoulder and upper arms and a lesser one to one side of her jaw that likely kept her throat from being lacerated.

The suspect had worked himself into a frenzy and had been quite vocal during his attack. In short order the older man had run up from the basement shop area to intervene. He attacked the suspect and drove him off his wife and daughter. In the ensuing minutes he was slashed a dozen times and sustained permanent damage to his hands from the severity of the lacerations. The mother had managed to call 911 as her husband continued to grapple for control of the weapon for many more minutes until help had arrived. That old man had more sand than any person I ever met and the whole family came to the station a month later to thank all the police officers who helped them.

The suspect was wired on some kind of mind-altering substance and he had a few nicks where he had cut himself during his wild slashing. I dumped him onto a two-man unit that promptly locked him up with a request for denied bail to the Crown after we threw the book at him. I even called a buddy over at Immigration to see what he could find out and it wasn't a real long time before he got a free trip back to Cambodia.

I saw courage in another form under the very strangest of circumstances. It still bothers me although it was a long time ago. I was a Staff Sergeant working downtown on a permanent desk job that went with the rank and I had capitalized on one of those rare opportunities to get out of the building on a day shift as there was another person of the same rank working the overlap day in my office.

I liked to walk down Portage Avenue and show the flag a little and see all the places that had grown so familiar to me twenty-odd years before when I was walking the beat down there on a full-time basis. I made it up to Donald Street and decided to sneak a little look into the back lane around the corner behind the Portage Village Inn. The PVI was a hub for criminal activity of all kinds—drugs, stolen goods—whatever—day or night. The professional shoplifters would hit Eatons store across the street and head right on over to the PVI to dump their haul for some cash or drugs. As if on cue, I took a quick look and a low-life was leaning into the driver's side window of a parked U-drive sedan doing a deal with the driver of a foursome of rodents in the vehicle. I got right up to the male outside the car before he saw me and I grabbed the cash and cocaine packets right out of his hand.

I'd seen the left rear passenger dump something under the driver's seat and I unsnapped my holster and told everyone inside to get their hands up on the dash and seatbacks. There was a little hesitation, but I barked it out quite a bit louder the second time and they complied. I cuffed the pedestrian and parked him belly-down on the hood. I couldn't shake him right down for weapons but at least his hands were secured. It wasn't a comfortable situation being alone like that but I'd been there before and I was in control—at least for the time being—as long I could keep them all right where they were. I always had maintained that it was most important to show no fear. It also worked well to your advantage if the suspects believed you would shoot them if they gave you half a reason to. Naturally, I was comfortable knowing that the intelligently legislated Canadian Firearms Laws would have precluded any possibility of any of these criminals—or any others in the country—being armed. I was also equally comfortable knowing that pigs could fly. I had a radio and got on it with location and circumstances with a request for some backup—as in immediate backup. Within ninety seconds or so, I heard the siren and my first backup unit came from the Training Division.

It was in the form of a Sergeant Instructor that I always liked and respected and a recruit that was still in his first phase of Recruit Training. They had been en route from the Police Academy out in the west end of the city to the Deputy Chief's (Administration) office for an appointment. I hadn't even been able to get the suspect vehicle shut off or to do much else but watch, wait and look mean until assistance arrived, but within a couple of minutes and the help of another backup unit, we got them all shook down and recovered more drugs from inside the car. A bonus pair of prohibited weapons in the form of a push-dagger and a switchblade knife came from two of the four parolees in the car.

The recruit had been front and center in it from the moment he arrived—and all by the book. His officer safety consciousness looked good as were his searches and general observations. I was impressed to say the least. He seemed like a good kid too, although that was the first time I had seen him. When the smoke cleared, the car was towed and the five members of The Dregs of Society were hauled off to the downtown station. I thanked the Instructor for bailing me out. I also apologized for making him and his recruit late for their appointment. It was then that I learned he was taking the kid to see the Deputy Chief as he was being terminated. I went over and shook the kid's hand and wished him well. It seemed pretty feeble in the face of watching that young man perform his final duty knowing his dream was gone.

Another incident that really hit home with me occurred within a few blocks of where I grew up. I never felt worse than I did for the poor guy that showed what he was made of. One of the old Vice detectives that had been around even in the "home brew days" came up to me one evening shift when I was still in my first year in the Drug Squad. He lived in Westwood and I had gone to high school with his daughter. He gave me a name on a piece of paper and told me that kid was selling drugs at my old high school. It really annoyed me because BOTH of the guys that had tried to sell drugs at Westwood Collegiate when I went there got their asses kicked by assorted members of the senior grades. They were draftees that had come to the school from other places where they had been suspended for being assholes. My neighbourhood was BEER country.

I did a dial-a-dealer on the kid who turned out to be an adult, and lined it up to meet him in the parking lot of The Village Inn at Portage Avenue and Westwood Drive. He had a snazzy new Camaro when he picked me up in front of the pool hall and he wanted to talk about it for a bit before he sold to me, so we went for a ride. He cruised up and down some side streets and asked a few questions before he finally pulled out a match box crammed with purple micro-dots of LSD. He said he needed "a deuce" to make it happen. I peeled off a pair of C-notes from the roll I had and pocketed the acid. He was an obliging type and dropped me off right where he had picked me up. I had "made" four of the five take-down units during the ten minute ride with the dealer but somehow he missed them all—even the plain four-door Plymouth with the visible antenna on the back fender as we drove right up behind it on the way back.

I bailed out of his Camaro and took my glasses off—which was the pre-arranged signal that I had scored to the fifteen or so cops that were covering me—and the world went crazy. The kid tried to bolt. He made it out onto Westwood Drive and was simultaneously rammed from six different angles by Drug Unit cars. One of the boys had just reefed the dealer out of his somewhat caved-in muscle car when suddenly a lone figure waded into the melee and tried to fight with the dozen or so cops that were grinding the kid and his car into a fine powder.

It was the kid's father—the nicest, most honest and law abiding—human being on the face of the Earth. He'd been at the liquor store just off the corner picking up a bottle of wine for dinner. He'd made the turn southbound off Portage Avenue onto Westwood Drive when he drove right into Junior being murdered by numerous long-haired and filthy-looking assailants. With only the courage that fatherly love could muster, he attacked. Fighting with a lion's heart he was flung to the pavement with his son and got to "speak into the mike" about six times as various Colts and Smith and Wessons were parked on his nose.

I died for that man. He was Father of The Century and he and his wife agonized through the aftermath in our office. He listened to what I had to say. Then he shook my hand—apologized for attacking fifteen armed cops—and held up his sobbing wife as they walked out. The kid got a year—only because he had no record.

CHAPTER 27 Jail

Early in 1982 I was sitting around the Vice Division's back Drug Office with my partner of six months—Hokie—who was on his way out of the Drug Squad and back to uniform in the pending Spring Transfers. He was a king-sized Norwegian and a top notch drug-enforcement officer that did several hitches in the unit before and afterwards. We were knocking off some reports and just contemplating where we'd grab some dinner when Hino—the Drug Sergeant—walked in and shut the door.

We'd all heard about the case. It was national news on a daily basis even in those long weeks after it happened. A beautiful teenaged girl with a future full of promise had been working—alone—in the late evening hours when she was murdered. She had been sexually assaulted and then strangled in the doughnut shop's washroom. Her life had been crushed out and then discarded by the killer like a used cigarette butt and the Winnipeg Police Department began the manhunt of the decade.

As Drug Unit cops, we did not often stray into the world of homicide on purpose. However, I believe every cop on the job—regardless of his or her specialization—was so outraged by the killing of this young woman that they spot-checked anyone who remotely resembled the police sketch of the tall and gaunt cowboy that had been seen loping away from the coffee shop. Volumes could have written about exactly what had lead up to the arrest of a suspect in British Columbia and the nature of the evidence that supported that arrest, but in short, Hino informed us that an arrest had in fact been made. He also told us that the suspect would be arriving under escort in the jail on the fourth floor later that evening.

He finally got around to the "Why am I telling you this?" part. He had just left a lengthy conference held with the Crown Attorney's office, the bosses in the Robbery/Homicide Unit, and the Deputy Chief (Crime). It had been decided in the interests of maximizing the odds for obtaining a conviction on the suspect, a "jail-house" confession, in the absence of a formal one taken in writing was in order. He finished up by saying there was a time crunch to pull it off and that Hokie and I were going to jail.

He ran us through it. We were both going into "A Block". It was the maximum security area of the old jail reserved for murderers, rapists, and psychopaths who were lodged there between court appearances and whatever provincial jail or federal penitentiary they called home. I'd seen it lots of times in my first ten years on the department and had sat quite a few eight hour shifts in there on suicide watches on various prisoners. The lock-up stunk of human waste, stale smoke and fear. More than a few of the past invited guests had succumbed to the despair the place held and lynched themselves with strips of their own clothing. It was tough time to do.

We were both long-haired and dirty looking but we checked over the names and mug shots of the in-house population and we were both satisfied that no one already incarcerated there could recognize either of us. He didn't have to tell us the importance of being right about that. An eight-or-nine-against-two fourteen karat ass-kicking would be about the brightest possible result if we were wrong and we were a long way from the cavalry—especially since only the ONE Duty Officer on each shift from the Provincial Jail's staff would know there were two undercover cops in "A Block." None of the guards, nursing staff or kitchen support personnel were to be clued in about it. Hino did give us the option of refusing to go, but we both called our families and told them we were going for it and gave them Hino's pager number.

After hitting the Junior's across the street, and wolfing down a double chili-cheese burger and a large order of fries we went back to the office for some last minute preparations. Besides stashing our guns, badges, wallets, watches and money for safekeeping in our office, we each chugged down three or four really stiff hits off a bottle of Park and Tilford's Eight & Eighteen year old blend that Hino had in his drawer. Properly stinking of whiskey, it was decided that I'd go in first and come out last to maximize my time of exposure with the suspect. Hokie was along mostly for security if things got ugly, but he knew to play the suspect into whatever conversation possible if I wasn't able to. Then it was time.

A couple of the older Vice guys off the Gambling Squad handcuffed me and we took the back elevators up to the Fourth Floor. The steel door at the landing rolled back and Bert Ostrowski—drug trafficker of no fixed address—made his debut at the booking desk. The guys that took me up had all the required bullshit paperwork and plunked it down on the counter as a veteran jail guard the size of a garden shed searched me. In a small lull in the booking process when we were alone for thirty seconds or so, one of my coworkers winked at me and whispered, "Keep the cheeks of your ass clenched at all times." The guard came back and my last links to my regular side of the bars walked back out to the elevator. It went downhill from there.

The giant guard clamped a meaty hand on my shoulder and steered me into a side holding room and smirked, "Okay FREAK... Let's see where you hide your dope." Two of them skinned me down after they got on some disposable gloves and much to their credit did a full-body search that would have been a real challenge to circumvent with even the tiniest package of contraband. They looked all through my hair, armpits, between my toes, under my scrotum and then shone a bright light into my rectal cavity and mouth checking for "suitcased" drugs. I knew better than to act up or mouth-off for any added effect. They kept my boots and belt and then it was off to see the nurse. She turned out to have a sense of humour in about the same range as that of a Gestapo interrogator when the Nazis were proving that community-based policing was in fact an ill-received concept when they occupied most of Europe in WWII. Once she insured that I did have a detectable pulse and wasn't suspected of carrying the bubonic plague it was a wrap. One of the guards handed me a pouch of tobacco, a sheaf of rolling papers and one book of matches as we walked down the corridor to "A Block."

There were three empty steel bunks to choose from—no mattresses, pillows, blankets or anything else that could be lit on fire or fashioned into a weapon or a makeshift rope. Each bunk was in a tiny cubicle with a steel sink and had a rolling barred door. All of the cell doors were open and a half dozen inmates were sitting on the two steel picnic tables bullshitting and playing cards. The entire block had been painted an institutional cream colour and jailhouse graffiti ranging from moronic to magnificent was carved into every square inch of it. Mother, Christ and Fuck seemed to be the themes of the motivation that the various artists had gone with the most.

The door had clanged shut behind me when a very pudgy Indian got off one table and stomped over to me barefoot and shirtless with his massive gut bouncing up and down. He screamed into my face, "GIMME YER FUCKIN' SMOKES!" He looked like his entire being had been greased with liquid fat and he was perspiring heavily although it was fairly cool in the bull pen. When he got real close I got the immediate impression that he'd been sweating like that for at least several days. I said, "Fuck, Man, You STINK!" and I walked over to the tables. He followed me and I was watching him warily but he screamed at one of the Crazy Eights players, "GIMME YER FUCKIN' CARDS!" He was no threat.

I slowly took it up with the other inmates and was careful not to say that I had been in jail anywhere in case any of them had ever been there before. I volunteered nothing and when asked I said I was in for five charges of drug dealing and carrying a concealed weapon. Hokie came in about two hours later and I couldn't wait for him to notice the non-compartmentalized steel toilet out in the middle of the floor near the lone shower head sticking out of the wall.

Dinner was not on par with any of the city's better steak houses. It was a boiled potato, a thin slice of boiled ham and one piece of bread of dubious age—all eaten with a very rounded spoon off a shatter-proof plastic plate. The one cup of tea was a little weaker than I preferred. It appeared that the jail kitchen staff had perfected the art of making six thousand cups of tea out of one tea bag. Cream and sugar were apparently not included when High Tea was served. The coffee was only slightly better, but both beverages were served at room temperature so that they could not be utilized as weapons against the guards or other inmates.

Hokie and I kept it amicable—but detached—to try and avoid any continued association with the non-target inmates in view of the fact that when our target arrived we'd have to try and get close to him as quickly as possible. There were a couple of genuine badasses in the block but they looked and acted no different than the rest of us.

Our guy came in late with not much time left that evening before lock down, but two things became immediately apparent about the very tall West coast mystery man with the wild eyes. His defence team hadn't yet instructed him to speak to no one in jail and he was scared shitless. There was no swagger or bravado about him whatsoever and he looked about as predatory as a toy poodle. I said a very few words to him along with some of the other inmates, but it broke the ice.

Nightly lock down was a welcome thing. You were locked into your own bunk's cubicle and you could actually doze off a little—but only if you hadn't slept in the previous two weeks. I'd had some serious reservations about falling asleep in there and I just knew that if I did I'd likely wake up and be able to look up my ass and see the sky. I learned a lot about jail life that first night. Belching and flatulence were worn like belts of status by the population within, but snoring appeared to be punishable by death. I wasn't sleeping anyway because I was freezing to death and the steel bunk seemed to magnify the effects of the cold even more.

The target was pacing again before we all got let loose for breakfast. He'd done it just about non-stop the night before just after he arrived and he was obviously a man with some serious woes. He seemed responsive enough when some of the other cons spoke to him, but being a suspected "skinner"—a rapist or sexual predator—and the lowest rung on any prison's popularity scale excepting undercover police officers, was weighing heavy on him. At some point, I think he realized that for the time being anyway, no one in the block gave a damn about him either way. He relaxed just enough to where he would talk a little but it must have been a horrific experience for any man to endure.

I got into a foursome over cards with him and had just got rolling into some conversation with him when Greasy stomped over with his flat feet and screamed, "GIMME YER FUCKIN' SMOKES AND YER FUCKIN' CARDS!" The target almost fainted with fear. I couldn't believe it. I yelled at the Indian to fuck off and he went and sat at the other table and started to cry.

The con next to me did it for me. He asked the tall guy what he was in for. With no hesitation he responded that he'd been accused of killing a girl. I said, "What the fuck's with that shit?" He said he didn't know because he didn't do it. I wasn't exactly an old hand at eliciting confessions by subterfuge while being incarcerated, but I really started to wonder about the whole deal. I backed right off it, ignored him for a few hours and he came over and sat down with me at coffee time. He looked like ten miles of bad road. I told him if he was innocent he had nothing to worry about but if he was guilty he best be thinking of cooking up a good alibi. He repeated: "I didn't do it. "

Hokie got him into some one-on-one conversations over cards and I found out later he hadn't heard anything different out of him. They sprung us a couple of hours apart after what seemed like three life sentences but I decided to endeavor to pull something else out of the target if I could. By then, I believed he thought I was okay and I got exactly the same thing—a complete denial. No bragging. No macho bullshit. Just a statement of the facts.

The debriefing was over in a minute or two. The big boss from Robbery/Homicide was less than enamoured to hear my verbal report—especially when I told him I really saw nothing that lead me to believe or even suspect the target was guilty. It was purely gut intuition. I put it on paper and it played out over time. The prosecutor was one of the best of that era and was as passionate about the case as were the several homicide investigators that worked on it those long months. In my experience, I had found that people that were not passionate about their work were generally not worth a damn at it. All of these people really were—but they were wrong. Over time, the suspect was proven beyond any doubt to be innocent. I would have liked nothing more than to have come out of "A Block" and to have reported that the suspect had made a verbal admission of his guilt and that I had been able to elicit comments from him that proved he had knowledge of the circumstances that only the perpetrator could have known. It didn't happen.

In Reflection

In the writing of this book, I came away with a variety of thoughts on a gamut of subjects. All of them were based on what I had actually seen or experienced myself. I was just one of those guys that had to pee on the figurative electric fence himself.

Police officers, I believe, should always be supervised, managed and administrated to by police officers. It simply goes back to the old adage of "Never judge a man until you have walked a mile on his shoes." In my observation, the "civilian manager" is a practical concept—with civilian employees—but is at best highly ineffective when determining career paths or recognizing aptitude in people who carry badges. They don't have the hands-on experience and very rarely are respected for that lack of expertise in the same way police leaders have been. They have never seen a dead baby.

Unfortunately, but understandably, the "Cadet Program" was terminated in the police force nearly two decades ago. The Industrial Revolution lasted a lot longer than anyone ever imagined, as we were really the last children in the workplace. It was a "School of Hard Knocks" type of education that put the real world into perspective for a lot of us. It was "Initiation by Fire" and it worked. Police recruiting has, as of late, kept up to big business and today the trend is to hire better educated people with degrees in fields related to law enforcement and with positive and well-documented work experience.

Reflecting the demographics of society in the police ranks has become strangely more important than hiring the BEST possible candidates regardless of color, creed or sex. A crusty old Sergeant who ran the recruiting end of the former Personnel Division (now the trendier Human Resources) many years ago said it best with: "I don't give a Goddamn where your grandmother is from. Now you're BLUE first—then you can be any Goddamn colour you want." Some may argue that his words were not politically correct. Others like myself won't care.

I found that the old Chief that shook my hand when I started out was absolutely right. It only took me thirty-three years to see it clearly. Throughout this book, I believe I have made it fairly evident that a lot of us maintained and even nurtured our sense of humour in the face of an often unpleasant world. I had enough common sense to get street smart in short order and I accepted early in the game that you never learned anything when you were talking. I suppose it was enough.

As cops, I'm sure most of us had a least a modicum of that small degree of human compassion that the old Chief had also mentioned at the outset. Personally, I always felt some sadness for the drug addicts. It is truly one of the lowest points of human despair. I have always likened it to being buried alive. Without rescue, it was a lingering death with no way to dig one's self out. Contrarily, a lot of us loathed the dealers—the worst weeds in the societal gardens of the world. I hated them more than child molesters because with a clear mind they spread their poison with absolutely no regard for the shattered lives and deaths in their wake. At least some pedophiles were driven by demons perhaps beyond their control and were legitimately mentally ill. Drugs have changed this country and the rest of the world beyond imagination and are responsible for the vast majority of our crime. To even consider "de-criminalizing" some long-entrenched statutes because enforcement is too expensive is insane. It flies in the face of too many cops who gave it all they had.

In a nutshell, my police career was like a parade with a lot of people constantly moving but all going in the same direction with a semblance of order. The banners we all bore as individuals read

"Drugs" or "Homicide" or "Traffic" or "Fraud" or "General Patrol" and many others. There was always a steady flow of new faces and new signs that stayed in sight for a while, and then passed. Most of us had, at least for a time, the opportunity to do what we were passionate about. That was as good as it got.